Ranganathan Series in Library Science. 16

LIBRARY BOOK SELECTION

Ranganathan Series in Library Science

1 *Library movement in India* by P N Kaula
2 *Classified catalogue code* by S R Ranganathan assisted by A Neelameghan
3 *Library administration* by S R Ranganathan
4 *Colon classification* by S R Ranganathan
5 *Social science research and libraries* ed by S R Ranganathan and Girja Kumar
6 *Library manual* by S R Ranganathan
7 *Education for leisure* by S R Ranganathan
8 *Elements of library classification* by S R Ranganathan
9 *Reference service* by S R Ranganathan
10 *Documentation and its facets* ed by S R Ranganathan
11 *Decimal classification and Colon classification in perspective* by R S Parkhi
12 *Five laws of library science* by S R Ranganathan
13 *Pusthakalaya vigyan ki bhumika* (Hindi translation of S R Ranganathan's *Preface to library science*) by Umesh Dutta Sharma
14 *Library science today—Essays and felicitations offered to S R Ranganathan on his seventy-first birthday* ed by P N Kaula (Ranganathan Festschrift Volume I)
15 *An essay in personal bibliography:* Ranganathan Festschrift Volume II—*Bibliography of the writings on and by* Dr S R Ranganathan, compiled by A K Das Gupta (*In Press*)
16 *Library book selection* by S R Ranganathan assisted by M A Gopinath
17 *A descriptive account of the colon classification* by S R Ranganathan
18 *Granthalaya kaipidi* (Kannada translation of S R Ranganathan's *Library manual* ed 3) by N D Bagari
19 *From little acorns* by B I Palmer

In preparation

Prolegomena to library classification, ed 3 by S R Ranganathan assisted by M A Gopinath

Practical cataloguing by S R Ranganathan assisted by Ganesh Bhattacharyya

Library classification: retrospective and perspective ed by S R Ranganathan and A Neelameghan

Depth classification and its design ed by S R Ranganathan and A Neelameghan

Practical classification by S R Ranganathan and others

Social bibliography or physical bibliography for librarians ed 2 by S R Ranganathan

Library Book Selection

Edition 2

S R Ranganathan
National Research Professor in Library Science

Assisted By
M A Gopinath
Research Assistant

SARADA RANGANATHAN ENDOWMENT
FOR LIBRARY SCIENCE
Bangalore-560 078

Shiyali Ramamrita Ranganathan (1892)

Malur Aji Gopinath (1940)

Edition 2 Reprinted 1989
Reprinted 1992
Reprinted 1998
Reprinted 2006

2:1
N66

ISBN: 81-7000-463-2

Rs.750/-

Published By:
Ess Ess Publications
4837/24, Ansari Road,
Darya Ganj,
New Delhi-110 002
Ph.No. 23260807, 51563444, Fax: 51563334
E-mail: info@essessreference.com
url: www.essessreference.com

For:
Sarada Ranganathan Endowment for Library Science
702, 'Upstairs',
42nd Cross, III Block,
Rajajinagar,
Bangalore-560 010.
Ph.No. 23305109
E-mail: srels@vsnl.com

Printed in India at: Printline, New Delhi

TO

My Father

N RAMAMRITAM

who departed

before I was old enough

to know him

The Five Laws of Library Science

1. Books are for use
2. Every Reader his book
3. Every book its reader
4. Save the time of the reader
5. A library is a growing organism

CONTENTS

Part A

Introduction

Part B

Messages for Book Selection

Part C

Lines of Approach

Part F

Third Law of Library Science and Book Selection

Part G

Fourth Law of Library Science and Book Selection

PART H

Fifth Law of Library Science and Book Selection

PART J

Conflict of Laws of Library Science

CONTENTS

Part A

INTRODUCTION

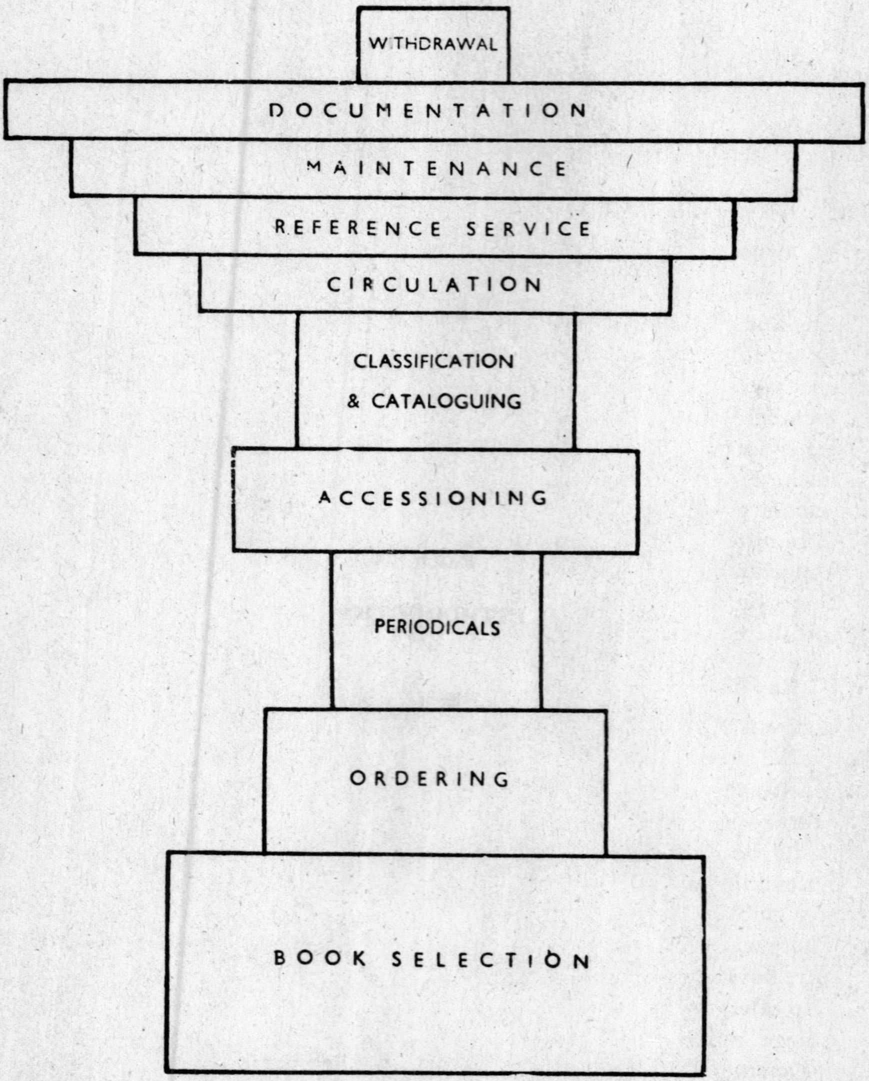

WORK FLOW IN A LIBRARY

Fig. 1

CHAPTER AA

PAST PRACTICES

1 Experience 1

It was 1925. I was visiting a Borough Library System in England. I was introduced to some members of the Library Committee. I was asking each one, "In which sub-committee are you — finance, or establishment, or book-selection?" One member said, "I am in the Book Selection Sub-Committee. I came into the Borough Council recently. I could not get a place in the Finance Committee or the Works Committee. There were seniors going into them. I could only get a place in the Library Committee. Even here, seniors occupied all the places in the important sub-committees. But I offered to go into the Book-Selection Sub-Committee, because I have not read many books. I can therefore be impartial in selecting books for the library!"

2 Experience 2

It was 1921. I had not then become a librarian. I was a member of the teaching staff of the Department of Mathematics of a constituent college of the University of Madras. The University Library had just then begun to develop. My Chief Professor was in its Book-Selection Committee. Neither he nor I knew of any systematic sources for book-selection. We depended mostly on any publisher's catalogue that might be sent to us voluntarily. There was no book shop in the city worth mentioning — at any rate, having books of the university standard. However, with the help of a young new professor, who had just joined the staff of the college after a distinguished career as a student in a foreign university, many worth-while advanced treatises had been acquired for the college library. My Chief Professor, therefore, said, "Make a list, for Rs. 1,000, of the costly mathematical books found in our College Library. I want to send it on to the University Library. That library has asked me to select books for it." I did accordingly. There were not many readers in the city at that time for these advanced books acquired in the College Library. Imprisoned behind glass doors they were simply pining away for readers. In spite of it, we recommended duplicating the set in the University Library too. Neither my Chief nor I knew anything about the social responsibility going with book-selection.

3 Experience 3

In 1958 I was visiting some of the libraries in a Constituent State of India. They were subscription libraries. Few of the subscribers were graduates. Few had tasted advanced books. Few could understand them. But I found in that library several copies of some very advanced books in Political Science, Economics, and Education. I asked the librarian whether he ever found readers for them during the preceding few months. He said that he had not. I asked him why those books were purchased. He said that the books were all by well-known authors and that a member of the Library Committee had recommended them. I asked, "But, why so many copies?" He replied, "Unexpectedly we had a good grant from the Government of India. We had to spend the money. The member of the Book-Selection Committee happened to go to Bombay at that time. He was asked to buy books at his discretion. He was also told about the amount that should be spent away. He selected the most costly books. But there were not many costly books to cover the amount. Therefore he bought a number of copies of one and the same book!"

4 Book Pedlars

In some cases, it is the book-sellers that settle book-selection. Enterprising book-sellers go round to the libraries as pedlars. They organise their work carefully. They notify the members of the Book Selection Committee. The members are entertained to tea. Bags of books are unpacked and displayed. Books are selected to the maximum amount available for purchase. Very often it happens that there are very few books left over in the pedlar's bag. In the absence of any reasonable method of book selection, beyond doubt these bookselling pedlars do some service.

5 Dependance on Book Exhibition

Sometimes, a combine of book-sellers arranges for a book exhibition at a vantage time in a vantage place. They somehow manage to bring in the influential members of the Book Selection Committees of different libraries. One of the members straightaway says, "Send copies of such and such books to my library". Prestige-contagion gets started. The members of the Book Selection Committees of several libraries vie with one another in bagging as many books as possible. The librarians have to accept the direction of the members meekly. They would not even dare to say, "We have got two copies of this book already in the library. Nobody reads them."

6 Antiquarian Member

It may be that a library is proud of its local collection. Then it may happen that there is a hunt for books for the local collection and that all the available book fund is turned on their purchase.

7 Consumers' Interests

Practices of these kinds may help the library to spend away its book fund to the last penny. But consumers of books come nowhere near this business. The consumer has no voice whatever in the selection of books. Not even the librarian who may know something about the consumers' interests.

CHAPTER AB

PAST AGENCIES

1 Legalistic Factor

A new Head took charge of a large academic institution. He was a medical man. Naturally he would like to have the goodwill of the colleagues in his profession. He asked the librarian of the institution to prepare a book selection list for medical books. "For how much?", the librarian asked. "What is the annual book fund?", the Head asked. "And what is the amount already committed for subscription to current periodicals?" After getting these figures, the Head ordered, "This year, spend the entire balance of the total book fund on medical books alone". The librarian explained that it was the practice to spread the money over several subjects. Then came the Head's reply, "I am the Head of this institution. The financial powers are vested in me. That is the legal position." The letter of the law was grasped by the Head and its spirit was driven out altogether. All the appointing powers of a government are constitutionally vested in the Head of the State. He can exercise this legal right. But he does not. He delegates it to different Heads of Departments, the Public Service Commission, and so on. A law enacted by the Parliament can have no validity unless it is assented to by the Head of the State. But no Head of the State takes power under this legal provision to deny assent to any law which he personally might dislike. If he does, he becomes a tyrant. Book Selection in libraries did fall a prey in the past in the hands of self-centred legalistic-minded Heads of the parent bodies of libraries.

2 Abuse of Power

In the past, Book Selection Committees have not infrequently used their power of selection as power for distribution of patronage. Preference is given to books published by particular agencies. Sometimes preference is given to only those books that certain favoured book-sellers can supply. Even worse considerations may prevail occasionally. Of course, unless a particular member of the Book Selection Committee carries a great weight with him, Book Selection often reduces at bottom to sharing the spoils among many.

3 Prestige Issue

Abuses of the kind mentioned in the preceding sections will be naturally of a high order in a newly established public library system in a new democracy — not accustomed to the exercise of public responsibility for a number of generations. In such conditions, the right to select books according to one's own fancy is lifted to the level of prestige. When prestige blinds, any argument may be pressed bare-facedly. In one case, the Chairman of a Book Selection Committee would not take any advice from the librarian in spite of his being the only person who knew the needs of the readers. His argument was that this power of selection would corrupt the librarian and he would use it as a means of patronage for his own purpose. And yet it was well known that he was the one most in need of being told, " Physician, heal thyself first".

4 Extreme Result

In extreme cases, such attitudes in members of Book Selection Committees often reduce the librarian to the status of a clerk. He can select neither books nor book-sellers. He has only to sign the orders. In some parent institutions, even this power of signing orders is denied to the librarian ! Who suffers ? Only the reading public. It cannot voice its feelings. At any rate, it does not. Is this all too cynical ? Look into the past history of Book Selection in the developed countries and look into the current practices in the newly developing countries.

CHAPTER AC

SHIFT IN RESPONSIBILITY

1 New Trend in Book Selection

Happily during the last decade or two, such things have begun to disappear in the developed countries. The Library Committee takes responsibility only to the

1 Laying down of the policy of book selection ;
2 Allocation of the book fund among books and periodicals ;
3 Allocation of the same among different subject areas ;
4 Allocation of the same again among different standards ;
5 Allocation of the same among different languages ; and
6 Appointment of a Panel of Experts in different subjects to be consulted by the librarian in making book selection.

Book Selection Committee reserves to itself also the right to

1 Review the books selected and acquired by the librarian on the advice of the experts ;
2 Check up if its policy has been deviated from ; and if necessary;
3 Introduce changes in its policy.

The librarian

1 Keeps informing himself, from week to week, of the books actually published and even merely announced during the week ;
2 Makes a preliminary selection from his sources ;
3 Sorts them out by subject fields, standards, and languages ; and
4 Places them before the appropriate Panel Members and takes their opinion on each book in the form of " selected ", or " rejected ", or " deferred ".

In making the preliminary selection, the librarian gives full weight to the

1 Actual needs of the readers ; and
2 Policy laid down by the Book Selection Committee.

He further makes a list, in which for each ultimate category of reading materials there are more items than what the library could afford to buy. This is done in order to allow the busy members of the Panel of Experts to choose between alternatives.

2 Newer Trend

In the advanced communities, the trend has gone even further. The librarian of a big library realises that it is futile for himself to do even the preliminary selection. He leaves this task to the reference librarians. For, these are the persons that are in touch with the readers. These are the persons that can read the pulse of the readers. These are the persons that find themselves in an awkward situation when the library does not have the books needed by the readers. The librarian comes in only after the reference librarians have done their work. He sits with the Experts in the Panel along with a reference librarian to finalise the book selection list.

3 Purification

When this stage is reached, book selection will be purified. It will be made free, as far as humanly possible, from the personal inclinations and prejudices of a few individuals. It will become more realistic in the sense that what is selected will be what is wanted by the consumers.

CHAPTER AD

A FAMILY OF BOOKS

O Necessity for the Family

For the library profession to carry out book selection in its purified form, it is necessary for it to acquire competence in evaluating books from two different angles — the angle of the consumer and the angle of the production of books. Accordingly, the first edition of this book was one of three books that came out together :

1 *Social education literature* ;
2 *Social bibliography or physical bibliography for librarians* ; and
3 *Library book selection.*

1 Social Education Literature

Of these, the first book is turned mainly on authors, publishers, and governments. It endeavours to formulate some principles which can be of guidance to the "new voices" which new India is throwing forth during the unfoldment of her present renascence. Without any intention of affecting the spontaneity which is of the very essence of true writing, it presses on the attention of authors the great social purpose which the writings of today are destined to serve. It also discusses how the publishing partner should do his work to make books acceptable to the whole spectrum of readers from the neo-literates onwards. Lastly, it examines how the lateness of the awakening of India finds her in an age which has left *laissez-faire* almost a century behind, which calls for planned, steady, action in almost every sphere affecting the life, not only of the community as a whole, but whenever unavoidable even the life of individuals. From this angle, it formulates principles of policy which the governments in the country should implement.

2 Physical Bibliography for Librarians

The second book elaborates, in a sense, what has been summarily indicated with regard to the physique of books in the first book. It is not a book for paper-makers, typecasters, printers, or book-binders. It is really meant for librarians who are essentially distributors of thought. Unlike teachers who transmit thought orally, librarians distribute thought packed or embodied in the form of books. The physique of books is therefore of vital interest to them. Their interest has to stem from the interest of the consumers — that is, the readers themselves. The second book therefore deals with book production from an angle which is of vital interest to those engaged in helping social education forward through books — either as leaders in social education centres or as workers in informal educational agencies which libraries are.

3 Library Book Selection

The present book, which is the third, assumes many of the details contained in the first two. At best it gives only relevant summaries of them in appropriate places. The fact that the other two books have already come out is utilised for making this book briefer than it would have been otherwise. This also implies that, for the fullest information, the three books should be read together.

4 Larger Family

In this sense, this belongs to a small family of books. In another sense it belongs to a much larger family. Indeed anybody can easily trace its ancestry to the first member of the family the *Five laws of library science* (1931 ; 1957). That book contains, in little, practically everything which is found more elaborately elucidated in all the succeeding books of the family.

5 Unity in Diversity

I owe this large family of books to Edward B Ross, my professor, who initiated me in the art of thinking in the six years he taught me mathematics. His development, not only of the lectures in the classes on any particular subject, but even of every conversation I have had with him — I have had them from 18 March, 1909, the year in which he captured my mind, to 14 April, 1932, when he retired and went back to his home-country — has produced a lasting impression on my mind. That impression had been given a name by another respected friend of mine Mahamahopadhyaya

Professor S Kuppuswami Sastriar. That name is *Ekavakyata* (=Unity). He used to say that all knowledge was one. The Vedas form, in a sense, a single "sentence" embodying a unit of thought. So does every chapter of it forms a single "sentence" embodying a unit of thought. Of course, every sentence in it is a single "sentence" embodying a unit of thought. *Ekavakyata* is seeing the unity hidden behind diversity.

51 Experience of Unity

When Providence transferred my field of interest from Mathematics to Library Science, this *Ekavakyata* tradition of the Vedic ancestors — demonstrated in daily life by my professor — came with me. When I spent a year wandering amidst diverse libraries in Great Britain in 1924-25 to prepare myself for my new life, the light of this *Ekavakyata* Principle was disclosing the minutest imaginable details in library practice. It illuminated each of them and at the same time threw them into a coherent whole. I felt the *Ekavakyata* pervading all that I saw in the British Library System and all that I read in the splendid library on Library Science found in the School of Librarianship of the University College, London. I still find it guiding me in all my thought and life. I often realise that even apparently trivial occurrences are organically fused into a single life-experience. Occasionally when immersed in thinking out ideas, all the long years of life fuse into a single moment. Such is the potency of *Ekavakyata*. It has helped me to realise the profoundness and the supreme truth embodied by Francis Thompson in the rapturous lines forming stanza 21 of his *Mistress of vision*:

All things by immortal power
Near or far
Hiddenly
To each other linked are,
That thou canst not stir a flower
Without troubling of a star.

6 Sub-families and their Development

I have described in my *Preface to library science* (Delhi University publication, library science series, 1), 1949, the struggle I have had in giving expression to this feeling, the help which my professor once again gave me in overcoming the struggle, and the great release I had when the ***Five laws of library science*** finally took shape in mind. That book is a verbal record of the ***Ekavakayta*** of library practice and science, as it revealed itself to me. As stated already, each one of my later books has come out as but an elucidation of one section or other contained in that first book. It is in this way that the family has been developing. It has developed along different lines — into different sub-families. There has been a considerable inbreeding among them. The result is that some friends find apparent repetition in several books and at the same time others find some elements of incompleteness in them. This book also may appear differently to different people. This is unavoidable when we look at a member of the latest generation of a family and compare him with the others in the lineage. It naturally embodies the features of all its ancestors. From the first ancestor downwards all the books of this group have family resemblance, each with its own individuality but bringing out, now more now less, of this or that characteristic of the original ancestor.

7 Facility to Development

The facility to live this particular branch of the subject a second time from 1947 to 1953, I owed to Sir Maurice Gwyer, one of the greatest friends of Education and Library Science I have known. It was his invitation to come to Delhi and his establishing a Department of Library Science which provided this facility to me. Pursuit of the branches of Library Science in Delhi was but a continuation of the thinking that had taken some shape prior to coming to Delhi. No doubt this pursuit took me into depths of greater and greater charm. But the present book marks a new line of pursuit which I was unable to explore till teaching this particular subject — Book Selection — at the University of Delhi opened it up for me. For, it is only contact with growing minds that generates the glow necessary to light up any line of intellectual pursuit.

8 Edition 2

In this edition, Shri M A Gopinath, my Research Assistant, has shared with me the work of revision. His assistance has been of immense help. He is mainly responsible for the revised version of Part K, "Sources for Book Selection". It has now become a policy with me to take the assistance of one or other of my younger colleagues in preparing new editions of books. This is done in the hope that it will help them to develop into competent authors. It will also give me the satisfaction that there is some competent young colleague of mine who can take care of the future editions of such of my books as may continue to be of value and in demand.

I should also record my acknowledgment of the help given by Shri A Neelameghan, my colleague and Professor of the Documentation Research and Training Centre, Bangalore, in the preparation of this edition.

The work of revising the text of Ed 1 and preparing the press copy of Ed 2 has taken about 400 man-hours. This does not include the time taken by secretarial work.

CHAPTER AE

CONSPECTUS

1 New Features

This edition differs from edition 1 in several respects. It has been completely rewritten. Its layout has been changed thoroughly. In the place of 8 chapters of edition 1 this edition has 100 Chapters. These have been grouped into 11 parts. This re-organisation has made each chapter short. The unity of the thought in it becomes obvious. Any later reference to any idea in the book may consequently become easier than what it was in edition 1.

2 New and Revised Chapters

The following chapter and part are newly added in this edition:

Chapter AC	Shift in Responsibility
Part B	Messages for Book Selection

The three chapters of Part C, the eight chapters of Part F, and the eleven chapters of Part K have been rewritten with more illustrations and brought up-to-date.

3 Conspectus

The chapters in Part B taken collectively display the principles of Book Selection derived from the different Laws of Library Science in the later parts of this book. When the same principle is derivable from different laws, it is repeated in the chapters of that part.

The last chapter of that part indicates the principles for different classes of libraries — such as public libraries, university libraries, and specialist libraries.

The chapters of Part C taken collectively explain the lines along which the Principles of Book Selection are searched — such as *a priori* approach and pragmatic approach. It also emphasises that in actual practice the principles found in different lines of approach should be blended together.

The chapters of Parts D to H taken collectively are devoted to the formulation of the Principles of Book Selection derivable respectively from each one of the Five Laws of Library Science.

The chapters of Part J taken collectively show how conflicts of the Five Laws of Library Science among themselves and with Finance arise, and how they may be reconciled.

The chapters of Part K give samples of sources for Book Selection in different classes and kinds of reading materials.

The chapters of Part L taken collectively describe the planning, the job analysis, and the routine of Book Selection in the day-to-day work in a library. In reality this part contains the reproduction of the relevant chapters of the *Library administration* (1935; 1959).

Though routine does not belong to theory, these chapters are included to make this book complete in itself.

4 Bibliography of Documents Used

In writing this book only a few documents had to be used. Therefore, each document referred to is mentioned in the text itself, where the reference to it is relevant. Thus, no bibliography is given as a separate list at the end of the book.

5 Numbering System

In our publications we have been of late making some experiments in the numbering of parts, chapters, and sections. In this experiment we use literal notation to represent parts and chapters and numeral notation to represent sections. This new practice appears to give elegant results.

51 Literal Notation

Roman caps are used to number the parts. They are also used to number the chapters in each part. Thus the number AE means "Chapter E of Part A".

52 Numeral Notation

Numerals are used to number the sections, sub-sections, and paragraphs, their numbers should be read as if they were pure decimal fractions — in other words a decimal point is taken as understood before the first digit. For example, in "Chapter FC

The New Helping the Old ", we have the following sections running consecutively :

1 Lure-effect
11 Message 1
2 Enhanced Lure-effect

Here it can be seen that " Sub-sec 11 " comes between " Sec 1 " and " Sec 2 ". This is possible only if the numbers are read as pure decimal fractions : If they are read as integers, the sequence will be 1, 2, 11

53 Advantage of Decimal Fraction Notation

The advantage of the decimal fraction notation is that the thought in each sub-section is subordinate to the thought in the parent section :

In the entries in the index for the headings in Sub-sec 52 will be as follows :

Enhanced Lure-effect FC2
Lure-effect FC1
Message 1
Third Law FC11

To facilitate the location of the correct section while working from the index, the index numbers include also the part and chapter numbers.

54 Inclusive Index Numbers in the Text

The index numbers are printed in the left hand top corner and the right hand top corner of an open double page. The index number in the left hand top corner is that of the section or sub-section to which the first line of the page belongs. The index number in the right hand top corner is that of the section or sub-section to which the last line of the page belongs. This inclusive system of Section Numbers enables the reader to know what sections or sub-sections fall within the open double page concerned.

55 Exception in Part B

In the chapters of Part B, however, each section number consists of two integers separated by a dot. This is not a decimal point. Thus, 1.69 means the " 69th section in the Messages of Law 1 ".

Part B

MESSAGES FOR BOOK SELECTION

CHAPTER BA

MESSAGES OF LAW 1

Note. At the end of each message, the sub-section in the text, where it is formulated, is mentioned. Its parent section in the text expounds the message.

Physique of Book

1.1 Select that edition of a work that has an attractive get-up. (Sec DB11).

1.2 Select that edition of a work that is cuboidal in shape. (Sec DB31).

1.3 Select that edition of a work, that has a height between 15 cm and 25 cm, a width roughly about seven-tenths of the height, and a thickness not more than 5 cm. (Sec DB41).

1.4 Select that edition of a work that weighs less than 1.5 kg. In particular, avoid an edition printed on loaded paper. (Sec DB51).

1.5 Do not select editions printed on India paper or mechanical pulp paper or art paper or feather-weight paper. Prefer editions on rag paper for books of permanent value, editions on esparto paper for the next order of permanence, and editions in chemical pulp paper only for books that are likely to have a comparatively short period of use, (Sec DB71), but never books printed on mechanical pulp paper.

1.6 If the book-trade sells a book in sheets, buy it and get it bound according to the library's specification. In the alternative, if an unbound, paper-covered stiched copy is available, buy it and get it bound according to the library's specification. If even this is not available, buy the copy with the cheapest binding and get it re-bound to the library's specification. If there is no suitable facility for binding, buy the copy with the strongest binding. (Sec DB83).

Printed Page

1.7 Select that edition of a work, that is printed in a type face that is readable, pleasing to the eye, and causing the least strain to it. (Sec DC11).

1.8 Select that edition of a work, that has type size of twelve points, or ten points in the absence of twelve points, in the case of a book mainly intended to be read by mature readers. Prefer bigger type in the case of books for children and neo-literates (Sec DC41).

1.9 Select that edition of a classic with a chain of commentaries on it, that prints them in parallel and subordinates them in succession by the use of different styles and sizes of type face. (Sec DC51).

1.10 Select that edition of a work, that has wide margins left plain or with soothing decorations and well leaded out printing, making the proportion of white and black unobtrusive and not tiresome. (Sec DC71).

1.11 Select that illustrated edition of a work, that has the illustrations and the letterpress in participative relation, neither subordinated to the other and both working together holistically. (Sec DC81).

Language

1.12 Keep yourself aware and extremely sensitive to going in for a book which is the embodiment of any given thought in the latest stage of the language. (Sec DD21).

1.13 Select books that are written in modern Tamil, modern Malayalam, modern Kannada, modern Telugu, modern Marathi, modern Gujarathi, modern Hindi, modern Oriya, modern Bengali, modern Assamese, and modern Urdu and reject books in the pedantic, medieval, and archaic forms of these languages except in libraries intended to promote linguistic studies or historical criticism. (Sec DD31).

1.14 Select the book which is written with flair in a simple clear style. (Sec DD81).

Illustration

1.15 Select a book which is illustrated adequately with well-drawn, well-printed, apt pictures, diagrams, histograms etc., whichever be appropriate to the standard, style, and subject of the book. (Sec DE15).

1.16 For infants and neo-literates, select books in which the proportion of letterpress to illustration in each page is very low, say, 10 per cent. For children of different ages and for adults removed from the stage of neo-literacy by different degrees, select books in which the proportion of letterpress to illustration in each page increases with the age or the stage of removal from neo-literacy respectively. (Sec DE16).

1.17 In selecting atlas, give weight to accuracy, clarity, functional use of colour, hachuring, producing a dimensional illusion, and overall attractiveness. (Sec DE41).

Index to Book

1.18 Select that edition of a work that contains an index in preference to one without an index. Among those with indexes, select the edition that has the fullest one. Among those with full ones, select the edition that has a Relative Index, and even better the edition that has an Expressive Index. (Sec DF41).

Standard of Exposition

1.19 Match the standard of exposition of books to the standard-scatter among the clientele. In the last resort, this may require scanning through the pages of books. (Sec DG81).

Reference Book

1.20 In selecting an encyclopaedia, pay attention to the names of the contributors, the extent of bibliography attached to each article, and the thoroughness of coverage. (Sec DH11).

1.21 In the case of a guide book, select the latest edition. (Sec DH21).

1.22 In the case of a statistical reference book, make the selection cover as much of the run of its earlier volumes, as the specialist collection in the library would demand. (Sec DH31).

1.23 Select that year-book, in a subject field, that has the maximum of

1 Reliability and up-to-dateness of information ;

2 Extent of coverage ; and

3 Provision of bibliography wherever warranted. (Sec DH41).

1.24 Have a decreasing scale of favoured countries, Constituent States, districts, and cities. The library's own city, district, constituent state, country, and world as a whole should naturally occupy the first five positions in the scale. In selecting national biographies and Who's Who. go down the scale so established as far as necessary, sufficient, and practicable. (Sec DH51).

1.25 Select linguistic dictionaries giving meanings of words and phrases respectively and a thesaurus in the language of the library. In the selection of bi-lingual dictionaries, select those with the language of the library as one of the languages and having for the respective second languages as many as found necessary down the scale of languages of the library. (Sec DH61).

1.26 Select an atlas with :

1 Up-to-date information embodied in it ;

2 Clear reference grids in addition to latitude and longitude, in order to facilitate location ;

3 Bias to home country or home continent, and with exhaustive index and pronunciation of place-names.

Prefer a loose-leaf atlas with follow-up of corrected leaves from time to time on an annual subscription basis, if available ; and, otherwise buy new editions at important epochs.

Select also special atlases with subject-bias such as physical, historical, economic, and so on. (Sec DH81).

1.27 For a generalist or a public library, select general bibliographies of wide coverage ; and for a specialist library, select the *ad hoc* closed bibliographies as well as documentation periodicals in the subject of specialisation, giving preference to abstracting periodicals over mere indexing ones unless the selection of both is financially possible, and to reviewing or trend-report periodicals. (Sec DJ73).

Appeal of Book

1.28 In a public library, select, in a suitable proportion, informative, elevatingly recreative, and inspiring books. In a specialist library, select books of the needed standards in the umbral subject of specialisation and in the related penumbral subjects. (Sec DK43).

1.29 Avoid books of bibliophilic value in an ordinary service-library, not meant for bibliophiles. But select them exhaustively for bibliotaph libraries. (Sec DL31).

Aid to Selection

1.30 The ideal is to select a book only after inspection and perusal. Conform to this ideal whenever and wherever facilities exist for it — either in the form of the chief book centre being not far from the library or of book-sellers or the agents of publishers taking the books from place to place. (Sec DM11).

Financial Factor

1.31 Allow seventeen months, from after the date of communication of the amount granted, to spend that amount, without enforcing the traditional limit of the end of the financial year. (Sec DM21).

1.32 Allow the unspent balance of the budget allotment for books in one year to be added to the normal budget allotment for books in the succeeding year. (Sec DM22).

Additional Aid to Book Selection

1.33 Whenever the available local experts are not sure of the standard and the value of a newly published book merely on the basis of the name of the author or of the publisher or of the series to which the book may belong, base its selection on reviews appearing in periodicals including newspapers. (Sec DM31).

1.34 As an aid to book selection, a librarian should develop special knowledge about the publishers and the publisher's series specialising in reliable, worth-while, and well-built books in different subject fields. He should also familiarise himself with the name of the outstanding authors of the past. He should further be on the alert to know the names of newly emerging reliable authors. (Sec DM41).

1.35 As an aid to book selection, a librarian should maintain a list of the special editions where the term 'Edition' is virtually equivalent to the term 'Series'. This is particularly necessary in respect of the Classics in Sanskrit. (Sec DM51).

Errors in Book Selection

1.36 Unless duplication is deliberately intended, do not select a new edition of a book without satisfying yourself that it is substantially different from its earlier edition in the library. Unless you have access to a copy of the new edition, insist on the vendor verifying the matter before supply is made. (Sec DM61).

1.37 Do not select a book merely on the ground of your own liking or for satisfying the liking of the individual members of the Library Authority, if it will not be of real demand among the clientele of the library. (Sec DM71).

1.38 In selecting books, have the stamina to resist the insistence of pressure groups. Remember that a sacred trust is being discharged so as to give the right books to the readers; do not allow your conscience to be weakened by indolence, or fear of any kind, or to proneness to bluffing born out of careerism. (Sec DM38).

Coverage of Subjects

1.39 Select books and periodicals from all the regions of knowledge. Vary the proportion among the diverse regions according to the nature of the library — generalist or specialist — and in the latter according to the mental age of the clientele. (Sec DN39).

1.40 In a generalist library, book selection should give dominance to subjects of emotional appeal — such as fiction, biography, travel, drama, poetry, other forms of Fine Arts, and Religion, in the sequence mentioned above. (Sec DP01).

Story Form

1.41 In a children's library, book selection should prefer the story-form of exposition of all kinds of subjects, whether falling within the range of humanities, or social sciences, or natural sciences, or their applications. (Sec DP11).

1.42 Book selection in fiction for neo-literates should prefer short stories to long novels. (Sec DP12).

Censorship

1.43 While book selection should not take up the responsibility for censorship, since a public library is a social institution for the betterment of society, book selection in a public library should abstain from including fiction with anti-social suggestions. (Sec DP13).

1.44 But in a specialist library devoted to research in the development of literature, book selection should include all fictions — elevating or otherwise. (Sec DP14).

Biography

1.45 In a children's library, next to story-form of exposition, book selection should prefer the biographical form not only in subjects falling within the area of social sciences and humanities but also of the natural sciences and their applications. (Sec DP21).

1.46 In a generalist library, book selection should cover the biographies of eminent persons in all the fields of knowledge. (Sec DP22).

1.47 In a specialist library, biographies of persons in the subject of specialisation concerned should form an important fringe area for book selection. (Sec DP23).

Travel and History

1.48 In a generalist library, book selection should pay special attention to impressionist books of travel and history. (Sec DP33).

1.49 In a specialist library, book selection should prefer objective, factual books of travel and history, and also books of an evaluating nature in history. (Sec DP34).

Drama

1.50 In a generalist library — be it for children, or neo-literates, or normal adults, — book selection should give full representation to collections of one-act plays, in addition to conventional plays of many acts. (Sec DP41).

1.51 In a specialist library devoted to histrionic art or movie production, over and above the dramas and the dramatised versions of poems, biography, travel, and fiction, book selection should also include the materials needed for the cultural-setting necessary for providing the correct historico-cultural setting for the dramas. (Sec DP42).

Translation

1.52 Book selection should include the translations, into the language of the library, of the best books written in other languages on diverse subjects. (Sec DP51).

Literature

1.53 Book selection should include anthologies of literary works. (Sec DP62).

1.54 The librarian should take the help of a literary connoisseur in the selection of books in the Main Class Literature. (Sec DP63).

1.55 In a public library and in an educational library, apart from specialist libraries in Fine Arts, book selection should include art materials reproduced in graphic form or in sound form. (Sec DP65).

Evaluative Books

1.56 In a college or a university library and in a specialist library devoted to literature, book selection should give full coverage to evaluative writings. (Sec DP72).

1.57 In a public library, book selection should include at least a small assortment of evaluative writings. (Sec DP73).

1.58 Book selection should give representation to writings embodying normative principles for the production of poetry, drama, fiction, and other literary forms. (Sec DP75).

Fine Arts

1.59 In a specialist library in Fine Arts, book selection should give full coverage to writings embodying normative principles in the Fine Arts concerned. (Sec DP76)

Mystics

1.60 In a public library, book selection should give a good representation to the lives, the sayings, and the devotional lyrics of mystics. (Sec DP81).

Religion

1.61 In a public library, book selection should give a balanced coverage of the books on diverse religions. (Sec DP82).

Linguistics and Philosophy

1.62 Book selection in linguistics and in philosophy will have to vary in coverage according to the library being a generalist or a specialist one. (Sec DP83).

Social Sciences

1.63 Books embodying scientific and statistical study of the subjects falling within the area of social sciences are suitable to a specialist or a university library rather than to a generalist one. (Sec DQ21).

Data Book

1.64 Books embodying statistical data and fact-finding reports of governmental and non-governmental agencies are suitable to a specialist or a university library rather than to a generalist one. (Sec DQ31).

Propaganda Book

1.65 Book selection should give a balanced representation to propaganda books of all groups, unless they can be totally excluded. (Sec DQ41).

Descriptive Book

1.66 In a generalist library, perhaps also in a specialist library, book selection should give a good coverage to the descriptive books in each subject in the social sciences. (Sec DQ51).

1.67 Book selection should give a balanced representation to all the systems of thought in the diverse subjects in social sciences. (Sec DQ61).

Book of Topical Interest

1.68 In any library — and particularly in a generalist library — selection of books of topical interest should be made quite promptly and in anticipation of the demand for them. (Sec DQ71).

1.69 Book selection may have to include several copies of books of topical interest in the measure of anticipated demand. (Sec DQ72).

Know-how Books

1.70 In a school library, book selection should include know-how books written in a low key with plenty of illustrations, in order to satisfy the abundant curiosity and the urge to do in children, and not confine itself merely to books covered by the curriculum. (Sec DR11).

1.71 In a public library and in a factory library, book selection should include know-how books for the use of workers not high up in the intellectual scale. (Sec DR12).

Books on Arts and Crafts

1.72 In view of the wide scatter of interest among people, book selection should give representation to every possible art and craft and to sports. (Sec DR21).

1.73 In a country such as India just recovering from cultural exhaustion, book selection should, as a transitory measure, include books in arts and crafts produced in a foreign language widely used in the country — for example, English in India or French in Algeria. (Sec DR31).

Hand Book

1.74 In the field of applied sciences, book selection should include the latest editions of the serial handbooks, giving data and specifications in their respective subjects and getting published annually or at other intervals. (Sec DR41).

Text book

1.75 In a college library, book selection should allot more money to a variety of text books and confine itself only to a few general periodicals and encyclopaedic treatises. (Sec DS31).

Periodical Publications

1.76 In a research library including a university library, book selection should allot more money to periodicals, serials, encyclopaedic reference books, and advanced treatises, than to ordinary book. (Sec DS32).

Popular Publications

1.77 In a generalist library — be it a public library or a children's library — book selection should include a good assortment of popular books and periodicals on the latest thought in the different subjects in the natural sciences — both physical sciences and biological sciences — written with flair and with plenty of illustrations but free from jargon or technical details and yet without loss of accuracy. (Sec DS41).

CHAPTER BB

MESSAGES OF LAW 2

Note. At the end of each message the sub-section in the text, where it is formulated, is mentioned. Its parent section in the text expounds the message.

Reader's Interest

Expert's Help

2.1 In a specialist library and a university library, prepare book selection cards for currently published books of the appropriate standard, group them under subject headings determined by the subject-field of specialisation of the experts, and circulate periodically each group of cards to the appropriate group of experts requesting each expert to express his selection or rejection in a specific place in the book selection card. (Sec EB11).

Pedlar Method

2.2 Play the pedlar by taking lists of currently published books to potential readers. This is essential in a specialist library. In a generalist library, approximate to this as much as possible. (Sec EB21).

Shop-keeper Method

2.3 Play the shop-keeper by discussing the book needs of each reader coming to the library, and by scanning with him the list of currently published books. (Sec EB31).

Reference Librarian's Help

2.4 Get the help of the reference librarian. Ask him to note the books needed by readers but not in the collection of the library. Make use of his notes. (Sec EB41).

Suggestion Book

2.5 Maintain a Suggestion Book. Help readers to understand the broad book selection policy of the library. Scan the Suggestion Book periodically and make the best possible use of it. (Sec EB51).

Subject Scatter

PUBLIC LIBRARY

2.6 In a public library, a vocational survey of the locality and the study of the subject scatter of the books used will jointly give much help in book selection. (Sec ED61).

SCHOOL OR COLLEGE LIBRARY

2.7 In a school or college library, the subjects prescribed for study and the subject-scatter of the books used will jointly give much help in book selection. (Sec ED62).

UNIVERSITY LIBRARY

2.8 In a university library, the subjects of research and the subject-scatter of the books used will jointly give much help in book selection. (Sec ED63).

SPECIALIST LIBRARY

2.9 In a specialist library, work out the subject-scatter in the Apupa region of the subject of specialisation, with several sub-divisions for the umbral subject, as the basis for book selection. (Sec ED91).

Standard-Scatter

SCHOOL OR COLLEGE LIBRARY

2.10 In a school or a college library, book selection should care for each of the standards at which pupils or students are found in the school or in the college respectively. Further, the proportion of the books of the different standards should be determined by the number of pupils or students found in the respective standards. Many copies of different text-books should be selected. (Sec EE11).

PUBLIC LIBRARY

2.11 In a public library, find out the few standards in which readers are found and select books in each of the standards. The proportion of the books of the different standards should be determined by the number of readers found in the respective standards. (Sec EE21).

UNIVERSITY LIBRARY

2.12 In a university or a research library, select only books of a high standard leaving books of a low standard to the college library or the public library as the case may be. (Sec EE31).

2.13 In a residential unitary university library, make book selection as for both a college library and a research library. (Sec EE32).

BUSINESS LIBRARY

2.14 In an industrial, or commercial, or other business library — a specialist library other than research library — select more books of application including trade lists, commercial catalogues, and statistical and descriptive publications than of books of high theoretical standard, of which only a few representative books need to be selected. (Sec EE41).

Language Scatter

PUBLIC LIBRARY IN A UNILINGUAL LOCALITY

2.15 In the public library of unilingual locality, give the greatest representation to books in the language of the area. Select also some books in the classical language of the area and in one or two modern foreign languages, including in countries such as India, the languages of the other States in the measure of the language scatter of the people of the locality. (Sec EF11).

PUBLIC LIBRARY IN A POLYGLOT LOCALITY

2.16 In the public library of a polyglot locality, the representation in book selection of the different languages in use should be related to the language scatter of the people of the locality. This applies not only to the public library system of a city as a whole but also severally to the branch library in each of its divisions or zones. (Sec EF21).

UNIVERSITY OR RESEARCH LIBRARY

2.17 In a university or other research library, book selection should also include important periodicals, reference books, classical works, and compendious treatises in the different foreign languages, in the measure of the importance of the communication in those languages and as indicated by the language scatter of the users. (Sec EF31).

VARIANT SCATTER

2.18 Pay attention to the variant scatter of the language of the library as determined by the impression of reference librarian and by field survey. (Sec EF41).

POTENTIAL WANT

2.19 Do not stop with the expressed want as inferred from the subject-scatter of accession, the subject-scatter of circulation, and other indications of the wants of the past; but use your knowledge of the changing social needs, the intellectual possibility, and the changing emotional wants of the community, and select books accordingly so as to serve and exploit such needs and possibilities. (Sec EG11).

2.20 Keep yourself ever alert to re-assess the potential unexpressed wants of readers from time to time.

Anticipated Want

SCHOOL OR COLLEGE LIBRARY

2.21 In a school or a college library, book selection should be done in consultation with the members of the teaching faculty at the end of each academic year so as to put on the shelves, from the beginning onwards of the next academic year, books necessary to meet the needs of the curriculum — not merely the prescribed books but also the books needed for preparatory, parallel, and follow-up study. (Sec EH11).

UNIVERSITY AND RESEARCH LIBRARY

2.22 In a university or a research library, book selection should be done from time to time in consultation with the members of the faculty or the research body, so as to put on the shelves the books needed in the anticipated change in the research activities, in good time before the changes take place. (Sec EH21).

GOVERNMENT DEPARTMENTAL LIBRARY

2.23 In a government departmental library including that of the legislature, contemplated development schemes, legislative measures, and policy-making should be watched with vigilance. The department concerned should take the librarian into confidence and alert him in good time. Book selection should be done immediately in collaboration with the persons concerned in the department. (Sec EH31).

BUSINESS LIBRARY

2.24 In a business library, the librarian should keep himself informed of all anticipated developments in each of the departments and select the books necessary to make the decision in the action of the department concerned conform to the latest theory and practice in the matter. (Sec EH41).

Public Library

2.25 In a public library, book selection should be made in anticipation in the light of the forthcoming international, national, and local events and occurrences. (Sec EH51).

Reference Book

Public Library

2.26 In a public library, select a good assortment of reference books such as biographical dictionaries and serials, directories of the locality and of other important cities, travel aids such as railway, shipping, and air guides, and tourist books, anthologies, linguistic dictionaries, and encyclopaedias of a general nature and in such of the subjects as are of local interest. (Sec EJ11).

University or Research Library

2.27 In a university or a research library, select as many as possible of authoritative reference books in each subject of study. These should include bibliographies, directories of learned world, encyclopaedias, linguistic dictionaries — particularly technical ones — trend reports, patents, standards, and specifications. (Sec EJ12).

Language

2.28 Select reference books in English to supplement those in Indian languages. Further, create public opinion for the production of reference books of all kinds in each Indian language. (Sec EJ21).

Survey Method in Book Selection

2.29 In a country, such as India, recovering from cultural exhaustion and just developing thereafter, book selection will have to be based for some years not merely on statistics of issue but essentially on field survey of and personal contact with potential readers. (Sec EK21).

Integrity of Librarian

2.30 High character and integrity on the part of the library profession should be brought to bear on the discharge of its duties in regard to book selection along with an all-round attempt to assess the potential wants of the readers — free from any sneaking tendency to please the whims and fancies of the individual members of the Library Authorities. (Sec EK21).

Periodicals

PUBLIC LIBRARY

2.31 In a public library, selection of periodicals should cover a few generalia periodicals of the popular variety and some specialised periodicals bearing on the chief vocations of the people of the locality as determined by field survey. (Sec EL11).

SCHOOL LIBRARY

2.32 In a school library, selection of periodicals should cover children's periodicals capable of entertaining and informing them on the one hand, and developing in them, on the other hand, the habit of perusing periodicals. (Sec EL12).

BUSINESS LIBRARY

2.33 In the library of a business organization, selection of periodical publications should cover the periodicals and the serials falling within the umbral region of interest of the parent body and also of a few appropriate ones falling within the penumbral region of interest. (Sec EL13).

UNIVERSITY OR RESEARCH LIBRARY

2.34 In a university or a research library, selection should cover periodical publications falling within the purview of the subject of their specialisation and also on the subjects auxiliary to them. (Sec EL14).

Continuity of Periodical

2.35 In a university or a research library, cutting down the subscription to a periodical in one year, restoring it in the next year, and cutting it down later will cause an inconvenient break in the set. Once the trial period is over and a decision is made to take the periodical, it should be continued until the standard of the periodical goes down abnormally. (Sec EL21).

BUSINESS LIBRARY

2.36 In an industrial or other business library, the continuity or otherwise of a periodical publication is best determined from year to year by the needs of the work in progress in the parent body. (Sec EL22).

Continuity in Periodical Selection

2.37 In a generalist library, be it a public or a college or a school library, freedom may be taken in the policy of continuity or otherwise in the case of a periodical not to be bound and preserved, according to the policy of the library. (Sec EL23).

Continuity of Serials

2.38 In the case of a serial, other than a statistical one, it may be possible to subscribe for it at intervals, say, every other year or once in three years. (Sec EL24).

2.39 In a library such as a research or a university library preserving a continuous set of volumes of a periodical, its successive cumulative indexes should be bought as and when published. (Sec EL31).

Newspaper

2.40 In a public library, make a balanced selection of newspapers — balanced in respect of their political, economic, and social leanings. (Sec EL41).

2.41 Avoid selecting common newspapers for a library other than a public library or a reading room. (Sec EL42).

Sub-normal Reader

Blind Reader

2.42 Bear in mind the humane responsibility to provide books in Braille or in sound records for the blind. (Sec EM11).

Cripple Reader

2.43 Bear in mind the humane responsibility to provide ceiling books for the cripple confined to bed. (Sec EM21).

Neo-literate

2.44 Select sound books for the neo-literates. If they are not already available, work for their production. (Sec EM31).

CHAPTER BC

MESSAGES OF LAW 3

Note. At the end of each message, the sub-section in the text, where it is formulated, is mentioned. Its parent section in the text expounds the message.

New book

3.1 Remember to include in the book selection list new and attractive books likely to lure their readers towards some of the books of the library, failing in their appeal to readers, and thereby to increase the probability for such old books to be put back into circulation. (Sec FC11).

3.2 To enhance the lure-effect of a new book on the old books, select such a new book as has a good bibliography. (Sec FC12).

Associated book

3.3 Select books so as to exploit the mutual dependence of books in cases, such as, a

1 Classic and the hierarchy of its commentaries ;
2 Original and its translations ;
3 Book on a theory and its applications ;
4 Expository book and the related laboratory handbooks ;
5 Law book and case studies on the law concerned ;
6 Source books and treatises ;
7 Original and its evaluations ; and
8 Books belonging to a publisher's series. (Sec FD21).

3.4 In a school library, select books so as to exploit the mutual dependance of pupil's books and the related teacher's handbook. (Sec FD22).

Exposition

LANGUAGE

3.5 Do not select books in a language not understood by the readers of the library. (Sec FE11).

STANDARD

3.6 Do not select any book of a standard, which has few readers among the clientele of the library. (Sec FE21).

SUBJECT

3.7 In a specialist library, do not select books in subjects not falling within the field of study of the library, including its fringe area. (Sec FE31).

3.8 In a generalist library, do not select books in a subject not likely to be of interest to any reader, either for intensive study or even for general acquaintance. (Sec FE32).

Misleading Title

3.9 Avoid selecting a book by the title alone without examining either the book itself or a review or an annotation on it, lest its subject should be outside the purview of the library or without any interest to any reader. (Sec FE41).

Responsibility

PUBLIC LIBRARY

3.10 In a public library, the responsibility for book selection should be vested in the library staff who alone can have the experience necessary to assess the probability for a book to find its readers. (Sec FF11).

ACADEMIC LIBRARY

3.11 In an academic library — be it a university, a college, or a school library — book selection should be the joint responsibility of the library staff and the teaching staff; they should be guided by the probability of getting readers for the use of the book selected. (Sec FF21).

BUSINESS LIBRARY

3.12 In a business library — such as industrial, commercial, government departmental library — book selection should be the joint responsibility of the library and the representatives of the different divisions of the parent body. (Sec FF22).

Patronage Motive

3.13 Book selection in any library should be based on the probability for readers, and should never be vitiated by consideration of patronage. (Sec FF31).

Foreign Books

3.14 In the utilisation of the fund of a library, set apart for books to be purchased from foreign countries, do not make a fetish of the absolute 31 March fixed by audit or budget. Work on the basis of the relative time limit of seventeen months after the sanction of the book fund. (Sec FG51).

Sacred Trust

3.15 A librarian should regard the responsibility for book selection vested in him as a sacred trust to be discharged in the best interest of the legitimate clientele of his library. (Sec FH41).

CHAPTER BD

MESSAGES OF LAW 4

Note. At the end of each message, the sub-section in the text, where it is formulated, is mentioned. Its parent section in the text expounds the message.

Rhythm of Work

4.1 Do not adopt the long leisurely rhythm of one year, six months, or even three months. Adopt the weekly rhythm, and in exceptional cases the monthly rhythm. (Sec GB21).

Elimination of Time Lag

4.2 To eliminate time lag, book selection may, with due circumspection, base itself on the advance announcements of books by publishers of repute. (Sec GB2).

Bibliography

4.3 Select up-to-date bibliographies of the subjects covered by the library. (Sec GC31).

4.4 Select that form of the bibliography available, which comes latest in the following list:

1 Author-list;
2 Chronological list;
3 Dictionary list by the name, authors, and subjects;
4 Subject list with broad subject headings;
5 Minutely classified list. (Sec GD11).

Annotated Bibliography

4.5 Select annotated bibliographies of books in all the subjects covered by the library. (Sec GD31).

4.6 The annotated bibliographies selected for a library, primarily to save the time of the readers, will serve also the secondary purpose of saving the time of the staff engaged in book selection. (Sec GE32).

Documentation List

4.7 In a generalist library such as a public or a college or a school library, select documentation lists giving a list of general and popular articles on the subjects covered by the library. (Sec GG21).

4.8 In a specialist library and in a university library, select as exhaustively as possible closed documentation lists on the subjects of specialization. (Sec GG22).

Documentation Periodical

Indexing Periodical

4.9 In a generalist library such as a public, a college, or a school library, select indexing periodicals giving a list of general and popular articles on the subjects covered by the library. (Sec GH71).

4.10 In a specialist library and in a university library, select as exhaustively as possible indexing periodicals on the subjects of specialization. (Sec GH72).

4.11 In a specialist library and in a university library, select the National Documentation List without fail. (Sec GH81).

Abstracting Periodical

4.12 In a specialist library and in a university library, select as exhaustively as possible abstracting periodicals on the subjects of specialization. (Sec GJ81).

Reporting Periodical

4.13 In a specialist library and in a university library, select as exhaustively as possible reporting periodicals on the subject of specialization. (Sec GK31).

Short Communications Periodical

4.14 In a specialist library and in a university library, select as exhaustively as possible 'Short Communication' periodicals on the subject of specialisation. (Sec GK42).

Pre-view Type Periodical

4.15 In a specialist library and in a university library, select as exhaustively as possible 'Pre-view' type periodicals on the subject of specialisation. (Sec GK51).

Reference Book

4.16 Select as many reference books as possible in all the subjects of interest to the clientele of the library. (Sec GL11).

Book of Topical Interest

4.17 Select a reasonable number of copies of books of topical interest in any library and of text-books in an academic library. (Sec GM21).

Anthology

4.18 Select a sumptuous assortment of anthologies to meet all interests. (Sec GN21).

Source Book

4.19 Select a sumptuous assortment of source books to meet all interests. (Sec GN31).

4.20 Select all multi-commentary editions. (Sec GP11).

4.21 Select variorum editions of the works of diverse authors. (Sec GP21).

CHAPTER BE

MESSAGES OF LAW 5

Note. At the end of each message the sub-section, in the text where the message is formulated, is mentioned. Its parent section expounds the message.

National Central Library

5.1 A National Central Library and a State Central Library should select the micro reprograph form for preservation and the conventional form for current use. (Sec HB31).

Local Service Library

5.2 In a local service library, book selection should resort to the selection of micro reprograph form of a publication only on grounds of :

1 Non-availability of a copy of the original publication in actual demand — either for purchase or for inter-library loan ; or

2 The cost being cheaper than that of the original publication, if needed only very sparingly by specialist readers. (Sec HB41).

Duplication

5.3 Book selection should be prepared to progressively change over to an increasing number of copies being selected in the case of an increasing number of books to meet simultaneous demand, by the readers. (Sec HB51).

Staggered Demand

5.4 Even if the increase of readers leads, not to simultaneous demand for the same book, but only to staggered demand, book selection will have to take extra-copies of the book, for replacing the copy worn out by use, if rebinding will not be cheaper, (Sec HB52).

Classics

5.5 Select new editions of classics from time to time. (Sec HC21).

Translation

5.6 Select translations, into the language of the library, of works in other languages — foreign as well as classical — to the extent available. (Sec HD11).

5.7 Select translations, into the language of the library, of a work in a classical language even though the original is in the library. (Sec HD12).

Foreign Language

5.8 For works in foreign languages, without any translations in the language of the library, select translations into the language coming earliest in the scale of languages of the library. (Sec HD21).

5.9 In a specialist library, make a liberal selection of books in foreign languages bearing on the subject of its specialization. (Sec HD31).

5.10 In a specialist library, make as complete a selection as possible, of periodicals in foreign languages bearing on the subject of its specialization. (Sec HD32).

5.11 In a specialist library, select translations, into the language of the library, of periodicals in foreign languages, wherever available and financially viable. (Sec HD41).

5.12 In a specialist library, selection of a periodical in a foreign language is not obligatory, if a translation of it into the language of the library is selected. (Sec HD42).

Bilingual Edition

5.13 Select bilingual and multilingual editions of works with the language of the library as one of the languages of the edition, wherever available. (Sec HD51).

Incomprehensibility

5.14 Don't reject a book because it is difficult. It may be difficult for the present generation but it may become comprehensible for a later generation. Include them in book selection. (Sec HE11).

Intangibility

5.15 Judge not hastily or light-heartedly. Reject not easily. Err on the side of selection rather than rejection. Beware of intangible qualities in writings of the highest kind. (Sec HE21).

CHAPTER BF

JOINT COMPROMISE MESSAGES OF THE FIVE LAWS

Note. At the end of each message the sub-section in the text, where the message is formulated, is mentioned. Its parent section expounds the message.

Capacity

SHELF-CAPACITY

6.1 Book Selection should go on without hindrance in all libraries. In a local service library, space will be found by the weeding out of no-longer-wanted and worn-out books, as its growth is adult-growth. In a National Central Library and in State Central Library, space will be increased to the necessary extent, as its growth is child-growth.
(Sec JB21).

STAFF-CAPACITY

6.2 Insist on a fraction of the fund — say twenty per cent. — to be set apart for the staff — viz, staff for selection, acquisition, accessioning, classifying, and cataloguing. (Sec JB31).

Stringency of Finance

MINIMISE MULTIPLICATION

6.3 Minimise multiplication of copies to the extent to which the rationing of the time of use — say by days and if necessary by hours — can be effected by Administration. (Sec JD11).

GAP IN SERIAL SELECTION

6.4 In a service-library, as distinct from a dormitory library, a serial may be acquired at suitable intervals instead of each year, if the information in it does not vary substantially from year to year. (Sec JD21).

CAREFUL SELECTION OF PERIODICALS

6.5 Restrict the acquisition of periodicals to those in which all the articles are in sufficient demand. For those only in occasional demand, depend on abstracting periodicals and if necessary on the acquisition of individual issues or of reprographs of the stray articles needed by the clientele. (Sec JD31).

Viable Unit System

6.6 Give up the old idea of having small independent libraries everywhere, but consolidate them into large Viable Unit Systems. Centralise and co-ordinate book selection and decentralise book-service. (Sec JE11).

Co-ordination

6.7 Federate the library systems in a Constituent State and make the State Central Library co-ordinate book selection and bring about inter-library loan for less frequently wanted books. (Sec JE21).

6.8 In a large country with many Constituent States, make the National Central Library and the State Central Libraries collaborate with the ultimate library systems. Bring about a Co-ordinated Book Selection Plan, so that books and periodicals published in foreign countries may be secured for the country as a whole in as full measure as possible. Bring about also Inter-State Library Loan both in respect of foreign books and periodicals and in respect of the books and periodicals in the languages of the different Constituent States. (Sec JE31).

Reprograph Service

6.9 Each country should have a National Documentation Centre to have charge of inter-library loan of learned periodicals and the supply of reprographs of micro documents whenever needed. (Sec JE53).

International Co-operation

6.10 Unesco should promote International Library Loan of books and periodicals only in occasional demand in the borrowing country. It should promote also International Reprograph Service. (Sec JE61).

Unbiased Selection

6.11 Do not allow the policy of Book Rejection, forced by finance, to be coloured or influenced by considerations of the orthodoxy or the heterodoxy of the idealogies presented in the book and by even the remotest propensity for censorship. (Sec JF21).

Economy Measure

6.12 As a first economy measure in a public library, reject low level fiction devoid of elevating literary merit. (Sec JF311).

6.13 Minimise, if not omit, selection of newspapers where community radio service is available, in case the book fund does not prove sufficient to take newspapers. (Sec JF411).

6.14 Minimise selection of non-literary, non-scientific, non-craft-centred, low standard, propaganda magazines, without jeopardy to the balance among all schools of thought, if the book fund does not prove sufficient to buy such magazines. (Sec JF421).

Austerity Measure

6.15 These austerity measures, forced by inadequate book fund, are not born out of contempt for the poor or for those lower down in the intellectual scale, but are based on a policy of long-term-return of social benefit to the community as a whole. (Sec JG51).

CHAPTER BG

MESSAGES OF THE FIVE LAWS AND THE STATUS OF THE LIBRARY

Note.

1 Only the numbers of the respective messages are given in this Chapter.

2 In the number of a message, the digit before the point denotes the number of the Chapter. And the integer after the point denotes the number of the message. For example the number 1.16 denotes the Sixteenth Message of the First Law.

1 All Libraries

1.1-26, 1.30-.38, 1.42, 1.52-.54, 1.58, 1.62, 1.65, 1.67, 1.69, 1.72-.74 .

2.2-.5, 2.18-.20, 2.28-.30, 2.38, 2.41 .

3.1-.3, 3.5-.6, 3.9, 3.13-.15 .

4.1-.6, 4.16-.21

5.3-.8, 5.13-.16

6.1-.3, 6.5-.7, 6.9-.15 .

2 National Library

5.1, 6.8 .

3 Public Library

1.27-.29, 1.39-.40, 1.43, 1.46, 1.48, 1.50, 1.55, 1.57, 1.60, 1.61, 1.66, 1.68, 1.71, 1.77 .

2.6, 2.11, 2.15-.16, 2.25-.26, 2.31, 2.37, 2.40

3.8, 3.10 .

4.7, 4.9 .

5.2 .

6.4 .

4 Academic Library in General

3.11 .

41 School Library

1.41, 1.45, 1.70

2.7, 2.10, 2.21, 2.32
3.4 .

42 College Library
1.56, 1.75 .
2.7, 2.10, 2.21 .

43 University Library
1.63-.4, 1.76 .
2.1, 2.8, 2.12, 2.13, 2.17, 2.22, 2.27, 2.34-.5, 2.39 .
4.8, 4.10-.15 .

44 Research Library
1.76 .
2.12, 2.17, 2.22, 2.27, 2.34-.5, 2.39 .

5 Specialist Library

1.44, 1.47, 1.49, 1.51, 1.59, 1.63-.4 .
2.1, 2.9, 2.23 .
3.7 .
4.8, 4.10-.15 .
5.9-.12 .

6 Business Library

2.14, 2.24, 2.33, 2.36 .
3.12 .

7 Special Library

2.42-.44 .

PART C

LINES OF APPROACH

CHAPTER CA

CHANGE OF OUTLOOK

1 Experience of 1956

It was the autumn of 1956. An unusual opportunity came to get a feel of a new awareness coming over the new generation of librarians. The opportunity came in the form of an invitation to visit and to teach in several schools of Library Science in the United Kingdom. This made possible a comparative study of the methods of teaching of the several branches of Library Science current in that country, the practices in some of the schools in India, and the practices observed in USA earlier.

2 Old Outlook

Before beginning the visit, a few hours were spent at the Chaucer House, London, in the company of some friends in the profession. An old friend asked, "What do you intend to teach?" I said, "I have no pre-determined plan. I seldom go to a class room with mind already made up as to what should be taught. I follow Field Psychology. Everything has to emerge from out of the immediate presence of the teacher and the taught together." My friend gave the advice, "Do not assume that our students know your Laws of Library Science." I said, "I assume nothing in advance."

3 New Outlook

I then went to the first School to be visited by me. There were about 50 students. I told the class, "Let us get started by one of you posing a problem for discussion!" The first response to this totally contradicted the estimate of the students' awareness of the latest ideas in the air, given by my elderly librarian friend at the Chaucer House. A student started the work of the class by saying, in effect, "We all enjoy your book on the Five Laws of Library Science. They provide a means to understand our subject with some human interest. I find that you have written books on several subjects in Library Science using the Five Laws as the starting point. You have written books of that kind on classification, cataloguing, reference service, organization, administration, and physical bibliography. Some of us have enjoyed them. They have made us like these subjects. But why you have not written a similar book on Book Selection. " I asked, " Are you sure that I have not done so?" A student replied in effect, " I know that some of the sections in your book *Five laws of library science* deal with book selection in that way. But so also have all the other subjects been dealt with in that book. Why have you not written exclusively a book on Book Selection based on your laws?" When I said that I had written, she replied that it was not in their library. However, somebody brought the book from the library collection. Its Chapter Headings were as follows:

1 First Law and Book Selection
2 Second Law and Book Selection
3 Third Law and Book Selection
4 Fourth Law and Book Selection
5 Fifth Law and Book Selection
6 Conflict of Laws and Book Selection

The student said, " Is there such a book? Then we shall read it ourselves. You need not use this hour to develop the theory of Book Selection. We shall discuss with you some other problems giving us difficulty."

CHAPTER CB

A Priori APPROACH

1 Effect of Formulation of Fundamental Laws

The change of outlook mentioned in Chapter CA is significant. This change in outlook is coming over the new generation of librarians, though overlooked and even resisted by the older generation. This change in outlook is the result of our now having Fundamental Laws governing every technique and practice in library science and library service.

2 Nature of Fundamental Laws

As in every other discipline the Fundamental Laws are elemental and general in this field also. They may be said to be almost trivial. Their potency in designing library techniques and organising the library service may not be obvious. And yet the fundamental laws include them all in a latent form.

3 Deduced Principles

To make an *a priori* approach to Book Selection on the basis of the fundamental laws, it is necessary to lay bare, in the form of derived principles, all the implications of the Fundamental Laws in respect of Book Selection. In other words, the Principles of Book Selection should be deduced from the Five Laws. These deduced principles will constitute the corpus of the theory of Book Selection.

4 Analogy

The theory of every other branch of library science is similarly made of principles deduced from the Five Laws of Library Science. The Principles are called "Canons" in the case of Classification. The Canons of Classification are enumerated in my *Prolegomena to library classification*, Ed 3 (1967). The corpus of the theory of classification is not determined directly from the Five Laws but through these derived principles called "Canons". Similarly in

Cataloguing we do not draw the theory directly from the Five Laws. What we do is to make use of the Canons of Cataloguing as the basis of the corpus of the Theory of Cataloguing. They are enumerated in Part B of my *Classified catalogue code*, Ed 5, (1964). So it is with every branch of library science including Book Selection.

5 Boundary Conditions

A library is a social institution. Library Science therefore falls in the area of Social Sciences. The social outlook, the social purpose, and the social range of any social institution or activity change from age to age. Therefore, the Fundamental Laws of any branch of social science may change with the boundary conditions set by society from time to time, on social outlook, social purpose, and social range. Even when they do not themselves change, the derived principles in respect of a branch of the social science may have to be varied with the boundary conditions set by the society. For our current use then, the principles of Book Selection should be deduced from the Five Laws of Library Science, subject to the boundary condition now prevailing in the society.

CHAPTER CC

PRAGMATIC APPROACH

1 Pre-Five Laws Period

The Five Laws of Library Science were formulated only in 1928 and published only in 1931. But Book Selection has been going on all along — even long before their formulation. Even in that period, some Principles of Book Selection had been evolved. They had been evolved not by deduction but by induction. The very early librarians should have made Book Selection with the help of their experience and flair.

2 Empirical Method

The empirical method would consist of field work in libraries. The way in which Book Selection is made would be observed in various kinds of libraries. The results of observation would be generalised. That would be a long and laborious process. This process was not readily available in India in the conditions prevailing till a generation ago. For, India had been in a state of cultural exhaustion for a few centuries. It was during this period that printing was invented and brought to a high level of efficiency. It was during this period again — indeed only during the last one hundred years — that education and library service came to be conceded as the right of every citizen. Therefore, India had few libraries till a generation ago. However, a tradition about Book Selection and a set of Principles of Book Selection had developed in some of the countries of Europe and America. These have formed the corpus of the Theory of Book Selection. India can and does draw help from this Theory of Book Selection.

3 Blending of the *a priori* and Pragmatic Methods

A discipline becomes a mature one when it outgrows the pragmatic stage and bases itself on fundamental laws admitting of *a priori* approach. When the stage of maturity is reached, further progress in the discipline is not based on either purely pragmatic or purely *a priori* method. On the other hand, the pragmatic and the *a priori* methods are blended with care. The method obtained by so blending generally proves helpful. It is such a method that is used in this book in developing a Theory of Book Selection. Each principle so derived is presented in the text as a message from an appropriate Law of Library Science. The messages so derived are 188.

Part D

FIRST LAW OF LIBRARY SCIENCE AND BOOK SELECTION

CHAPTER DA

FIRST LAW

1 Enunciation

The First Law of Library Science is "Books are for use". What is the message of this Law to the Theory of Book Selection? It would ask us in the first place to pay attention to each of the words "Selection" and "Book".

2 Selection

It would ask us to remember that selection automatically implies rejection. Selection and rejection are only two ways of looking at the same operation. It would also ask us to remember that selection would involve judgement. There may be near-equal alternative decisions about selection and rejection from among the books considered.

3 Book

When we look at the other word "Book", the First Law would employ the well-known rule of *Panchatantra* — Divide and Rule. It would ask us to recognise the composite nature of a book. Indeed it would bring back to our mind that a book is a trinity. It is a trinity of the

1 Gross body (the physique, the binding, the paper and the print);

2 Subtle body (the language, the style, and the standard of exposition); and

3 Soul (the thought-content or the subject matter) of the book.

The First Law would first break down the idea "Book" into these three sub-ideas. It will then pursue this breaking down process still further in each case until the principles of selection appear.

CHAPTER DB

PHYSIQUE OF THE BOOK

1 Attractive Get-up

Let us first consider a book as a physical entity. Let us imagine our approaching the book from a distance. The First Law will say, " A book is an artificial commodity. It has ultimately to appeal to the intellect in man. The intellectual interest is neither easily roused nor sustained for long. The soul of a book has therefore to invoke the potentiality of its physique to entice the primary senses. Make the book therefore as attractive, easy to handle, pleasing to read, and strong enough to stand use."

11 MESSAGE 1

The first message of the First Law to Book Selection is :

Select that edition of a work, that has an attractive get-up.

2 Easy to Handle

What are the factors that can make or mar the ease of handling a book as a physical entity ? What are the physical qualities of a book that will recommend its selection ? The same qualities, more or less, that play a prominent part in the selection of many things in life. Suppose we have to select a house. What are the physical qualities that will determine selection ? Surely we should like the house to have a convenient lay out and shape. Secondly, it should be of a comfortable size. A house of twenty rooms for a family of four members will be a burden rather than a help. Surely no wise man will select that house, nor can one select a single-room house for that family. Comfort in size is something which is definite and which is uniquely determined in each context. Or again take the case of determining physical qualities which normally weigh in the selection of personnel. We would all prefer a straight body to a hunch-back. We would reject a Brobdingian at one end and a Liliputian at the other. The optimum size for a human body goes perhaps with a height lying between $5\frac{1}{2}$ and 6 feet and the other dimensions in graceful proportion. Let us pursue the physical qualities of a book in a similar way. Surely three well-known qualities of any physical body are: 1 Shape; 2 Size; and 3 Weight. Let us examine what exactly is the message of the First Law of Library Science in regard to each of these three physical qualities of a book.

3 Shape

What are the possible shapes of a book? Since the last few generations have been accustomed to a particular shape of printed books, this question may appear to be unnecessary. But even today, we have certain books with an out-of-the-way shape. Take for example the maps. They are in the form of rolls. I saw in the Public Library of Philadelphia a whole Indian book in the form of a roll. The title of the book was *Horoscope of Rajah Fadhunathan Sinha, one of Tippu Sahib's Officers at Lucknow.* Before the discovery of printing, many books were in this difficult-to-handle shape — much to the chagrin of the First Law. In fact this shape gave those books the name " Roll ". We find that term still surviving in the designation of an important officer of Her Majesty the Queen of the British Isles — Keeper of the Rolls. Surely a shape like that is not conducive to use. The First Law will certainly reject that shape. The shape that has established itself as the most easy to handle is the cuboidal one.

31 Message 2

The second message of the First Law to Book Selection is:

Select that edition of a work, that is cuboidal in shape.

4 Size

Similarly to make books easy to handle, the First Law would ask for certain limits within which the size of a book should lie. Since we have decided cuboid as the favoured shape for a book, it is enough if we mention the height, the ratio between the height and the width, and the thickness which will make the book easy to handle. Extremes which are unacceptable to the First Law easily come to mind. A miniature book — 1″ in height, $\frac{3}{4}$″ in width, and say 1″ in thickness — will not be accepted by the First Law. Such books do exist. There are many such miniature editions of the *Koran* and the *Gita*. At the other extreme, I remember seeing a giant book in the Royal Library at Stockholm, Sweden. Its pages measured 76 cm by 48 cm. There are even bigger giants.

41 MESSAGE 3

The third message of the First Law to Book Selection is :

Select that edition of a work, that has a height between 15 cm and 25 cm, a width roughly about seven-tenths of the height, and a thickness not more than 5 cm.

5 Weight

To minimise the strain in the handling of books, care must be taken to see that a book is not too heavy. Undue weight may be due to two causes. Firstly, it may be a book of a great number of pages. Secondly, the paper used may be highly loaded with clay. The first cause for weight is usually found in books of reference — that is, books not meant for continuous reading. Webster's *New international dictionary of the English language* is an example. Such books are not likely to be held in hand while being consulted. At any rate, it is difficult to reduce the weight in their case. On the other hand, the second cause for weight can be avoided. In fact, the First Law would plead with the producers of books to abstain from using loaded paper.

51 MESSAGE 4

The fourth message of the First Law to Book Selection is :

Select that edition of a work that weighs less than 1.5 Kg. In particular, avoid an edition printed on loaded paper.

6 Durability

For any given use, or wear and tear, the durability of a book depends on two factors : 1 Paper ; and 2 Binding.

7 Paper

We can arrange paper according to a scale of durability. Arranged in the decreasing sequence of durability, we get hand-made rag paper, hand-made esparto or other grass paper, machine-made esparto or other grass paper, machine-made chemical pulp paper, machine-made feather-weight paper, machine-made loaded or art paper, and machine-made mechanical pulp paper. Apart from these primary grades, we may have many others interpolated in the above scale, according to the proportion in which the different kinds of pulp are mixed. Mention should also be made of India paper which is very thin, though tough and strong. An edition printed on India paper will be relatively thin and many pocket editions are printed on such paper. Books printed on such paper may be suitable for private ownership where the frequency of use will be small. But in a library where the frequency is large, the sheets of a book printed on India paper usually fold awkwardly. Several libraries in India have had this pestering experience when they bought the supplementary volumes of the fourteenth edition of the *Encyclopaedia Britannica* printed on India paper.

7' Message 5

The fifth message of the First Law to Book Selection is:

> *Do not select editions printed on India paper or mechanical pulp paper or art paper or feather-weight paper. Prefer editions on rag paper for books of permanent value, editions on esparto paper for the next order of permanence, and editions in chemical pulp paper only for books that are likely to have a comparatively short period of use, but never books printed on mechanical pulp paper.*

8 Binding

Unlike in the case of paper, the librarian has occasionally a greater freedom of choice between different qualities of binding given by the publishers themselves. But experience shows that even the so-called strong binding or library binding given by publishers is not generally as durable as reinforced library binding made according to the specification given for example in D Cockerell's *Book-binding and the care of books: A text-book for book-binders and librarians*, ed 4 (1934) or in my *Library administration* (Ranganathan series in library science, 3), ed 2 (1960) Sec 3959, or my *Library manual* (Rangathan series in library science, 6) ed 2 (1962) Sec 5624. A rational course will be to buy a book in sheets and get it bound according to the specification for reinforced library binding before putting it into circulation. But there are difficulties in the way. In the first place, except in France and other neighbouring countries, the publishers invariably refuse to supply books in sheets. I remember the great effort made by the

Director of Public Libraries of Norway in this matter. To minimise wastage of manpower in the repetition of the same work in all the libraries of the country, he had introduced a co-operative system. All the libraries sent their orders for books to the national centre. This centre bought copies of books in bulk to answer the number of orders received from several libraries, classified and catalogued them, and also had them bound before transmission to the libraries. When I visited the centre on 2 July 1948, I was amazed to find some half a dozen girls engaged in peeling off the publisher's casing from hundreds of copies of the same book. I was told that this waste of manpower as well as binding material had to be gone through, as the publishers refused to supply books in sheets even to such an influential and large-scale buyer as that National Co-operative Organisation.

81 Publisher's Case

In these circumstances one has to decide which binding should be selected if more than one binding is offered by the publisher. If the library has to replace the publisher's case either immediately or after a short spell of circulation by its own reinforced binding, it is more economical to go in for the cheapest binding.

82 A Practical Difficulty

There are, however, certain practical difficulties in the way, due to an *ex cathedra* attitude adopted by sanctioning authorities. I know of cases where the provision under the heading " Binding " is grudgingly made in the budget. The library profession in India has not yet developed enough coherence and stamina to educate the sanctioning authorities in matters like this. Perhaps it is so in other countries too. The fun is that the sanctioning authorities seldom detect or object to the selection of an edition which is made more costly on account of the slightly better binding given by the publishers themselves. In a situation like this, expediency would make a librarian select the more costly editions. This may amount to budgetary trickery. For, in the allocation of the expenditure, the extra cost of binding in such a case will be absorbed in the cost of books and not shown against cost of binding. With proper understanding and reasonableness, these anamolies can be eliminated.

83 MESSAGE 6

The sixth message of the First Law to Book Selection is:

If the book-trade sells a book in sheets, buy it and get it bound according to the library's specification. In the alternative, if an unbound, paper-covered stitched copy is available, buy it and get it bound according to the library's specification. If even this is not available, buy the copy with the cheapest binding and get it re-bound to the library's specification. If there is no suitable facility for binding, buy the copy with the strongest binding.

CHAPTER DC

PRINTED PAGE

1 Readability

Next in order of grossness, in the embodiment of a book, is the appearance of the printed page. Here an important element is the type face. There are various styles and sizes in type face. The Roman script is more common than any other. In India many classics are being brought out in several editions. In their selection, therefore, the quality of the type face can play a great part. But sufficient experiment or even observation has not yet been made by the library profession or by the book-trade to set up a scale of readability for the different styles of type face. This may be traced to historical reasons. The decadence in Asian countries and the renascence in Western Europe, increased in intension ever since printing from movable metallic types was invented. This continued even through the nineteenth century when machinery was invented to mechanise printing. The neglect of improvement of type face went with the neglect of everything else in our land. But some thought has been bestowed on the subject in western countries. Some authors, such as William Blake and William Morris, appear to have devoted much thought to this question. Perhaps their approach was more subjective than objective. Typographers themselves have, perhaps, done some work in this matter. However, a standardised scale does not seem to have been set up from the angle of the anxiety of the First Law to intensify the use of books by every possible means. In the absence of the help of such an objective and accepted standard, book selection on the basis of type face has to be largely a matter of opinion and flair.

11 Message 7

Even so the seventh message of the First Law to Book Selection is :

> ***Select that edition of a work, that is printed in a type face that is readable, pleasing to the eye, and causing the least strain to it.***

2 Indian Script

In the application of the above principle, we are not faced with many alternatives in the case of books printed in Indian scripts. Generally speaking, what are called white faces are more pleasing to the eye. It may be preferable to select the editions printed in such faces. In the Indian book world today, book selection based on the look of the printed page is more operative than in the West. This is due to the fact that much of India's book production consists of re-publishing of classics. The proportion of modern works is low. Book selection in their case is one of Hobson's choice. But it is not so with classics. They are available in diverse editions. Therefore, Indian librarians have to exercise much judgment in book selection from the point of view of typography. It will be advantageous not only to book selection but also to the improvement of Indian typography, if the library profession, the printers, the publishers, and typecasters could jointly study the problem of readability of type face and fix a scale of standard. The phase of renascence into which India and other Asian countries are now entering calls for organised and planned acceleration of achievement in several directions. Typography is one of those directions. In 1959, the Ministry for Works, Mining, and Power invited me to serve on a Committee on Typography. Some preliminary discussion happened in the first meeting. But I have not heard any thing more about it. I wish that the Indian Association of Master Printers takes up this problem of typography, so vital to the spread of the use of books in the country.

3 Other Asian Scripts

I do not have familiarity with other Asian scripts. But I should expect that from the point of view of book selection conditioned by typography the position is similar to what it is in regard to Indian scripts. Perhaps the Semitic script has problems of its own which will require even greater investigation to set up standards to aid book selection based on type face.

4 Type Size

In determining readability, type size comes next to style of type face. Here, it is not so much the absolute size that counts, as the

Gestalt value of the type size as printed — that is, readability is not determined by type size taken in isolation. The length of the line and the space between lines go a long way in determining the most comfortable and at the same time economical type size. For ordinary reading matter of, say, Royal or Demi or Crown Octavo pages, ten point type composed in single column with lines leaded out reasonably appears to be quite readable. Twelve point type is certainly even more readable. But the cost of the latter is bound to be higher. In a library open to the public, it is desirable that if there can be a choice between editions in twelve and ten point types the former should be selected. Type sizes larger than twelve point may have the defect of including within a sweep of the eye much less matter than comfort requires. However, in books intended for children and neo-literates, books with larger type faces should be selected.

41 MESSAGE 8

Stated in general terms, the eighth message of the First Law to Book Selection is:

> *Select that edition of a work that has type size of twelve points, or ten points in the absence of twelve points, in the case of books mainly intended to be read by mature readers. Prefer bigger type in the case of books for children and neo-literates.*

5 Indian Classics

The scale of type sizes for Indian script is slightly different. It also appears to be different for the different Indian scripts. A systematisation of the scale awaits to be done. Many of the general principles stated in Sec DC4 will be applicable here also. But there is one peculiarity in Indian classics, which, as stated already in Sec DC2, get often printed by different publishers at the same time and thus offer considerable scope for book selection. Many Indian classics consist of a basic text with a commentary of the first remove, second remove, third remove, and so on. A tradition has been established to print all of these in the same page in parallel, instead of putting each member of this hierarchy of associated books continuously as separate parts. Printing them in parallel has proved itself to be more helpful. The readability has been increased still further by using different type faces or type sizes for the text and the commentaries of the successive removes. Difference in the size of the type as well as the style of the face is resorted to in producing readability by this device.

51 Message 9

The ninth message of the First Law to Book Selection is :

Select that edition of a classic with a chain of commentaries on it, that prints them in parallel and subordinates them in succession by the use of different styles and sizes of type face.

6 Make-Up Of The Page

Another element in the printed page of a book which should weigh with Book Selection for libraries may be named as "Proportion of black and white". For determining this proportion, it is an open double page that should be taken into account. The general quality of the make-up of the page is determined by the colour contrast between the printed lines and the paper, the space between lines, and above all the margins. In recent years some investigation has been made in the first of these factors, for the type face of Roman script current in the West. No work appears to have been done on this factor in India or in other Asian countries in regard to their scripts. It needs to be done and a scale of standards needs to be established ; for, guidance based on flair should be replaced by an objective method.

7 Margin

The margin is of considerable importance in the view of the First Law. Large margin encourages the use of books. Narrow margin is depressing ; it discourages the use of books. The margin was hit hard during the war years. But it is now recovering. The ideal is shown by the illuminated books of the middle ages. The big black letters of the small space of the text are surrounded by large margins with beautiful and delicate pictures and decorations — brightly coloured scrolls and leaves and flowers or landscapes and portraits that illustrate and illuminate the text.

71 Message 10

The tenth message of the First Law to Book Selection is :

Select that edition of a work, that has wide margins left plain or with soothing decorations and well-leaded out printing, making the proportion of white and black unobtrusive and not tiresome.

8 Illustration and Letter Press

The spatial relation to the letterpress and the illustration printed with the text is another important, though subtle, factor which can make or mar the use of books. In the first half of the nineteenth century when wood cut was largely in vogue, some very good results were produced by printers. After the introduction of modern methods of illustration, this problem does not seem to have been worked out with much care. Objective tests to evaluate a book on this basis are not available. Dependence on flair appears to be the only course.

81 MESSAGE 11

The eleventh message of the First Law to Book Selection is :

> *Select that illustrated edition of a work, that has the illustrations and the letterpress in participative relation, neither subordinated to the other and both working together holistically.*

91 Hobson's Choice

It may be repeated that none of the principles of book selection derived so far from the angle of the physical body of the book can come into use, if there is only one edition of a book. For it is then a case of Hobson's choice.

CHAPTER DD

SUBTLE BODY OR EXPOSITION OF THE BOOK

1 Librametry

If the paper, the binding, and the print constitute the physical body of the book, the language, the style, and the illustration constitute its subtle body. The extent of choice in Book Selection from the point of view of the subtle body is greater than the one from the point of view of physical body. For the subtle body is a purely mental creation. It is therefore more protein and capable of great variation. On the other hand, the physical body is less subtle than the mind. In spite of this, the opportunity for choice between alternatives is not very great in the case of advanced books of a specialised nature intended for confirmed intellectuals whose intellect functions and looks for food, as it were, spontaneously and accepts it without the need to be coaxed by factors relating to the physical or the subtle body in which the thought is embodied. But the opportunity for the exercise of skill in Book Selection is vast in regard to the books intended for the common reader — be it for his recreation, information, or inspiration. The regression from spontaneity of intellectual interest is as varied as the scatter of age among men and of intellectual capacity among men in the same age group. There is therefore both varied supply and varied demand in regard to the subtle body of books. This implies that among diverse books on the same subject, great judgment should be exercised in matching the diverse standards of their subtle bodies with the readers of various kinds. The First Law whose concern with use is more statistical than individualistic will therefore put a great strain on Book Selection work. There is need for a grasp of the frequency distribution of demand and the matching with it of the frequency of the books selected on the basis of the qualities of the subtle body.

11 Multiple Correlation

It is a case of multiple correlation as in the draper's trade. This trade has taken the fullest advantage of modern statistical methods and of correlation ever since Karl Pearson showed the way at the turn of the present century. One of the government publications of the United States is solely on the selection of varied sizes by drapers in correct proportion to meet the demand of the community. The book is *Body measurements of American boys and girls for garment and pattern construction*, (United States, Department of Agriculture, miscellaneous publication, 366) (1941) by Ruth O'Brien etc. This was possible because Biometry was forged as a discipline more than half a century ago and it is being fully exploited. But a corresponding Librametry is yet to be forged. This concept itself was isolated and clothed with the term Librametry only a few years ago — when I was addressing the Aslib Conference at Lemingten Spa, England, on 18 September 1948. In its application to the problem brought up here, Librametry is likely to be involved. But if the library profession is not merely that of a store-keeper, if it is to fulfil its possible role in making library service a social institution for the perpetual unfolding of the personality of one and all, the library profession cannot rest on its oars. It should be ever blazing new trails. It will have to press into its service all disciplines — and indeed create a new brand of them suited to its peculiar needs. If this is not done, the library profession will be failing in its duty to society. It will have no right to complain that it is not getting the same respect as many other professions. In the absence of work along such lines having been taken up, we can only state here what are perhaps truisms.

2 Language

The most trivial truism which may pose itself as a principle in Book Selection derivable from the First Law is "Select the books only in the language which the present and the prospective users of the library can read". In applying this principle, we have to interpret language not only in the commonly understood way but also as the stages in the evolution of the language. Most languages in which there is a considerable literature have been growing through several centuries. Though the same name is still retained and though the change from one century to another is too mild to be noticed, it is well-known that the common man born today within a language group is unable to understand its prototype of a thousand or two thousand years ago. For purposes of book selection, stages of language, separated by large spans of centuries, should be treated as virtually different languages. King Alfred's English, Chaucer's English, Shakespeare's English, and Bernard Shaw's English should be distinguished in Book Selection. For a public library, an edition of Shakespeare in Elizabethan English will be a wrong selection. It will be in its place only in a specialised library intended for scholars pursuing either English linguistics or Shakespearean studies. In the developed countries there is a considerable endeavour to re-write old classics in modern language There is thus opportunity to select editions in either language and indeed in the languages belonging to each of the successive stages. The well established democratic force in the developed countries is pulling books forward towards the language of the common man, though this does not mean towards the level of slangs or dialects. The standard language itself is therefore being pushed further and further, from where it was to what it is in the mouth of the common man. It is indeed a delight to watch and examine the nimbleness with which the language keeps growing.

21 **Message** 12

The twelth message of the First Law to Book Selection for a Public, School, or any generalist library is :

> ***Keep yourself aware and extremely sensitive to going in for a book which is the embodiment of any given thought in the latest stage of the language.***

3 Indian Languages

The First Law would urge paying special attention to this factor in the libraries of India which are sprouting here, there, and everywhere today. Book writing as well as Book Selection is prone to a great danger in India today. Due to the exhaustion of society and the consequent political handicaps, our languages have been paralysed during the last few centuries. They have not been used as media for current thought during this period. They have been used by the common man, only for the trivial needs of life in physical and vital planes and of outbursts in emotional plane.

What little intellectual work had been done in the country had been clothed in a foreign language. Those that did not change over to a foreign language have been clinging to the medieval or even to the ancient stage of our language. Their vocabulary is archaic; their morphology is complex; their syntax is involved; and their literary productions are intelligible only to their own peers. Fortunately, however, as a concomitant to the slow emergence of new life which burst out into political independence in August 1947, new voices have been appearing in the arena — new voices which write in the language of the common man. These new voices have begun to increase in number during the last few years. Still there are enough old voices left hugging the old stage of the language. During the life time of one or two generations, therefore, the stage of language will play a large part in Book Selection work in Indian libraries.

31 MESSAGE 13

The thirteenth message of the First Law to Book Selection in respect of books in Indian languages is:

> *Select books that are written in modern Tamil, modern Malayalam, modern Kannada, modern Telugu, modern Marathi, modern Gujarathi, modern Hindi, modern Oriya, modern Bengali, modern Assamese, and modern Urudu and reject books in the pedantic, medieval, and archaic forms of these languages except in libraries intended to promote linguistic studies or historical criticism.*

4 Style

Next to the need for modernity of language comes the need for an appealing style. Books in a simple, transparent, dynamic style are to be preferred to those in a heavy, involved, ornate one. The style of a piece of writing is like the personality of a human being. It is the total effect of several qualities. It is un-analysable. If we analyse it into its diverse features, it may be possible to set a scale of standard for each of them. Even if a style is at its bes- in each of its features, the total effect may not be so. The intant gible something, which produces the total effect, plays a prepotent part in determining the effectiveness of style. It is very much like the trace element in food or manure. It is like flavour. It is difficult to lay down, in words, standards for this intangible something. But a truly good style is usually good in each of its features. It is possible to have standards for such features as can be isolated. We shall therefore deal with some of them.

5 Words

A book using simple short words is preferable to one using long pedantic ones. Modern words which are current among people are to be preferred to those of yesterday, lingering among conservative writers far beyond their time. This is about the ordinary terms in a piece of writing. Among technical books, those using the correct technical terms are preferable to those playing indiscriminately between technical terms and non-technical ones.

51 Morphology

A language usually grows, as it has been already said, in the mouth of the common man. His tendency is to reduce morphological variations, and to replace them with uninflected words along with auxiliary words if necessary. In the Indian languages the old habit of printing with the full effects of *Sandhi* Rules (=Rules of phonetic changes in the end-letter of a word, determined by the first letter of the succeeding word) usually causes a considerable difficulty for the ordinary reader. The severe grammarian may still insist on them. Some authors conform to the grammarian's dictum. Others boldly deviate from *Sandhi* Rules into the direction of what is comfortable to the ordinary reader. In a public library, books of the latter kind are preferable.

52 Coalescence

Some of the Indian languages have not yet completely outgrown the classical *Samasa* Rules (=Rules of coalescence according to which compound words are formed by dropping the morphological endings and fusing the component words into a long chain-like single word). There is a tendency, however, for such coalesced words to be eliminated in modern writing. Books in which this elimination is greater are to be preferred in a public library. Some writers go half way in this affair and hyphenate freely — that is, they insert a hyphen between every two consecutive components in a coalesced word. Books in which there is hyphenation should be preferred in case those without coalesced words are not available.

6 Sentence

Books with simple short sentences are to be preferred. One of the results of the masses having been kept illiterate till so late in the day has been that the Indian languages have not had the benefit of the pressure of the common man on the length of sentence. Absence of this corrective by the common man has been responsible for the use of long-winded sentences. New writers are however emerging from the grip of this tendency.

7 Paragraph

A book is readable if it is arranged in short paragraphs observing the Principle of Unity of Thought. Similarly, chapters too should respect this principle. The book itself should be properly focussed. In fact the words should pile up to a sentence. The sentences should roll into a paragraph. The paragraphs should mount up to a chapter. The chapters should culminate in the book. The Unity Principle should characterise each one of these elements at its own appropriate level. If books are to be widely used with comfort — not merely by the intellectuals who can cross any hurdle, but by one and all — those which respect the Unity Principle should be selected in preference to those which are diffuse.

8 Clarity and Flair

The Unity Principle is a characteristic of the style of writing. In the opening verse of the *Raghuvamsa*, Kalidasa says, "Language and thought are inseparably fused". Considerable work has been done in investigating the psychological and the logical foundations of this dictum. Attempts are being made almost endlessly to examine if thought can exist without words and if words can exist without thought. Whatever be the findings of psychology or logic, so far as style is concerned, there is no doubt that language and thought are inseparable. To make books used, it is not only necessary that there should be simplicity of language and Unity of Thought, but there should also be Clarity of Expression. Books in a clear style should be preferred to those in a confused one. As stated in Sec DD4, conformity to all the above considerations is necessary but not sufficient to make the style of a book helpful and even to determine the degree of helpfulness of style. Another necessary but intangible quality is Flair.

81 **Message** 14

The fourteenth message of the First Law to Book Selection is:

> ***Select the book which is written withflair in a simple clear style.***

CHAPTER DE

ILLUSTRATION AS SUBTLE BODY

1 Pressure of Race-Habit

Next to language and style, illustrations form an important feature of the subtle body of a book. Often they are more effective in making a book used. For, a picture or an illustration takes the idea directly to the mind unmediated by words which are higher up in the scale of abstraction than pictures. Even those, long established in the habit of reading, give first preference to pictures and charts. When the weekly magazine arrives, we first turn to the pictures, instinctively. We defer looking into the letter-press. This must be because it involves less strain to capture an idea through pictures than through words. Perhaps there is pressure of race-habit behind this. For, literacy on a mass scale is a very recent affair. On the other hand, seeing the things themselves had been in use ever since man acquired the power of sight. So also recognising a plane-picture of three-dimensional objects has been practised by humanity very much longer than writing and reading. Communication of idea through pictures had come into use centuries before communication through phonetic symbols. Whatever be the reason, the First Law would like us to remember that pictures and diagrams make a quicker and greater appeal than letter-press. At any rate, they illumine the letter-press. They facilitate reading. The First Law would therefore vote for illustrated books. Even in advanced books for scholars, schematic diagrams help their use considerably. Histograms are equally helpful. They reduce the strain involved in capturing the thought. They make the use of books easier.

2 Standard

In order to exploit the potency of pictures and diagrams to promote the use of books, the First Law would naturally plead for books in which these are well produced. The effectiveness of an illustration depends upon :

1 Its appropriateness to the thought illustrated ;
2 The artistic quality of the original ;
3 The quality of the block used for its reproduction ;
4 The skill of the printer in producing its impression ; and
5 Its insertion at the right place amidst letter-press.

It is not possible to go here into the principles of art criticism or art economy. Here again, a knowledge of what is good or bad in each of the above factors in regard to illustration, though necessary, is not sufficient. It is only the flair of the librarian, cultivated no doubt by his own reaction to illustrated books and by his observing the reaction of the readers to the same, that can form a reliable guide.

21 MESSAGE 15

The fifteenth message of the First Law to Book Selection is :

> ***Select a book which is illustrated adequately with well-drawn, well-printed, apt pictures, diagrams, histograms, etc, whichever be appropriate to the standard, style, and subject of the book.***

3 Children and Neo-Literates

Good and profuse illustration is of the very essence of books for children and neo-literates. The art and the technique of book illustration has improved by leaps and bounds during the last few years. All that is best in this art and technique should be pressed into the service of the First Law in making books accepted by children and neo-literates. The proportion of illustration to letter-press will have to begin very high — 80 to 90 per cent — in the case of books for children and neo-literates and slowly decrease until it is reversed in the case of highly educated people in whom literacy has become part of their nature and capture of ideas through phonetic symbols has become nearly involuntary. Coloured illustrations will be even more effective and therefore preferable according to the First Law.

The proportion of illustration to letter-press in books for children and neo-literates has been examined in detail in my book *Literature for neo-literates* (1953) (Indian Adult Education Association, English series, 6).

31 MESSAGE 16

The sixteenth message of the First Law to Book Selection is :

For infants and neo-literates, select books in which the proportion of letter-press to illustration in each page is very low, say, 10 per cent. For children of different ages and for adults removed from the stage of neoliteracy by different degrees, select books in which the proportion of letterpress to illustration in each page increases with the age or the stage of removal from neo-literacy respectively.

32 VICIOUS CIRCLE

In India there is a great dearth of illustrated books for children and neo-literates. One of the means of stimulating their production is for libraries to go in for them, whenever produced. A vicious circle has to be cut thereby. Well-illustrated books are naturally costly to produce. The sale-price will be proportionately high. The only means of reducing it is to have mass production. Mass production will be possible only if there will be mass purchase. Neo-literates can neither find the money nor develop the willingness to spare money to buy costly books. This will make the book trade hesitant to produce well-illustrated books. One means of cutting this vicious circle is in the hands of libraries. Though we do not now have a sufficient number of libraries *qua* libraries, there are cropping up a large number of Social Education Centres. These are expected to maintain collections of books suited to neo-literates. They have to be maintained even for the very purpose of preventing relapse to illiteracy and thereby for the purpose of saving the public money spent on social education. If the book selection for all these centres is done in unison and is done in conformity to Message 15 of the First Law given in Sec DE21, the vicious circle will be cut and the country can hope to have illustrated books of a standard pleasing to the First Law and particularly to the common folk.

4 Atlas

The subtle body of the Atlas requires special care in the selection of Atlases. Many technical factors are involved in the compilation, drafting, and reproduction of Atlas-maps. The quality of the Atlas is largely dependent upon the specialised knowledge and artistic skill of the cartographer. Accuracy, clarity, and attractiveness are the most desirable features. Maps over-loaded with names or a heavy background of shading to show relief should be avoided. The use of colour in cartography is primarily functional. Poor colouring not only offends the eye but it may also obscure much of the underlying line-work. In the case of topographical maps, those using coloured border lines to show political divisions instead of contrasting colours are preferable. There are three methods of showing relief on maps :

1 Hachuring to produce a third dimensional illusion with contrast between hills and valleys ;

2 Combining contours and altitude tints with a gradation of colours ; and

3 A combination of these two.

In Atlas Selection, its effectiveness in the portrayal of relief should go a long way. It is well known that the projection of the earth's surface on a flat map cannot avoid distortion. There are various modes of projection. For a good reference Atlas, one using different projections best suited to each different objective should be preferred. For example, equal area projection should be preferred for showing distribution of any entity over the world or a region of it.

41 MESSAGE 17

The seventeenth message of the First Law to Book Selection is :

In selecting atlas, give weight to accuracy, clarity, functional use of colour, hachuring, producing a dimensional illusion, and overall attractiveness.

CHAPTER DF

INDEX AS PART OF THE SUBTLE BODY

1 Need for Index

According to the First Law, the use of a book depends not merely on continuous study but also by a frequent return to it to pick up some specific information or to check up a vague impression or to verify memory. To get into a book without an index is like getting into a forest without a trained guide. There is no greater authorial sin than releasing a book without an index. It should be even made an indictable offence. British and American lawyers had proposed that an author publishing a book without an index should be deprived of the benefits of the Copyright Act. About the middle of the nineteenth century Lord Campbell was at the point of introducing a bill in the Parliament to implement this idea. Such an Act can be enforced only on future authors. It is hoped that, even without such an Act, authors of today will provide indexes to their books. Many of the modern books do have an index. But what about books of the past — particularly the classics being brought to print now and again? The different editions of such old works have different kinds and lengths of index.

2 History of Index

In the early days, an index was usually meagre. It was of the block variety as illustrated in Sec DF32. The meagreness persists even today not only in several current books but also in current editions of old books and classics. Some at least of these editions, however, have a more sumptuous index. Further, a considerable improvement is being made today in respect of the quality of the index. Melvil Dewey introduced the idea of a relative index. In this kind of index, a concept is indexed in relation to several others, instead of all the references being given in one block under the primary concept. I have myself experimented on various kinds of indexes in my books. The structure and the quality of my latest style of indexing may be described as "expressive and featured". The expressiveness consists in the indication not only of the secondary concept as in Dewey's relative index but also of indicating the relation between the primary concept and the secondary concept and further indicating whether the primary concept is merely mentioned or described or reinforced by reference to some other authority or even by quotation from it. The Documentation Sectional Committee of the Indian Standards Institution has worked out a Standard on Index. It has been published as *Indian standard: Rules for making alphabetical indexes,* (IS: 1275—1958).

3 Kinds of Indexes

Here are some illustrations. The Arabic figures used as index numbers indicate the pages to be looked up. They are supposed to occur in a book in which the *Classified catalogue code* occurs as an index heading.

31 Ordinary sparing index:

Classified catalogue code 180

32 Ordinary full index:

Classified catalogue code 12, 18, 30, 36, 60, 180, 300, 360, 400

33 Relative index:

Classified catalogue code

Arrangement 12, 30
Described 180
Style of writing 18, 36
Types of entries 60, 300, 360, 400

34 Expressive index:

d = described. *irt* = in relation to.
q = quoted. *r* = referred.

Classified catalogue code

d 180

dirt

Style of writing 36
Types of entries 360

i r t
Arrangement 12
Types of entries 60
q i r t
Arrangement 30
Types of entries 400
r i r t
Style of writing 18
Types of entries 300

4 Efficiency of the Index

The efficiency of the index and the comfort in the use of a book — for reference as distinct from continuous study — will surely be least in ordinary Sparing Index and greatest in Expressive Index. From this point of view, an ordinary Full Index is better than an ordinary Sparing Index ; while, a Relative Index is better than an ordinary Full Index though not as good as an Expressive Index.

41 Message 18

The eighteenth message of the First Law to Book Selection is :

> *Select that edition of a work that contains an index in preference to one without an index. Among those with indexes, select the edition that has the fullest one. Among those with full ones, select the edition that has a Relative Index, and even better the edition that has an Expressive Index.*

CHAPTER DG

SOUL — STANDARD OF THOUGHT

O Range of Standard

We have seen in Chapter DC that the scatter of standard in regard to the physical appeal of books is often limited and that book selection based on physical standards may often turn out to be Hobson's choice. We have also seen in Chapters DD, DE and DF that there is usually a slightly larger range — a greater variety — out of which book selection can be made on the basis of the language and the style of books and the extent o. illustrations in them. But in most of the developed countries, the range for book selection is beginning almost to be unlimited when based on the soul (thought-content) of books.

01 Standard of Thought

In book selection, one should recognise that books — covering the same subject, with equally inviting physique with similar style, and equally well illustrated and indexed — may differ immensely in standard of thought. The scale of standard of thought is something continuous; one standard shades into another imperceptibly. However, it is necessary to have a scheme of standard — not including very many in number. When I was thinking about such a scheme in 1939, Swami Turiananda Brahmendra Saraswati, disciple of Swami Svayamprakasa Brahmendra Saraswati of Senthamangalam, happened to call on me and mentioned four standards of exposition recognised in Vedic tradition. This put me on a helpful track.

1 Seminal Material

First in the scale is Seminal Material. This is a contribution of a fundamental nature. It emanates occasionally from a master-mind. It helps the fertilisation of several minds. It indicates a way of thinking. It affords a tool for use in furtherance of thought.

This is called *Prabhu sammiṭa* in Vedic tradition. This standard obtains in communication from one of the highest order of intellect and intuition to those of lower orders.

Example: Sir C V Raman's paper entitled *New radiation* (1928), which appeared in the *Indian journal of physics*, is a Seminal Material.

Another universally known example is Darwin's first contribution on *Origin of species*. The account of Foci, Facet, and Phase in *Library classification: Fundamentals and procedure* has perhaps some claim to this class.

2 Research Material

Second in the scale of standards is Research Material. This is a contribution embodying the results of investigation in a specialised field. It is made from time to time by whole-timed or part-timed research-workers. It is made available for circulation among co-workers in the same field so as to facilitate team-work and avoidance of unintended duplication. This is called *Suhrith sammita* in Vedic tradition. This standard obtains in communication to intellectual equals or peers.

Example: The hundreds of papers listed in the *Indian journal of physics* (1930-32) under the title *Bibliography of Raman effect* consist mostly of Research-Contributions. So are the thousands of papers on evolution and other related problems, which have appeared in biological periodicals since Darwin's days. Many of the papers appearing in the *Annals of library science* and in the *Library science* (1964—) belong to this class.

3 Expository Material

Third in the scale of standards is Expository Material. This is a contribution of an expository nature. It emanates from time to time from persons with special flair for exposition. It is so illuminating as to light up the field even for non-specialists in such a way that they can take an intelligent interest in the progress of thought in general. This is called *Kanta sammita* in Vedic tradition. This standard obtains in communication to intellectuals, say, up to half way down the third quartile, of the intellectual scale, on subjects in which they do not specialise.

Example : Raman's own account of the Raman effect forming his Nobel Lecture or his contribution to the *Malaviya commemoration volume* is an Expository Contribution. The delightful talks on Raman Effect which the Madras audience was accustomed to hear from Prof J P Manickkam is also a contribution of that kind. So are the various papers that Huxley wrote on Darwinism and the popular expositions of relativity by Eddington and Jeans. Some of the articles in the *Herald of library science* are of this class.

4 Elementary Material

The fourth in the scale of standards is Elementary Material. It is a contribution of an elementary nature. It seeks to give an extremely popular exposition of particular topics. It brings them to the level of the man in the street or even of the child. Not infrequently, it is even in the form of stories. This is called *Sisu sammita* in Vedic tradition. This standard obtains in communication to immature persons, whether they be children, or neo-literate-adults or adults among the last quartile and the lower half of the third quartile of the intellectual scale.

Example : An account of Raman Effect or of Origin of Species in any of the school or college magazines forms an Elementary Contribution.

5 Reporting Material

To the four standards found in Vedic tradition, we should add a fifth which has been evolved during the last two centuries. The fifth in the scale of standards is Reporting Material. It is a contribution giving brief reports of facts and information without attempting elucidation or exposition at length. This standard obtains in most of the reference books described in Sec DH2 to DH91. Newspapers too belong to this class.

6 Wilson's Example

The decision about the standard of a book is not easy. It is difficult to be totally objective. In regard to current books, a method of deciding whether the standard is popular or too severe is being experimented upon by H W Wilson & Co for several years now. When I visited them in September, 1950, I spent some time in finding out how they selected the titles for their *Book review digest*. A permanent staff uses its own experience in making a preliminary selection. Proof-copies of the selection are sent to a large panel of public librarians for their votes to be marked against each item. The slugs for the entries are kept standing till the replies come. After the replies are collated, the slugs of the rejected entries are melted down, while those of the retained entries are assembled in formes, struck off, and preserved for the successive cumulative editions. This is said to work fairly well in book selection on the basis of standard.

7 Stamping by National Bodies

The question is whether a similar procedure is practicable to determine standards on a national or international basis as a help to book selection. Can each nation set up an Assessing Academy to assess the standard of each book as it comes out of the press and put the stamp of standard on it before it is ready for marketing. Assuming that this can be done, it has to be further examined how far this procedure will add to time-lag or whether pre-natal stamping — that is stamping even at the proof stage — is possible. These are moot questions. Until any such aid on a national basis is set up, book selection will involve judgment and estimating in relating the several national standards to the particular levels obtaining among the clientele of a particular library.

8 Message 19

The nineteenth message of the First Law to Book Selection is :

> ***Match the standard of exposition of books to the standard-scatter among the clientele. In the last resort, this may require scanning through the pages of books.***

CHAPTER DH

SOUL — KIND OF APPEAL

O Kinds of Books

Three important kinds of appeals of books may be recognised — information, recreation, and inspiration. It is seldom that information is totally absent in a book. In a story book which usually passes for a recreative book *par excellence*, there are always some "inclusions" of information. The famous *Pancha tantra* tales are repositories of political wisdom and ethical standards. Even the poorest type of modern fiction, that does not amount to true literature, communicates at least some psychological information, though it be by implication and suggestion. With regard to books which inspire, they are global in their appeal. They serve all the three purposes. Information of eternal value is the characteristic of the greatest books of inspiration of the world — the so-called revealed books — the *Vedas*, the *Pitakas*, the *Talmud*, the *Bible*, and the *Koran*. Though they are generally vast and encyclopaedic, they do contain also many cases of considerable recreative value. The stories of the Upanishads and the parables of the Bible are for ever being reproduced in the form of independent books. One reason for this is their unexampled recreative value. Thus it is not possible to classify books as exclusively informative, or exclusively recreative, or exclusively inspirational. And yet we can throw books into these three groups on the basis of that quality which dominates over the others. Books are sought for use on account of each of these forms of appeal. Each man is in need of each of these appeals at one time or other. Indeed his interest alternates between these three modes of appeals. A public library should therefore care equally for all the three classes of books.

01 Informative Book

Informative books are of two kinds :

1 Ready Reference Books ; and

2 Ordinary Books.

02 Ready Reference Book

Ready Reference Books may be of any one of the following kinds and may pertain to any class of knowledge whatever, as broad as the entire universe of knowledge or as narrow as, say, Ice Cream : 1 Encyclopaedia ; 2 Guide Book ; 3 Case Study ; 4 List ; 5 Statistics ; 6 Year Book ; 7 Biography; and 8 Table. There may also be other forms of Reference Books, such as Concordance, Dictionary, Atlas, and Gazetteer. Of these, concordances are found most often for classics in any class, the sacred books of religions, and works in the main class 'Literature'. Atlases and Gazetteers figure greatest in the main class 'Geography'. Each of these kinds of ready reference books calls for certain distinctive factors to be borne in mind in book selection work.

1 Encyclopaedia.

Generally speaking, it is the latest edition of an encyclopaedia that should be selected. However there are instances where an earlier edition is superior in value though information is not up-to-date. This factor would suggest the selection of the latest edition for the sake of up-to-dateness of information, and of an earlier edition — even if it could be had only as a second hand copy — for the sake of the sumptuousness of information. In the *Encyclopaedia Britannica*, for example, the ninth edition has articles by the foremost experts of the day and most of the articles were of the monograph type and very informing. The tendency in the later editions is to atomise.

11 Message 20

The twentieth message of the First Law to Book Selection is :

In selecting an encyclopaedia, pay attention to the names of the contributors, the extent of bibliography attached to each article, and the thoroughness of coverage.

2 Guide Book

In the selection of guide books or handbooks, the reliability of information, the extent of coverage in respect of details, and the mention of the original sources where fuller information can be had, should form the guide in book selection. Above all, up-to-dateness is of the very essence of a guide book.

21 MESSAGE 21

The twenty-first message of the First Law to Book Selection is :

In the case of a guide book, select the latest edition.

3 Statistics

Unlike in the case of guide books, it is not only the latest edition but the earlier editions also are of value. In fact the value of a statistical reference book depends essentially on the completeness of the set. For, such reference books are mainly of help in tracing events and data through a series of years. It is only then that a reader can form a correct judgment of the trend of events and use the latest edition to the fullest advantage and without any risk. It is particularly so in a specialist library. But in a generalist library, this may not be necessary to the same extent.

31 MESSAGE 22

The twenty-second message of the First Law to Book Selection is :

In the case of a statistical reference book, make the selection cover as much of the run of its earlier volumes, as the specialist collection in the library would demand.

4 Year Book

As in the case of guide books, it is the current edition of a year book that should be selected. Indeed this is a case where, it is ideal to buy the new edition every year.

41 MESSAGE 23

The twenty-third message of the First Law to Book Selection is :

Select that year-book in a subject field, that has the maximum of

1 *Reliability and up-to-dateness of information* ;
2 *Extent of coverage* ; *and*
3 *Provision of bibliography wherever warranted.*

5 Biography

The selection of biographical dictionaries and Who's whos should be guided by the

1 Extent of information furnished ;
2 Extent of coverage ; and

3 The provision of bibliographies of the ' by ' as well as the 'on' type.

Today there are biographical dictionaries and Who's whos covering each of several countries, Constitutent States, counties or districts, and cities. There are also Who's whos covering each of the diverse subjects and even of the learned world as a whole. There are also international Who's whos. In our own country, this kind of reference material has just begun to develop.

51 MESSAGE 24

The twenty-fourth message of the First Law to Book Selection is :

Have a decreasing scale of favoured countries, constituent states, districts, and cities. The library's own city, district, constituent state, country, and world as a whole should naturally occupy the first five positions in the scale. In selecting national biographies and Who's who, go down the scale so established as far as necessary, sufficient, and practicable.

6 Linguistic Dictionary

Linguistic dictionaries should be selected for many languages. The selection of dictionaries in the language of the library should cover a wide range from exhaustive historical dictionaries, typified by the monumental *New English dictionary* for the English language, down to single volume or concise dictionaries. Dictionaries giving meanings not merely of words but also of phrases and proverbs should be selected. Dictionaries of the type of thesaurus should also be selected. It is also necessary to extend book selection to technical dictionaries specialising in the terminology of particular subjects or groups of subjects. A library should also select bi-lingual and multi-lingual dictionaries both of the ordinary and of the technical kinds.

61 MESSAGE 25

The twenty-fifth message of the First Law to Book Selection is :

Select linguistic dictionaries giving meanings of words and phrases respectively and a thesaurus in the language of the library. In the selection of bi-lingual dictionaries, select those with the language of the library as one of the languages and having for the respective second languages as many as found necessary down the scale of languages of the library.

7 Atlas

Atlases form an important class of refernce books, perhaps next in importance only to linguistic dictionaries. Kipling once observed that "As soon as men begin to talk about anything that really matters, some one has to go and get the atlas". I remember the great part played by maps and atlases in World War II. The telephone calls from newspaper offices were never ending in the Madras University Library in which I was then working. Every event in the progress of the war needed, for its being communicated to the public, a specification of its location. As we did not have a very good collection of atlases and maps, we had to hunt for the little, isolated, inset maps appearing in diverse books. Indeed, the many and varied demands for information during the war brought home to us the importance of liberality of book selection in regard to atlases. Indeed, I developed a yearning to be rich in atlases. This yearning was fulfilled, vicariously though, when I went in August 1948, into the colossal, nearly exhaustive, and unique Map Division of the Library of Congress. Atlases have to serve many purposes. The commonest is location of countries, cities, rivers, or mountains. To fulfill this locational demand a general world atlas is needed. A general atlas consists of maps, predominantly locational, of the countries of the world on as large a scale and with as many names of places as possible together with a sprinkling of maps relating to climate, ocean currents, physical features, vegetation, economic resources, trade routes, human distribution, changes of political boundaries, and so on. A world atlas should, strictly speaking, include maps of all parts of the world with a good number of place-names. No single atlas can be so complete, of course, as to include every geographical name on the earth. We should select an atlas which is comprehensive enough to answer most of the locational questions basic to an intelligent understanding of world affairs. The relative amount of map-space devoted to the various parts of the world is another factor that weighs in book selection. Most of the existing atlases are suited primarily to domestic markets and consequently maps of the homeland predominate. Many so-called 'world atlases' consist of a series of large scale maps for the country of publication, supplemented by a few small scale maps for the rest of the world. This factor should warn one in book selection from being misguided by the title "World Atlas". While a library should necessarily go in for such an atlas which is predominantly biased to its own home-country, it is also necessary to go in for atlases published in other countries so that the atlas collection may be a balanced one. This is the only way for a detailed coverage of the world, because the ideal reference atlas truly international in its concept has not yet been produced.

Though the object of this book is not to suggest any particular book for selection, an exception is made in the case of atlases. This is because few Indian libraries know of the few comprehensive atlases which exist, either of world or of local coverage. Here is a list. Select the latest edition now available.

71 LOCAL COVERAGE

711 *Atlas of road maps* published by the Survey Office of the different Constituent States of India.

712 One inch maps published by the Ordnance Survey of India.

72 WORLD COVERAGE (BRITISH)

721 *Times survey atlas of the world* prepared at Edinburgh Geographical Institute under the direction of J G Bartholomew. 112 double plates; 12+259 p of pronouncing index and gazetteer. London: The Times. 1922. 17 pounds. 12½ x 18 inches.

722 *Citizen's atlas of the world,* Edinburgh: John Bartholomew & Son, Ltd. Ed 8. 1944. 12+200 pages of maps. 90 index pages. 14½ x 10 inches. 5 pounds.

723 *Philip's international atlas* designed and compiled by George Philip. Interim edition. Ed by George Goodall, London: George Philip and Son, Limited. 1944. 158 p of maps; 94 p of index. 8½ pounds. 16½ x 11 inches.

73 WORLD COVERAGE (ITALIAN)

731 *Grande atlante geografico, storico, fisico, politico, economico* by Mario Baratta, Plinio Fraccaro, and Luigi Visintin. Novara: Instituto Geografico de Agostini. Ed 4. 1943. 205 plates; 115 pages of index with more than 140,000 names. 16½ x 13 inches.

74 WORLD COVERAGE (FRENCH)

741 Vivien de Saint-Martin (Luis) et Schrader (F). *Atlas universal de geographie*, dress sous la direction de F Schrader d'apres les sources orginales et les documents les plus recents. Paris: Librairie Hachette. 1930. 80 plates, 88 pages of index. 22 x 17¾ inches.

75 WORLD COVERAGE (GERMAN)

751 *Stielers hand-atlas*, 254 haupt-und nebenkarten in kupferstich. Zehnte auflage, hundertijahr-ausgabe, von grund auf neubearbeitet unter leitung von Prof H Haack Gotha: Justus Perthes. 1926-27. 108 plates; 336 pages of index including 320,000 names. 12 pounds. 16×10 inches.

752 *Andrees allgemeiner handatlas* 123 haupt-und 211 nehenkarten. Mit vollstandigem alphabetisschen namenverzeichnis in besonderem bande. Herausgegeben von Dr Ernst Ambrosius. Bielefele und Leipzing: Velhagen & Klassing. 1930. Ed 8. 224 plates; separate index volume of 664 pages. 17½ x 12 inches; (index 11 x 9 inches).

76 WORLD COVERAGE (RUSSIAN)

761 *Bolshoi sovetski atlas mira* (*The great soviet atlas of the world*). Moscow: Scientific Editorial Institute of the Great Soviet World Atlas. Vol 1. 1937. 168 plates. 21 x 14½ inches. Vol 2. 1939. 143 plates. Vol 3 to follow.

77 WORLD COVERAGE (AMERICAN)

771 *New world looseleaf atlas*. New York: C S Hammond & Co 1922 and later. 360 plates with index. 19 pounds. 21 x 14 inches. Rs 240. Correction sheets on annual subscription basis.

78 SCHOOL ATLAS

781 *Goode's school atlas*. Chicago: Rand McNally Company. Revised and enlarged. 1933; later imprints to 1943. 173 p of maps; 110 p of index. 11½ x 9 inches.

782 *Oxford advanced atlas*. London: Oxford University Press. Ed 5. 96 p of maps; 32 p of index. 15 x 10 inches.

783 *University atlas*. London: George Phillip and Son Limited, 1937. 96 p of maps. 14¾ x 11 inches.

8 Atlases of Other Kinds

Book selection as applied to atlas does not end with the atlases of the kind mentioned above. From the point of view of the thought-content, atlas selection should also extend to those of specialised varieties such as physical, cultural, economic, social, ethnographic, historical, political, and so on.

81 MESSAGE 26

The twenty-sixth message of the First Law to Book Selection is :

Select an atlas with : and

1 Up-to-date information embodied in it;

2 Clear reference grids in addition to latitude and longitude in order to facilitate location;

3 Bias to home-country or home-continent, and with exhaustive index and pronunciation of place-names;

Prefer a looseleaf atlas with follow-up of corrected leaves from time to time on an annual subscription basis, if available; and, otherwise buy new editions at important epochs.

Select also special atlases with subject-bias, such as physical, historical, economic, and so on.

CHAPTER DJ

BIBLIOGRAPHY

1 Importance of Bibliography

Among reference books, special mention should be made of bibliographies — particularly, subject-bibliographies. Bibliographies are like relief maps of the world of knowledge. Without them it is difficult to traverse the world of knowledge so as to satisfy the First Law. To use a book, one should know of its existence. When a reader asks for books on a specified subject, the library catalogue will of course tell him what book the library has. It may happen that the books on the subject are out on loan or it may happen that the library has no book on the subject. What is more, it may happen that even if the library has a book on the subject, it is not up-to-date or it is unsuited for the purpose on hand. In all these cases the use of the library would suffer. This is against the First Law, particularly because there is every chance that the information sought by the reader forms part of some other book or periodical lying hidden on the shelves of the library. To locate such information and thereby put books and periodicals to fuller use, the First Law would urge that bibliographies should not be fogrotten in book selection work. The alternative of providing exhaustive analytical entries in the library's catalogue will prove prohibitively costly. In bibliography selection, various factors should be borne in mind and each library should decide what will suit its requirements.

2 Time and Material Factors

Viewed from the angle of time, a bibliography may be an *ad hoc* one or a periodical. An *ad hoc* bibliography is usually published as an independent book or as a part of another book or periodical. But from the point of view of book selection, we are concerned here only with a bibliography published as an independent book. A bibliography book of this kind is said to be "closed". A bibliographical periodical, whose issues are planned to occur at regular intervals and can be bound into a volume at stated intervals, is said to be "open". Sometimes, a bibliography in the form of a book may also be rendered "open" by supplements brought out from time to time, which may or may not be cumulated from time to time. Bibliographies can also be distinguished by the nature of the document forming the unit of entry. It may be a whole book, a whole periodical, or articles in periodicals, and parts of books. The *Indian national bibliography*, the *British national bibliography*, and the other national bibliographies are examples of bibliographies listing whole books. The "closed" variety of bibliography is more common in the humanities and social sciences. Evisch and Shucking's *Shakespeare bibliography*, Rand's *Bibliography of philosophy, psychology and cognate subjects*, and Cole's *What to read in economic problem of today and tomorrow* are examples of the "closed" variety. On the other hand, documentation periodicals — that is, bibliographies listing articles also and getting published periodically — are found largely in the mathematical, physical, and biological sciences, and their applications. Now a days, Unesco is promoting the publication of documentation periodicals in the social sciences too. A documentation periodical may be one of three kinds — indexing periodical, abstracting periodical, and trend-report or reviewing periodical.

3 Indexing Periodical

Certain bibliographies merely list the documents. Each entry gives only the author, the heading, the location if it is a periodical or the collation and imprint if it is a book. This variety is the least helpful in promoting the use of books as it can serve only as a finding list and contains neither any evaluation nor any indication of the nature of the contents.

South's *Index of periodical literature in testing* which is a bibliography of personality measurement and *Index medicus* published by National Library of Medicine, USA are examples.

4 Abstracting Periodical

There are also bibliographies — particularly among those which are run as periodicals — in which each entry is backed by an abstract or an annotation. These are of greater use than bare lists. Sometimes they even serve as substitutes for the originals for readers who do not have the need to know all the details of the original or who are hard pressed for time. This species of bibliography is more common among the natural sciences, though it cannot be said that every scientific subject is provided with an abstracting periodical. *Mathematical reviews*, *Science abstracts*, *Chemical abstracts*, and *Biological abstracts* are well-known examples.

5 Trend Report

There are also bibliographies which are midway between indexing or abstracting periodicals on the one side and bibliographical essays on the other. These are usually published annually. The information about published documents is arranged so as to read continuously and disclose the development of new thought during the year. But the extent of description of new thought is not as much as in a bibliographical essay. Well-known examples are: *Year's work in librarianship*, *Annual report on the progress of chemistry*, and *Annual review of biochemistry*.

6 Bibliographical Essay

While lists and abstracts are more suited for ready reference, they do not attempt evaluation of the thought on the subject. A bibliography which does it will certainly have greater potentiality to promote the use of published literature. *Select topics in algebraic geometry* published by the National Research Council of the United States is an example.

7 Kinds of Library

71 Generalist Library

During the last half a century, bibliographies are being published on diverse subjects even of a general nature, such as those which fall within the purview of a generalist or public library. In the English-speaking world, H W Wilson & Co have been pioneers in this respect. Their *Essay and general literature index* first published in 1931 in four volumes and continued as a cumulative annual from 1934 is an outstanding example of the kind of bibliography whose selection in a public library will provide a master key to unlock many of the tomes lying closed on the shelves. There are also other bibliographical indexes of this kind of coverage.

72 Specialist Library

In specialist libraries — such as university and business libraries, book-selection must pay great attention to bibliographies. Although the total number of bibliographies currently produced is large, in most of the sectors of knowledge there may not be more than one such bibliographical aid. Whatever it be, the First Law would press the claim of bibliographies and particularly of those of abstracting variety on the book selection work in libraries which are to serve specialists, whether they are of the university or business variety.

73 Message 27

The twenty-seventh message of the First Law to Book Selection is :

> *For a generalist or a public library, select general bibliographies of wide coverage ; and for a specialist library, select the* ad hoc *closed bibiiographies as well as documentation periodicals in the subject of specialisation, giving preference to abstracting periodicals over mere indexing ones unless the selection of both is financially possible, and to reviewing or trend-report periodicals.*

CHAPTER DK

ORDINARY BOOK

1 Range of Interest

In regard to ordinary books the First Law would emphasise the old adage *Bhinna ruchir lokaha* (=diverse are the fields of interest of the public). This dictum is literally true for the people of the world taken as a whole. As we narrow the geographical extent, its validity becomes lessened. When it comes down to a local library, this dictum will have to be applied with great circumspection and local knowledge. Again when it comes down to an institutional library, the First Law would ask for even greater care in book selection work. For it does not want any service-library to select any book for mere preservation unless there is a reasonable chance for its use. The First Law would therefore ask us to look critically for the sectors of the universe of knowledge, the books in which will find use. It is all a question of the range of interest of the clientele of the library. Generally speaking, the range is widest with children and it progressively narrows down with age in the case of adults. The inference is that book selection for children may have to make a wide coverage of the universe of knowledge but without much intension. Book selection for adults may have to restrict itself to particular sectors and to particular degrees of intension of knowledge. This can only be determined by local surveys. The Second Law is even more interested in this. We shall deal with this in greater detail in Part E.

2 Recreative Book

Travel Books, Biographies, and Fiction form the chief sources of recreation in generalist libraries. The direct information-content decreases in them as we go down the above list. The proportion, which these books occupy in the issue of books from a balanced collection in a generalist library, has been often discussed. Generally speaking, it begins at a high figure in a community which is new to library service, and it goes down gradually as the service of the library itself demonstrates to the readers the existence of informative and inspirational books and that in the long run it pays to care for them. This proportion and the gradual change in it should, according to the First Law, be reflected in Book Selection. " To be reflected " does not mean " To be reproduced in exact measure ". Similarly the proportion in the use of the three types of recreative books should also be reflected in book selection. At no time the selection of fiction which has true literary merit will be questioned. A good deal of controversy goes on, however, in regard to fiction of lower order, which gratifies the grosser urges and passions of men particularly of those who spend their time in muscular work or in repetitive work which creates a sense of boredom, and which de-intellectualises or de-humanises. Such fiction induces " addiction ". It botches up. It does not elevate. It is not truly recreative. Its effect is depressing, dissipating, or degrading to personality. The controversy is about the selection or rejection of such a stuff. At one extreme, the clauses on fundamental rights in the Constitution are invoked in defence of the demand for them ! At the other extreme, the great social responsibility of the library as a social institution to sublimate the passions of citizens, to turn their mind to whatsoever is elevated, and to rescue them from deadening addictions of all kinds, is stressed. A middle course is neither to refuse what a reader wants nor to take up the attitude of saying " Yes. Have it if you must, I hate it though." This attitude may arise out of superiority complex and contemptuousness or inferiority complex and resignation. Each of these attitudes offends the Laws of Library Science. The proper course should be to move with the readers, to accustom them by demonstration and persuasion to look for fiction of a better kind, to offer better recreative books, and to help them on to accept them in preference to what they had been led into. The library is neither a monitorial body nor a helpless one. It should never usurp censoring function ; and yet a certain opportunity for good influence goes with it. The vexed question of harmful anti-social fiction can be by-passed in book selection, if this opportunity for good influence is used. Its use depends on the existence and the personality of the reference staff and the librarian on the spot and their frequent personal contact with readers on a footing of equality — neither of condescension nor of subservience.

3 Books for Inspiration

It is one of the essential duties of a generalist library as a social institution to provide opportunity for people to read books of an inspiring kind, books that stir the soul, sublimate emotion, and lift one to a higher level of existence. Those seeking them voluntarily should be served with them. To those whose sensitiveness to their value is too feeble, their value should be demonstrated. The basis for discharging this duty has naturally to be the existence of books of that nature in the library's collection. This implies that books of this kind should figure in book selection. Such books are more numerous in the Main Class "Literature" — profound poetry, penetrating drama, and fine fiction. Next in sequence, particularly among ancient and medieval Indian books, come devotional lyrics by realised souls. Sections of sacred books and lives of saints also belong to this category. It does not, however, mean that inspiring books are exhausted by literature, mysticism, and religion. A book written by a master, whatever be the subject matter — even if it be dry-as-dust mathematics — can be a source of inspiration, which stirs the soul via the subject matter which it embodies.

4 Kinds of Libraries

41 Public Library

Let us remember that a public library is a social institution charged with the work of helping universal self-education. Let us also remember that education is helping the development of one's personality towards its own fullness, along its own lines, and at its own speed. Let us further remember that personality is a trinity of body, mind, and soul, and that in the present mental age, education has to be varying enough to work on all the phases of the mind — intellect, emotion, and intuition. Book Selection in a public library should therefore provide equally for informative, recreative, and inspirational books.

42 Specialist Library

In the case of other classes of libraries like the university or the business or other specialist libraries, which are institutional, book selection will depend very much upon the state of library development in the country. If these happen to be the only libraries, as it is in most places in India today, the book selection policy in them should be broad — almost approximating to that for a public library. While they may not be able to give equal emphasis to all the three classes of books as public libraries should, they should not exclude any of the classes. On the other hand, if there is a public library in the neighbourhood to take care of recreative and inspirational books, it is but proper that all the resources of an institutional library should be turned on books devoted to the subjects in which the institution specialises.

43 MESSAGE 28

The twenty-eighth message of the First Law to Book Selection is :

> *In a public library, select, in a suitable proportion, informative, elevatingly recreative, and inspiring books. In a specialist library, select books of the needed standards in the umbral subject of specialisation and in the related penumbral subjects.*

CHAPTER DL

BIBLIOPHILISM

1 Fourth Kind of Appeal of the Soul

In Chapters DH to DK, we dealt with three kinds of books as viewed from the appeal of the soul of a book. Sometimes the appeal of a book is based upon its ancientness. Book Selection often takes this into consideration. This appeal cannot be said to belong strictly to the soul of the book and yet it gets connected with the soul or the thought-content remotely. We shall therefore deal here with this unusual fourth appeal.

2 Definition

Book selection in public and academic libraries often suffers abberration by the influence of a tradition formed in the days when the anti-First Law — Books are for Preservation — reigned supreme. Perhaps the genesis of this Anti-First Law was scarcity of books. Books of the pre-printing and early printing days, often acquire rarity value. During the last century, collection of incunabula and of books printed two or three centuries ago has become a cult with some libraries. This has given rise to the following terms :

Bibliophile = Lover of books especially of their format
Bibliopole = Seller of rare or curious books
Bibliotaph = Who hides books in a tomb.

Bibliophilism appears to have taken possession of them. The mania for possession of curios is often the motive for selecting such ancient books. They are not selected chiefly for their thought-content; for, either they may have been much outmoded by now, or if they had lasting or permanent value, they would have come out in new editions or as new books.. They are selected for the sheer oldness of their physique — which at bottom is equivalent to their rarity.

3 Service Library *vs* Bibliotaph Library

Book selection on this basis with only secondary emphasis or no emphasis whatever on the usefulness of the thought-content — in practice they are seldom put to use but are only displayed — may be in its place in a specialist library founded for this very purpose — in a bibliotaph library — but not in a service-library. There is a certain narrow strip of scholarship which needs libraries of that nature — and exhaustive collection of materials produced in or on a particular period or person or subject. Book Selection in such libraries may well be to the satisfaction of not only the Anti-First Law but also of the First Law. The Huntington Library in Los Angeles, the Folger Shakespeare Memorial Library in Washington DC and the Gandhi Memorial Library in Delhi are examples of libraries where Book Selection of this kind should reign supreme.

31 Message 29

The twenty-ninth message of the First Law to Book Selection is:

> ***Avoid books of bibliophilic value in an ordinary service-library, not meant for bibliophiles. But select them exhaustively for bibliotaph libraries.***

CHAPTER DM

OVERALL EVALUATION

O Judgment

The overall evaluation of a book from the point of view of the physical body, the subtle body, and the soul, to make Book Selection to the satisfaction of the First Law, requires considerable judgment. There are various means by which this may be done. These are not all equally satisfactory; but it often happens that more satisfactory methods are not available.

1 Personal Inspection

Evaluation is best done by an actual examination of each book. For this the books themselves must be seen, perused, and assayed, and not merely a description of them and still less their titles alone. As the book trade is concentrated often in one city — for example, Paris in France, Frankfurt, and Leipzig in Germany, London in Great Britain, and New York in the United States — it is difficult, if not impossible, for each library to find facilities to examine personally even the books published in its own country. Although it is said that at one time the publishing firms in certain countries sent round sample copies from place to place, this is not now happening. All that we find is travelling agents of just a few publishing firms. Even they often canvass with prospectuses only or concentrate on text-books rather than on general adult books. In newly developing countries such as India, it does not happen that the book trade is concentrated in a single city. This is equally unhelpful. There is no single place to which librarians can go to examine personally all new books. Indeed in a country such as India, books are published in all sorts of places and very often by the authors themselves. These are not easily accessible. Personal visit is nearly impossible. Thus both in developed and undeveloped countries personal inspection of all books becomes impracticable. It may be possible to get books on approval in some cases, but not in all. The more worthwhile books seldom come that way for evaluation. Even when it is possible, the period of time allowed often proves insufficient. Generally speaking, evaluation by personal inspection and perusal is seldom possible. But wherever possible, it must be resorted to.

11 MESSAGE 30

The thirtieth message of the First Law to Book Selection is:

> *The ideal is to select a book only after inspection and perusal. Conform to this ideal whenever and wherever facilities exist for it — either in the form of the chief book centre being not far from the library or of book sellers or the agents of publishers taking the books from place to place.*

2 Self-Deception

An enterprising book seller may present to a librarian, on a dish as it were, either in his own shop premises or even in the library itself, copies of the books he had selected from his own angle of marketability. It may even be that he does so with the dead stock in his hands refusing to move out. To inspect these books alone and exhaust Book Selection on their basis alone amounts to abdication of the right and duty of the librarian to the enterprising book seller. This is nothing short of self-deception. Unfortunately this often happens today in newly developing countries such as India. This abdication is resorted to under the pressure to spend out the book-fund of the year, before the end of the year without surrendering any part of it. So long as our main book markets are thousands of miles away, the account and audit rules should be amended in respect of surrender of unspent balance, if librarians are to be saved from resorting to such abdication and self-deception. As Chairman of the Library Committee of the University Grants Commission, I raised this issue. The Commission accepted my suggestions on this point. It has recommended them to the universities. We get two messages based on these recommendations.

21 MESSAGE 31

The thirty-first message of the First Law to Book Selection is:

> *Allow seventeen months, from after the date of communication of the amount granted, to spend that amount, without enforcing the traditional limit of the end of the financial year.*

22 MESSAGE 32

The thirty-second message of the First Law to Book Selection is:

Allow the unspent balance of the budget allotment for books in one year to be added to the normal budget allotment for books in the succeeding year.

3 Dependence on Review

In the absence of facility for the book selector to peruse a balanced collection of worth-while books, the next best is to depend upon evaluation by other competent persons. This is found in reviews in periodicals and in special weekly editions of newspapers. This evaluation itself should be evaluated with care. For some reviews may be polemical and biased for or against the author. Young, inexperienced reviewers find pleasure in decrying the faults than mentioning the merits. They are even called "scorpions" on that account. Cases of the authors furnishing reviews of their own books are not unknown. A dangerous review is the interested one. On the other hand, a review may merely give the contents or reproduce some of the sentences in the preface without giving any positive lead or evaluation. Such neutral reviews may not be of much help. To keep clear of these dangers, one should evaluate the reviewing periodicals themselves. Even in cases where we do get a reliable evaluation in reviews, the time-lag often makes them useless. Even in the case of weeklies, it often takes a few months before a book is reviewed except in the case of books of popular topics for which advance copies — even galley proofs — are sent out well ahead of publication. But specialised books often get reviewed only in learned periodicals which are monthlies or quarterlies. Before their reviews appear, the books get widely distributed. To wait for their evaluation in reviews will amount to a disservice to the First Law. This has to be said in spite of the fact that very often reviews in such learned periodicals are balanced and trustworthy. But the time-lag often exceeds a year. In India most of the dailies have review columns in the Sunday editions; but except in a few cases these columns are filled up haphazardly. There is a good deal of drifting. Often it is author's pressure that brings out a review. The dangers of such happenings may be minimised by a comparative study of the review of the same book in several media. But this means time-lag, if there is no special staff for the purpose. The time-lag may be so much that a book goes out of print before it is selected. If the First Law is to be satisfied, a good library should provide the necessary staff for it. I found the Library of the Department of Agriculture of the United States setting apart quite a team of review-scanners to aid book selection.

31 MESSAGE 33

The thirty-third message of the First Law to Book Selection is :

> *Whenever the available local experts are not sure of the standard and the value of a newly published book merely on the basis of the name of the author, or of publishers, or of the series to which the book may belong, base its selection on reviews appearing in periodicals, including newspapers.*

4 Dependence on Genesis

In the absence of opportunity for personal evaluation and when time-lag between the publication of a book and the appearance of its reviews is inordinate, Book Selection has to depend upon evaluation by other means. Except in the case of "new voices", the reputation of the author is often of help in determining both the authoritativeness and the standard and style of the book. The name of the publishers may similarly be a help in evaluating the physique of the book. The name of the publisher is also often a reliable index of the quality of the subtle body and the thought-content of the book. Another reliable means of evaluation is the name of the series to which a book may belong. In their own days a mathematical book by Hardy, a physics book by Eddington, a biological book by Huxley, a drama by Bernard Shaw, a psychology book by Titchner, and an economics book by Cole were accepted on the mere announcement by publishers. Of course this method is not available for authors who are just appearing in the horizon. In India, imprints of the Oxford University Press, MacMillan and Longmans, have generally led to unhesitating acceptance. Nowadays, the imprint of Asia Publishing House is generally a recommendation, though there are occasional miscarriages. Familiarity with publishing backgrounds will, it can be said, go a long way in helping evaluation. Even greater help will be found in familiarity with the subjects of specialisation of well known publishers. Library Science, Mathematics, Technology, Religion, Law, and Children's books, for example, are important subject fields of publication with which certain publishers have long been identified. A librarian should build up a knowledge of such specialisation both by experience and by the intelligent study of source books such as *Reference catalogue* and *Cumulative book index*, and the issues of National Bibliographies. Again books which belong to the same series have the same physical characteristics and often imply sameness of standard and authoritativeness. Home University Library and Everyman's Library are widely known examples, covering the entire universe of knowledge. It is so particularly in subject series such as : Cambridge Tracts in Mathematics and Physics, Recent Advances Series, Loeb Classical Library, World Classics, Library of Philosophy, Modern World Series, and Heath Social Science Series. Many of the university presses also are floating series with their hall-marks. The *English catalogue* gives the names of many such series. A librarian should familiarise himself with the qualities of these series.

41 MESSAGE 34

The thirty-fourth message of the First Law to Book Selection is :

> *As an aid to book selection a librarian should develop special knowledge about the publishers and the publisher's series specialising in reliable, worth-while, and well-built books in different subject fields. He should also familiarise himself with the name of the outstanding authors of the past. He should further be on the alert to know the names of newly emerging reliable authors.*

5 Edition in the Sense of Series

The term "Edition" may prove to be a pitfall in book selection. In the first place, edition has several meanings. One of its original meanings — in names like Aldine edition of British poets, or Globe edition of Shakespeare — had been what is now denoted by the term "Series". Many Sanskrit classics are being reproduced in diverse editions where the term "Edition" is used in the sense of "Series". Each such edition guarantees a certain standard in the physical get up and in the trustworthiness of the text.

51 MESSAGE 35

The thirty-fifth message of the First Law to Book Selection is:

> *As an aid to book selection, a librarian should maintain a list of the special editions where the term "Edition" is virtually equivalent to the term "Series". This is particularly necessary in respect of the classics in Sanskrit.*

6 The Unreliable Term "Edition"

The meaning of the term "Edition" as "the total number of copies printed and published at one time" is not relevant to the present context. But often the term "edition" is used to denote a new impression or a new issue which is got by a later printing from undistributed types or unchanged plates. In other cases, a new edition may not mean anything more than that the book was printed from newly set types or plates but without any substantial change from the earlier edition. On the other hand, it can also mean substantial change in the text. The change in the text may be of various degrees —from a slight change to a total transformation. Particularly in Law and Medicine, there is a tradition to prolong the name of a book through several editions which together cover two and even more than two generations. These are subjects in which new facts accumulate rapidly and a new edition almost amounts to a new book. A "School edition" may mean nothing more than printing from existing type on cheaper paper. It may also mean a different edition to which notes are added. Edition *de luxe* is meant to be one of high artistic quality though this name may have been wrongfully usurped. It is generally printed on rag paper or other special paper. The number of copies of such an edition is usually limited. It is consequently of high price. Very often the number of copies is fixed by booking orders before publication. Public libraries can seldom afford them. Bibliophilic libraries will always go in for them. Facsimile edition is an exact copy of an earlier edition made by photographic methods. But a "Facsimile reprint" only means that the original text has been re-set in types of identical character. In recent years, certain publishers like Edward Brothers are specialising in the reproduction, of out-of-print reference books and advanced treatises, by new reprograph methods. They are also called facsimile editions. The ambiguity of the term "Edition" lands Book Selection in difficulty in the avoidance of unintended duplication. The book trade does not always indicate how far a later edition differs from the original edition or one edition from another. There appears to be no means of satisfying oneself about this except by physical verification. As personal verification is not often practicable, it is usual to throw the burden on the standing vendor, by inserting a special clause in the terms of agreement to the effect that if a book order mentions in a note that a particular edition is already in the library, the vendor should supply a copy only if the newly announced edition is substantially different and that in all cases of doubt the question must be settled by a reference to the library before the supply is made.

61 Message 36

The thirty-sixth message of the First Law to Book Selection is:

> *Unless duplication is deliberately intended, do not select a new edition of a book without satisfying yourself that it is substantially different from its earlier edition in the library. Unless you have access to a copy of the new edition, insist on the vendor verifying the matter before supply is made.*

7 Subjective Selection

One of the practices to be avoided in book selection is for a librarian to select a book for personal subjective reasons or other wrong reasons, without any reference to probable use by the clientele of his library. I know, for example, the callous way in which the librarian of a government departmental library went on investing the book-fund largely on complete sets of different editions of Shakespeare's works. This was because the librarian was interested in Shakespeare studies. In another departmental library books in subjects totally irrelevant to the department were bought often, because the then officer was known to be personally interested in those subjects, and the acquisition of those books put the librarian in his good books.

71 MESSAGE 37

The thirty-seventh message of the First Law to Book Selection is :

> *Do not select a book merely on the ground of your own liking or for satisfying the liking of the individual members of the Library Authority, if it will not be of real demand among the clientele of the library.*

8 Irresponsible and Indolent Selection

Another equally objectionable way of selecting books for a library is to select only from or all of those books of which copies are pressed upon the librarian by the book trade; or, for the librarian to accept books picked up from the market by persons immediately or remotely connected with the library without any reference to the policy of the library or the previous holdings of the library. This fault in book selection is often traceable to indolence and sometimes to lack of stamina to resist pressure. Even worse things may happen if the librarian is a careerist and public opinion is not healthy enough to act as a check. I know a case where a pretentiously long book selection list was produced for a public library in India. The intention was to bluff — to produce the impression on the authorities concerned that great work was behind such a balanced and exhaustive book selection. The list was obviously too good to be a true book selection list. Apart from that, it was totally unrelated to the needs of the community. The First Law was in a rage and said "Surely these books are not for the use of the readers here. They might be quite suited to the common reader in the United States." Moreover it was possible to guess that several of the books in the list were out of print. The librarian was asked to produce the source from which he copied the list. After some evasion, the list was produced and it turned out to be a printed catalogue of some public library in the United States. In a case like this there was no evaluation of any kind. Book Selection work of this sort sins against the First Law and indeed against all the Laws of Library Science. It sins against the public.

81 MESSAGE 38

The thirty-eighth message of the First Law to Book Selection is :

In selecting books, have the stamina to resist the insistence of pressure groups. Remember that a sacred trust is being discharged so as to give the right books to the readers; do not allow your conscience to be weakened by indolence, or fear of any kind, or to proneness to bluffing born out of careerism.

CHAPTER DN

A HYPOTHESIS

0 Introduction

To reconcile conflicting claims in doing book selection in diverse kinds of libraries, some hypothesis of a theoretical nature may prove to be a help. This hypothesis may be taken by some to belong to the sphere of metaphysics and by others to that of psychology. Whatever that be, the following hypothesis has been of help to me. I stated it in explicit terms for the first time in my inaugural talk to the Unesco-Ifla International Summer School of Librarianship held at Manchester in September 1948. It had been stated earlier at the Chaucer House, London, before a large gathering of British librarians. It was recorded *in extenso* in the *Indian librarian* 1948. A summary was given in Sec 7231 of my *Library tour* (Indian Library Association, English series, 1) (1950). Here is the hypothesis.

1 Personality

Man's personality is dynamic. It is ever in flux. It seeks unfoldment at its own speed, in its own way, and towards its own fullness. Such unfoldment is true education. To understand this process of unfoldment, we may mentally analyse the physically unanalysable personality. Three constituents may be recognised : the vital, the mental, and the spiritual — arranged in increasing sequence of intangibility and decreasing sequence of cognisability. They may be schematically represented as co-axial sheaths lying one within another, the spiritual constituent taken to be the innermost and the least reachable and the vital or the body-constituent being the outermost or the most reachable.

We may recognise three sub-sheaths in the mental sheath : the lower emotions, the intellect, and the sublimated emotions. Thus we may conveniently think even of five sheaths in human personality.

2 Forces Acting on Personality

The growth or unfoldment of personality is under three forces :

hereditary or biological force, environmental or ecological force, and a third — not easily granted but well-known in traditions not obliterated by the anti-occult European drive of the last few centuries — psycheo-genetic force which gains in momentum as the soul marches on from embodiment to embodiment. While all the three sheaths are amenable to all the three forces, there is a specificity in their relation. The spiritual sheath is most susceptible to the psycheo-genetic force and least to the others. The biological force has the greatest incidence on the vital sheath and the least on the spiritual sheath. The correlation of the mental sheath and the ecological (physical as well as social) force is most pronounced.

3 Possibility of Manipulation

Further, the hereditary force is not easily subject to manipulation. Though with the aid of powerful radiations the scientific man has begun to influence the biological force acting on lower organisms like the banana fly, to manipulate their gene perhaps and to derive monsters with three eyes from normals with two eyes, it is unlikely that this scientific mastery will ascend to the level of the human body; at any rate we do not wish for such a success in the scientist.

The psycheo-genetic force is denied by many and even those who grant it hold that it is not amenable to manipulation by human organisations such as we are familiar with. It is only the environmental force that can be manipulated and, as we have said, it is predominantly incident on the mind.

4 Switch-Board

So to speak, there is a switch in each of these sheaths. By working the switch in the vital sheath it is only its own growth or unfoldment that can be regulated. By working the switch in the mental sheath, the growth of the vital as well as the mental sheaths can be regulated. By working the switch in the spiritual sheath, the growth in all the three sheaths can be manipulated. But the working of the switch in the spiritual sheath is known only to a few adepts. It is not reachable by social organisations. And so we shall have little to do with it. This in its turn may quiet the mental disturbance induced in those who question the existence of this sheath. Of the two switches workable by social organisation, the one in the mental sheath is the more potent.

5 Activation

Each of these is ever-growing. In the evolution of the human race, there is a parallelism to the growth of an individual. Phylogeny is imitated-in-little by ontogeny. The vital sheath or the body is activated first ; it also attains maturity or adulthood earlier than others. Next in order comes the sheath of lower emotions. Then comes the intellect. It is slower than the other two in getting activated, but it is earlier than the sublimated emotions and the soul in man. The soul is very lethargic in getting activated. In most persons, it does not visibly get activated at any time. But there are exceptions like Buddha, Jesus, Sambandar, Sankara, Muhammad, and a few others. In modern times, we know in India of Ramakrishna, Ramalingaswami, Sadhu Sundar Singh, Sai Baba, and Ramana Rishi. In regard to the activation of the mind, just a few finish their lives without its getting activated at all. Psychological statisticians would postulate that about 10 per cent of a normal community finish off like this and that as if to balance this, about 10 per cent are precocious. The remaining 80 per cent are evenly spread out between these two extremes. There is a correspondence to all this in the evolution of the human race. The following diagram shows the march in the five sheaths of human personality. The thick portion of each line represents the relative lateness in the activation of the sheath.

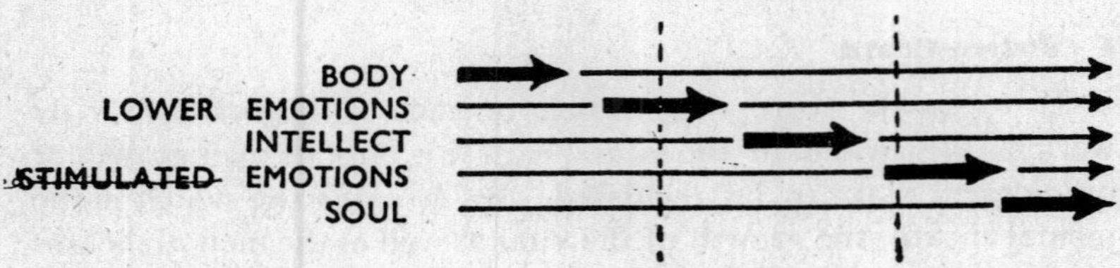

Fig. 2

While there are exceptions at all stages, the human race as a whole is now in the region enclosed by the dotted verticals. It is predominantly mental. It has entered this stage in comparatively recent times. It therefore still prefers the testimony of the primary senses. Its reasoning power, which has to make abstractions and generalisations, is still immature, unstable, fleeting, and easily overpowered and extinguished by passion. It has not developed stamina to persist against obstruction.

6 Leisure Time and Its Use

The mind, if established in a state of activation, is not exhausted as quickly as the body. It recovers from exhaustion much earlier than the body. When the body is still exhausted, mind is to be fed. This is true leisure time; and it is this time that public librarianship should fill profitably. During this time the mind can be fed with stuff that satisfies the lower emotions — the kind of detective stories or sensational news items which one forgets as rapidly as one reads and which, in the long run, leaves one degraded. Or it can be fed with intellectual pabulum or material of higher emotional value. These make men more efficient and elevated when the body recovers. The public library has to choose between these two. The soul, when activated, knows no exhaustion. It is ever in ecstasy and it radiates.

7 Degrees of Abstraction or Generalisation

The above hypothesis makes us infer that among potential library-going public — about 90 per cent of the people of a locality — we can recognise three groups :

1 Those the approach to whose intellect has to be through emotional appeal ;

2 Those who feel at home, without effort, in descriptive account of concrete things and situations which they can handle and experience ; and

3 Those that can find interest in thought of various degrees of abstraction or generalization.

Corresponding to these groups, we can divide the Universe of Knowledge into four regions arranged in ascending degree of abstraction or generalisation :

1 Humanities ;
2 Social Sciences ;
3 Arts and Crafts ; and
4 Pure Sciences.

Every reader will be interested in all the four fields but what he can enjoy reading in the different fields will be of different orders. Even the commonest man whose favourite is passion-fiction will, in certain moods, manifest curiosity and interest in pure sciences. Conversely even the severe scholar who normally revels in abstractions of the highest kind will in certain moods like to enjoy purely descriptive books which calls for very little of his abstractive capacity. This fact should be reflected in Book Selection work.

71 MESSAGE 39

The thirty-ninth message of the First Law to Book Selection is:

> *Select books and periodicals from all the regions of knowledge. Vary the proportion among the diverse regions according to the nature of the library — generalist or specialist — and in the latter according to the mental age of the clientele.*

CHAPTER DP

HUMANITIES

O Introduction

Fiction, Biography, Travel, Drama, Poetry, other forms of Fine Art, Linguistics, Religion, and Philosophy including Metaphysics and Esthetics may be labelled Humanities. Of these, Fiction to Fine Arts involve the least abstraction. They are nearly global. Their emotional appeal often takes off the edge from their intellectual content. Therefore they have a universal appeal. They will form the channels through which the minds of ordinary men can be taken to more abstract and intellectual subjects. They are subjects on which even the most severe intellectual worker may find solace. These are therefore to be given a permanent place in book selection for public libraries.

01 MESSAGE 40

The fortieth message of the First Law to Book Selection is :

> ***In a generalist library, book selection should give dominance to subjects of emotional appeal — such as fiction, biography, travel, drama, poetry, other forms of Fine Arts and Religion, in the sequence mentioned above.***

1 Fiction

Yarn-spinning and story-telling have been the oldest pre-occupation of man and the earliest attraction of children. It has been the chief method of filling up leisure time as well as means of relief from boredom. It still remains so. The colour with which fiction is dyed may range through the entire spectrum of knowledge. Science, relativity and fourth dimension have formed subjects of entertainment. Religion has always been a theme. Psychology, love, and crime characterise the most widely sought fiction. Historical personalities as well as common man's life give life to another class of fiction. In fiction-selection representation should be given to all such interests. Not only long drawn out ponderous novels but also short stories should be selected. The short stories will appeal to anybody on account of their rapid movement and the narrowness of their canvass. Such stories are particularly suited to neo-literates. Before the strain, caused in the exercising of newly acquired literacy, begins to over-power emotional interest, the story will be rounded off if it is a short one. This is one reason for giving representation to short stories in Book Selection. The action, the conversation and the personification possible in the story-form of exposition make it the most effective medium for books meant to give children information on diverse subjects. Even abstract subjects can be concretised by this method. Indeed the lower the age of the child the more extensive will have to be the proportion of the story-form in Book Selection.

11 MESSAGE 41

The forty-first message of the First Law to Book Selection is:

In a children's library book selection should prefer the story-form of exposition of all kinds of subjects, whether falling within the range of humanities or, social sciences, or natural sciences, or their applications.

12 MESSAGE 42

The forty-second message of the First Law to Book Selection is:

Book selection in fiction for neo-literates should prefer short stories to long novels.

13 MESSAGE 43

The forty-third message of the First Law to Book Selection is:

While book selection should not take up the responsibility for censorship, since a public library is a social institution for the betterment of society, book selection in a public library should abstain from including fiction, with anti-social suggestions.

14 MESSAGE 44

The forty-fourth message of the First Law to Book Selection is:

In a specialist library devoted to research in the development of literature, book selection should include all fictions — elevating or otherwise.

2 Biography

Biography, including autobiography, is only second to fiction in its general appeal. The hero of physical prowess has always been the centre of attention and his life-story has therefore a personal appeal. In modern times the hero of physical prowess has begun to share his place in popular imagination with heroes in other fields. Men of eminence, industrial magnates, persistent explorers, great educators, penetrating psychologists, discoverers in biology, inventors of machinery, chemists, physicists, and even mathematicians make an appeal to the common man. Such biographies are also written in modern times with considerable literary insight. To read the adventures of heroes in any field gives vicarious satisfaction. The thrill of vicarious satisfaction can be as real as that of personal satisfaction. This psychological fact gives importance to biography in Book Selection. The biographical form is so human that in order to exploit the inborn anthropomorphism of children, preference is given in Book Selection for children to books in biographical forms whatever be the subject of exposition. In modern days a hybrid which may be called biographical fiction is coming into vogue. In this realism, psychology and fiction meet in an effective way. This hybrid-form is highly helpful to the First Law. Two particularly fascinating and intimate variant forms of biography which should not be omitted in Book Selection are reminiscences and letters of correspondence.

21 Message 45

The forty-fifth message of the First Law to Book Selection is :

In a children's library, next to story-form of exposition, book selection should prefer the biographical form not only in subjects falling within the area of social sciences and humanities but also of the natural sciences and their applications.

22 Message 46

The forty-sixth message of the First Law to Book Selection is:

In a generalist library, book selection should cover the biographies of eminent persons in all the fields of knowledge.

23 Message 47

The forty-seventh message of the First Law to Book Selection is:

In a specialist library, biographies of persons in the subject of specialisation concerned should form an important fringe area for book selection.

3 Travel and History

Fiction and biography paint life in communities, and lives of individuals, in a way fit for use by those who prefer understanding things as wholes and even by others when they are in a mood to see things as wholes. When things are so presented, intuitive insight and grasp are necessary and abstraction is at a minimum. But the presentation is deeply flavoured with the personality of the author. In one sense, such a flavour acts on the imagination of the reader. It lessens the intellectual effort involved in reading. Travel and history describe life in communities, and incidentally portray lives of individuals too, in a way that is far less personal. This impersonal presentation takes the description nearer to what may be called public description. It is objective, as it is called. In this, the reader escapes the influence of the author. This implies that he has to go without the help of the aroma of the author. The result is that he has to lose the help of imagination and lean much more on his intellect. Objective or sense-dependent concreteness implies some abstraction. For it abstracts what is nearer to the grasp of the primary senses and a varying degree of intellectual comprehension, and leaves out what may be subtle and intangible. It is the absence of this intangible element — the trace element — in the objective accounts of travel and history that makes them appeal to the intellect rather than to imagination and makes reading less attractive. However, the gross wholeness of the situation is not shattered too much. That is why travel and history come next in popularity to fiction and biography. Travel covers a shorter range of time and is more impressionistic, more objective, and less thorough in detail than history. History may cover any range of time and is more objective and detailed than Travel. Moreover, there are writings — plenty of them — which belong to the region in which fiction and biography from one side and travel and history from the other meet and overlap. Examples of works which are near the factual end of this region are the histories by Froude and Macaulay and travels like the ***Eothen*** or the ***Man eaters of***

Tsavo. Works which are near the fiction end of this region are called biographical fiction and historical fiction. *The Edwardians* by Sackville-West and the *Baladitye* by A S P Ayyar are examples.

31 TRAVEL

Travel books can have all the charm of fiction and all the thrill of biography. Their lightness of touch and concreteness are elusive and yet science, geography, history, and anthropology can lie imbedded in travel books. Here again the vicarious statisfaction given by a travel book makes a great appeal. The more brilliant the writer is and the more delicate the fusion of literary merit and penetrating insight is, the greater becomes that satisfaction. There is also a great social service which travel books can do. If they are written in a spirit of tolerance, fair-play, and appreciation of the culture and the ways of life of the people visited, they can become a powerful medium for promoting international understanding. Therefore by giving a good representation to travel books in Book Selection not only will the travel books constitute a part of the library which is widely used, and in addition they may even stimulate greater use of other books.

32 HISTORY

The more chronicling history is, the more abstract it becomes, and the less appeal it has to the non-specialist. Social and cultural history is more global and less abstract, and appeals to the common reader. *Outline of history* by H G Wells is an example. So is the *Discovery of India* by Jawaharlal Nehru. These facts determine the range to be covered by Book Selection in the field of history. Book Selection, in this subject should also aim at world coverage. This does not mean merely selection of volumes on the history of the world but an extended selection of independent histories of the various countries of the world.

33 MESSAGE 48

The forty-eighth message of the First Law to Book Selection is .

> *In a generalist library, book selection should pay special attention to impressionist books of travel and history.*

34 MESSAGE 49

The forty-ninth message of the First Law to Book Selection is :

In a specialist library, book selection should prefer objective, factual books of travel and history, and also books of an evaluating nature in history.

4 Drama

Drama and *Natya* including *Kathakali* (story-rendering-dance) form a bridge between Fine Arts in literary form and other forms of Fine Art. Folk drama dates from primitive ages. Even the most evolved man finds a pull towards drama. The First Law would urge Book Selection to harness this popularity of drama among people of all intellectual grades. It would emphasise that dramatic books can in the case of some persons provide the preparation necessary to enjoy witnessing a performance with intelligent appreciation. It may also happen that in others the written drama is sought after the performance is witnessed. In either case there is use for written drama. There is still another class of people who come in directly to written dramas, without any reference to performance, and enjoy reading them. But ordinary people may not be able to do so. This is because, the words in dramatic literature pre-suppose supplementing by histrionic art. It is not everybody that can supply this supplement from imagination. All the same, dramatic works appeal to all grades of people. The great zeal with which neo-literates turn to dramatisation suggests that dramatic literature can be used as a means for inducing reading habit in them. Dramas present all the varieties which fiction presents. The colour with which drama is dyed may range through the entire field of knowledge. Religion, Psychology, History, and Social Criticism can form the theme. In drama-selection representation should be given to all such interests. Not only long-drawn-out plays but also one-act plays should be selected. One-act plays lend themselves for amateur performance as leisure-time occupation after the day's work. Those whose day's work is repetitive get their total personality blossom forth by such performances. In organised communities, through this use, one-act plays can be easily popularised. All that has been said about dramas are equally applicable to sound-pictures. The revival of interest in drama and the shooting of sound-pictures are helping the use of books in a variety of subjects. Search for background material, costume appropriate to the age represented, geographical setting, and several other factors, needed to make drama or picture-shooting realistic, often influence and enrich Book Selection in a purposive manner.

41 MESSAGE 50

The fiftieth message of the First Law to Book Selection is:

In a generalist library — be it for children, or neo-literates, or normal adults — book selection should give full representation to collections of one-act plays in addition to conventional plays of many acts.

42 MESSAGE 51

The fifty-first message of the First Law to Book Selection is:

In a specialist library devoted to histrionic art or movie production, over and above the dramas and the dramatised versions of poems, biography, travel, and fiction, book selection should also include the materials needed for the cultural-setting needed for providing the correct historico-cultural-setting for the dramas.

5 Translations

"The world nowhere is other than what it is here" is an old Indian saw. This is certainly true of human nature. Therefore the appeal of the master-pieces in fiction, biography, travel, drama, and poetry often transcends national limitations. They are universally enjoyable. This makes the First Law press the claim of translation in Book Selection. It has been said that next to the Bible, the *Panchatantra* the ancient book of Indian tales is the most widely translated book in the world. It may bear diverse titles in diverse languages — for example, Arabian Nights. Translations of such classics go some way in bringing about a glimpse into the oneness of mankind. It is believed by Unesco that promotion of translation can help the emergence of one world. As a means of rapid internal cultural integration, India is now promoting the translation of the best books in each of its languages into every other of its languages. The First Law supports this belief and recommends selection of translations. Modern developments in communication tend to eliminate distance and intermix people belonging to different nations. This brings mankind into closer relationship. This relationship can be made amicable by books acting as messengers of light. This closer relationship also creates a longing to enjoy the classics in other languages. For this reason also the First Law recommends selection of translations. In the earlier years there was a tendency for the translations to lean on verbal faithfulness. In recent years, the tendency is to care for faithfulness to the whole thought. Of course both varieties have been co-existing in some proportion all along. Generally speaking, translations which are free renderings are preferable. Translations which are free renderings shade imperceptibly into adaptations. Adaptations themselves shade into reproductions or fresh creations in the new language by master-writers. Several such renderings of the classics in Sanskrit literature are to be found among the modern Indian languages. The *Ramayana* and the *Mahabharata*, have been re-told in the modern languages by first rate masters of style and literary insight. No doubt the impress of these authors is unmistakable in such reproductions and fresh creations. So also a reflection of the changed social values may also be there. These, however, are not distractions. On the other hand they are enrichments. Indeed they render the ethos and the flavour of the original far more intelligible to their contemporaries than orthodox translations. On this ground their selection is justified both on their own merit as a piece of literature and on their being vehicles for the classics in other languages. Book Selection should cover translations of ancient classics as well as of contemporary literature.

51 MESSAGE 52

The fifty-second message of the First Law to Book Selection is:

> *Book selection should include the translations, into the language of the library, of the best books written in other languages on diverse subjects.*

6 Fine Arts

While fiction, biography, and travel feed at once the

imagination and sublimate the emotion, they have a frame of reality and concreteness which is more or less self-contained, and further, the author acts as a guide. He does not hide himself. He makes his presence felt directly. He steps in often to explain, underline, and even give a helping hand when we falter or have difficulty in seeing the heart of things. On the contrary, in the dramatic form of writing, the author hides himself from the reader, as it were. He makes his creatures move and talk. Unless their doing is witnessed in a performance, communication may prove incomplete in the case of certain readers. Thus, the gap formed by the hiding of the author proves a barrier except to those whose imaginative capacity has been well-developed. The theatre, where the words of the drama are uttered and supplemented by action and dowered with life, brings drama within the grasp of the primary senses. It is in this sense that drama is a bridge between invisible and visible art.

61 Poetry and Prose

Pure literary art is most invisible. Poetry and Prose are least mediated by primary senses. The fact, that the content of such pure literary art has no frame of reality and concreteness such as the primary senses are accustomed to, and that even in the use of words it seeks to depend more on their flavour than on their normal meaning, and that it seeks to captivate the reader by suggestion rather than by expression, makes it more elusive than any other form of Fine Arts. The perfect economy of first class Poetry and Prose is the result of the ineffability of the penetrating global experience of the highly gifted author, But it is so packed with unending layers of experience and it scintillates such a cascade of suggestions, that one is made to go back to it again and again throughout one's lifetime. Each time, it reveals more and more of its depth and concreteness in the measure of the actual experience in life, that we turn to it to check up, as it were. It is so benign that it interprets our experience and soothes and confirms and reassures us. It thus induces in us a greater degree of self-confidence and sends us back to live our life a little more fully, with greater zest and delight, and come back to it to get a further push. Verily, verily, works like the *Ramayana* of Valmiki, the *Iliad* of Homer, the *Aeneid* of Virgil, the works of Kalidasa, Tulsidas, Shakespeare, Blake, Bernard Shaw, Tagore, and Subramania Bharathi are like cyclotrons pushing up our life potential to higher and higher levels in each round. In respect of form, Poetry and Prose of this order shade into each other and share in common a large overlapping region which is described as prose-poetry or poetic-prose. What is common to all of them is their infinite amplitude of appeal and a transparency which has given rise to the expression "art conceals art". It taps the secret currents of life and turns the mind of the reader inwards into itself. The artist just stops short of, or stops just out of, the threshold of the unspeaking — because their experience is unspeakable — of the unspeaking *muni* and *mauni* (=mystic). The artist has not yet lost his power of expression or has just regained it and uses it to entertain us with a vision of his profound experience and to communicate to us something which our soul longs to share. It bombards our inner self with its radiation and make us radiate. Book Selection should take full care of this highest reach of human expression. It is too much to expect a single person, however gifted, to assess all such gems. Nor is it possible to categorise tests with which Poetry and Prose can be assessed by librarians engaged in Book Selection. It is here that Book Selection has to lean inevitably on the connoisseur reviewer. Even the physical accessibility of the book may not be of avail in this case. The critic and the reviewer must be brought in to make Book Selection bring in books of this order, which have the greatest and ever-lasting potency for use. It should take care not merely of collected works and whole pieces — which may soon cause surfeit in many — but also anthologies. Selections which are garlands woven, as it were, to fit the diverse temperaments are not only better used, but they also promote the use and appreciation of the whole works.

62 Message 53

The fifty-third message of the First Law to Book Selection is:

Book selection should include anthologies of literary works.

63 Message 54

The fifty-fourth message of the First Law to Book Selection is:

The librarian should take the help of a literary connoisseur in the selection of books, in the Main Class Literature.

64 Other Fine Arts

As a community is helped by library service to spend leisure in finding joy in reading, it is found that people look to the library not only to be helped with books but also with other materials which give satisfaction to esthetic craving. Paintings, drawings, pictures of sculptures, graphic representation of embroidery work, musical scores, and sound records of music are now recognised to come within the purview of libraries. Book Selection should recognise this fact. During recent years many public libraries have formed departments of Fine Arts. I found in my visits to the developed countries of the West that the loan of gramaphone discs and speaking-books has now widely come into vogue. This means that these materials are ungrudgingly selected. I also found a new service by libraries. Members are given loans of framed pictures for long periods like six months and one year. I found it very much in vogue in university and college libraries. Students living in hostels appreciate this service. But in India today even the traditional book service as a public project has not yet fully established itself. But it does not mean necessarily that the time-interval between the inclusion of books and that of art materials in Book Selection need be as great as it has been in the developed countries. The great contemporary musical awakening and signs of possible awakening for other forms of Fine Arts as a result of the zest for life released by political independence may justify the inclusion of Fine Arts materials in Book Selection even from the very beginning.

65 Message 55

The fifty-fifth message of the First Law to Book Selection is :

In a public library and in an eductional library, apart from specialist libraries in Fine Arts, book selection should include art materials reproduced in graphic form or in sound form.

7 Auxiliaries

Book Selection in the field of humanities is not exhausted by the selection of original or positive writings of the kind considered so far. A considerable amount of auxiliary writings has grown about them. They are of two kinds — aids to appreciation and aids to authors themselves.

71 EVALUATION WRITINGS

Those that are aids to appreciation are called evaluative literature. I prefer to call them evaluative literature instead of criticism. They are abstract and intellectual. They help a more understanding use of the originals, though their appeal is not to imagination but to the intellect. We have evaluating literature bearing on poetry, drama, fiction and prose. We have also evaluative literature on the visible and audible forms of Fine Arts like sculpture. graphic arts, painting, music etc. We have evaluation of individual authors and artists too. The upper quartiles in a community seek their use. Indeed a study of any original piece induces in them a desire to look up the associated evaluative literature. Conversely too, study of evaluative literature leads them to the study of the originals. This mutual dependance makes the First Law ask for Book Selection covering evaluative literature. Book Selection should therefore care for them.

72 MESSAGE 56

The fifty-sixth message of the First Law to Book Selection is :

In a college or a university library and in a specialist library devoted to literature, book selection should give full coverage to evaluative writings.

73 MESSAGE 57

The fifty-seventh message of the First Law to Book Selection is :

In a public library, book selection should include at least a small assortment of evaluative writings.

74 NORMATIVE WRITINGS

Applied evaluative literature implies also the existence of Canons of Evaluation. There are books on them. This class of books transitions imperceptibly into the class of those that are mainly normative in intention. While it is true that creative artists are born and not made, there are also persons who may be called "near-artists" and who can be helped to develop into artists, if they are guided by norms distilled out of spontaneous creative art by the intellectual analysis and examination. Books on Canons of Evaluation, and on norms for literary writings and other forms of Fine Arts for the guidance of authors, reach an abstraction of a higher order. But if such books are not produced and included in Book Selection, it will be like not ploughing and manuring the field or sowing seeds.

75 MESSAGE 58

The fifty-eighth message of the First Law to Book Selection is :

Book selection should give representation to writings embodying normative principles for the production of poetry, drama, fiction, and other literary forms.

76 MESSAGE 59

The fifty-ninth message of the First Law to Book Selection is :

In a specialist library in Fine Arts, book selection should give full coverage to writings embodying normative principle in the Fine Arts concerned.

8 Other Humanities

Spiritual experience and mysticism, religion, philosophy, and linguistics form the residue of the humanities to be considered. Of these, books belonging to the class, "Mysticism and Spiritual Experience" charm many a reader. Lives of saints and accounts of their miracles, and expositions of their teachings, make a great appeal to many. Book Selection should bear this in mind. The sacred books of religions have had perhaps the longest hold on people. Theology, Church History, and Sermons are widely sought. The *Puranas* and the *Itihasas* have been from the most ancient times relayed to the people by word of mouth. This is happening even today in villages as well as cities. The First Law would urge the need for the library providing for follow-up study by including this class of literature in Book Selection. Philosophy including dogmatic and speculative Psychology is perhaps the most abstract branch of humanities. But among the intellectuals in any community there is considerable demand for Philosophy. Perhaps it is true — at any rate it is visible in India — that the interest in the study of Philosophy increases with one's age. A count made at one time in the Madras University Library confirmed this conjecture. For the sake of the older people then, Book Selection should include Philosophy. This is apart from the requirements of specialists in Philosophy.

81 MESSAGE 60

The sixtieth message of the First Law to Book Selection is:

In a public library, book selection should give a good representation to the lives, the sayings, and the devotional lyrics of mystics.

82 MESSAGE 61

The sixty-first message of the First Law to Book Selection is:

In a public library, book selection should give a balanced coverage of the books on diverse religions.

83 MESSAGE 62

The sixty-second message of the First Law to Book Selection is:

Book selection in linguistics and in philosophy will have to vary in coverage according to the library being a generalist or a specialist one.

CHAPTER DQ

SOCIAL SCIENCES

1 Abstraction

As we passed from the first to the last sub-section of "Chap DP Humanities", we passed gradually from something profoundly concrete to something increasingly abstract. The abstraction reached its climax in Philosophy. This mode of regression from concrete wholes is characterised by omission of particulars and the insertion of generalities of higher order. Blake describes as follows in *Jerusalem* (Section 10 lines 7 to 16) what brings about this abstraction.

> " It is the Reasoning Power,
> An Abstract objecting power that Negatives every thing.
> This is the Spectre of Man, the Holy Reasoning Power ;
> And in its Holiness is closed the Abomination of Desolation "!

11 Atomisation

There is another way in which aberration from holism can happen. It is the way of atomisation. It is the way of breaking up a whole into parts and concentrating on each part severally. Atomisation also lends itself in abstraction. In his *There is no natural religion*, Blake recognises the two modes of abstraction followed by Philosophy and Science respectively and emphasises that when compared to what is seized by spiritual, poetic, or intuitive insight, what is understood by experimental or scientific analysis and study, is itself an abstraction. He lays it down. " If it were not for the Poetic or Prophetic character, the Philosophic and Experimental would soon be at the ratio (=mental abstraction) of all things." Abstraction is reached largely via atomisations in the region of Social Sciences.

12 Impact of Mathematical Statistics

The invention of the method of the mathematical statistics in recent years has equipped man with a tool with which he can analyse, compare, and test social phenomena in a way comparable to what the physical sciences do with material phenomena. The result is the emergence of Social Sciences. These include Education, Geography, Political Science, Economics, Sociology, and Law. The scientific method in Social Sciences is akin to, though not identical with, that for Natural Sciences. This is further examined in Chapter JH. It has now crystallised and made itself recognisable. It is man himself and groups of men that form the subject of study in the Social Sciences. It is therefore difficult to isolate facts totally from the wishes and wills of the observers. This has been responsible for the delay in the admission of these subjects to the jurisdiction of scientific methods.

2 Scientific Books

Consequently, a new kind of books is coming to existence in the region of social sciences. These can only appeal to specialists. These are too abstract to the common man or the generalist.

21 Message 63

The sixty-third message of the First Law to Book Selection is:

> *Books embodying scientific and statistical study of the subjects falling within the area of social sciences are suitable to a specialist or a university library rather than to a generalist one.*

3 Data Books

The State has to play an intensive part in the sphere of Social Sciences. Much of the observational work is done by the State. The results emanate as publications of governments — be they local bodies or governments of constituent States of a Federation or national governments or approximations to world governments — such as the late League of Nations or the United Nations and their specialised agencies. At the higher levels of government, and particularly those of national and world governments, we have publications not only of observational data but also of the result of the digesting of the data and the distillation therefrom of principles of varying degrees of abstraction. The various departments of the United States are the most prolific in this regard among national governmental agencies. The annual output of the United Nations and its specialised agencies is becoming so great in quantity and so extensive in its coverage of the Social Sciences that the Library of the United Nations has to issue special Book Selection aids.

Several non-governmental agencies — such as large industrial concerns, Chambers of Commerce, and Foundations — have also begun to produce similar publications fit to form the basis for the scientific study of some of the regions in the Social Sciences.

31 MESSAGE 64

The sixty-fourth message of the First Law to Book Selection is:

> *Books embodying statistical data and fact-finding reports of governmental and non-governmental agencies are suitable to a specialist or a university library rather than to a generalist one.*

4 Propaganda Books

As already stated in Sec DQ12, since human beings themselves are the subject of study in the Social Sciences, there are naturally books produced under the pressure of the wish and will of persons with partisan views, these are naturally books not presenting balanced views. They are really partisan books. Partisan books are not censored by governments unless they are violently stimulating group hatred and public disorder. Therefore propaganda books are widely available in the market. It also often happens that they are freely thrust on libraries by power groups. Here, as an institution primarily intended to promote social understanding, good will, and well being, libraries have a difficult task to perform. There are plenty of instances when librarians have been hauled up by this party or that for the admission of propaganda books in the library.

41 MESSAGE 65

The sixty-fifth message of the First Law to Book Selection is:

> *Book selection should give a balanced representation to propaganda books of all groups, unless they can be totally excluded.*

5 Descriptive Books

Ever since books came to be published, descriptive books have been appearing in Social Sciences all along, coloured by personal opinions and prejudices to varying degrees. Such descriptive books continue also after the advent of scientific methods in the Social Sciences. After the advent of scientific method a new kind of descriptive books have come into existence embodying a popular version of the results reached by scientific study and the outlook born of such results without showing how the results were reached. These descriptive books in Social Sciences form an important link between specialists and non-specialists. This fact should be given full weight in the selection of books in the library.

51 MESSAGE 66

The sixty-sixth message of the First Law to Book Selection is :

> *In a generalist library, perhaps also in a specialist library, book selection should give a good coverage to the descriptive books in each subject in the social sciences.*

6 Systems of Thought

The advent of scientific method into the sphere of Social Sciences has brought some clarity in the mind of specialists and this is capable of spreading slowly into the minds of non-specialists as well. It is now becoming a little more easy for a man to know what he is talking about and to communicate it clearly to others, and for the others to pick up the communication in a less foggy condition and to check it up with his own idea, with less confusion. This advance is still in an incipient state. Much of the tension in the world can be traced in the first instance to the poor degree of clarity, that has been attained today, in man's knowledge of the subjects forming the Social Sciences. If clarity attains the same degree as it has done in the Physical Sciences, then only can be true springs of tension, if any, built into the very nature of man, be laid bare. As a social institution charged with the promotion of universal self-education, the library should help progress towards this clarity. The first step for this has to be taken at the stage of Book Selection. Book Selection should recognise that, as a result of the introduction of scientific method, recognisable systems of thought are emerging in each branch of the Social Sciences. For example, in Education we have two groups of systems of thought. One group may be said to emphasise "Transmissive Education" and "Mass Method". The other group may be said to emphasise "Creative Education" and "Individual Method". In each group there are many systems. Book Selection should see that all the systems of thought are represented in the collection of the library. In the politico-economic field, systems of thought exist which belong to one or other of two groups. One of these groups seeks to solve the antithesis between the individual and the community by upholding the individual. The other group regards the community as paramount. In each group there are several systems of thought with varying shades of difference. Capitalism and socialism, democracy and dictatorship are examples of antithetic sub-groups. Book Selection should see that all the systems of thought are represented. So it is in Sociology, and so it is in Law. About each system of thought, Book Selection should care not only for severely abstract and scientific monographs and treatises, but also for popular relays of the finished results contained in such severe treatises and for books which picture the immediate and remote consequences of such finished results. There is use for all such varieties of books in Social Sciences. Book Selection is said to be unbiased or balanced, and to conform to the Canon of Reticence only if it covers all such varieties of books. This kind of books is different from the propaganda books mentioned in Sec DQ4.

61 MESSAGE 67

The sixty-seventh message of the First Law to Book Selection is :

Book selection should give a balanced representation to all the systems of thought in the diverse subjects in social sciences.

7 Topical Interest

Since man himself is the subject of study in Social Sciences, the pressure of "topical interest" reaches unusually high levels of potential in regard to topics falling in the area of Social Sciences. Moreover, the interest may be short-lived and fade away quickly. This does not happen so much either in the Humanities, or the Arts and Crafts, or the Pure Sciences. In the first place any interest that gets created in topics falling within the area of any of these latter groups, persists for a long enough time. Nor does the interest get intertwined with passion and thereby step up its potential.

Perhaps it is also true that the consequences of the emergence of a topic in the area of any of these groups do not impinge upon or affect the physical and vital well-being of man, or the political, or economic, or legal make-up of his social setting, as intensively as a topic that emerges in the area of Social Sciences. The consequences is that Book Selection in Social Sciences should be very sensitive and resilient so that no interest that develops among readers goes unharnessed for the benefit of the First Law. One practical consequence of this is that in the Social Sciences Book Selection should be prompt. Another consequence is that Book Selection should be prepared to support several copies of a book being taken in Social Sciences — much more frequently than in any other fields of knowledge. For example, at one time the libraries in India had to buy several copies of the *Mission with Mountbatten*. I saw dozens of copies of Churchill's *Second World War* piled up behind the screen in several of the British libraries in 1948, awaiting to be released on the day fixed for it by the publishers. This demonstrates the way in which Book Selection should react to books of "topical interest" in the sphere of Social Sciences.

71 MESSAGE 68

The sixty-eighth message of the First Law to Book Selection is :

> *In any library — particularly in a generalist library — selection of books of topical interest should be made quite promptly and in anticipation of the demand for them.*

72 MESSAGE 69

The sixty-ninth message of the First Law to Book Selection is :

> *Book selection may have to include several copies of books of topical interest in the measure of anticipated demand.*

CHAPTER DR

ARTS AND CRAFTS

1 Know-How Books

In the field of Arts and Crafts, Engineering, Technology, Agriculture, Animal Husbandry, and Hygiene, the concrete in the physical sense — that is the concrete not far removed from the reach of primary senses, not veneered or deeply coloured or flavoured by traces of intangible something and not needing spiritual awareness to become manifest — the concrete as it is commonly understood — dominates. Books on them are usually read either with a fresh memory, or in the immediate presence, or physical materials. Moreover, the books themselves give visual aids by appropriate photographs, schematic diagrams, and other illustrations. Thus the edge of the abstraction involved in any written communication is taken off considerably. Therefore books in these subjects can be used even by those who are not accustomed to abstract thinking and intellectual flights. This means that Book Selection in these fields should bear the non-specialists in mind. It should go in not merely for advanced theoretical books for specialists but also for practical books of the "Know-how" type. In regard to this latter popular variety, Book Selection should provide for two sub-varieties — those suited to children and those suited to adults.

11 Message 70

The seventieth message of the First Law to Book Selection is:

> *In a school library, book selection should include know-how books written in a low key with plenty of illustrations, in order to satisfy the abundant curiosity and the urge to do in children and not confine itself merely to books covered by the curriculum*

12 Message 71

The seventy-first message of the First Law to Book Selection is:

> *In a public library and in a factory library, book selection should include know-how books for the use of workers not high up in the intellectual scale.*

2 Subject-Scatter

The Subject-scatter to be covered by Book Selection in this group is far more extensive than in any other group. Time was when knowledge of subjects in this group was not much represented in books. The time-honoured method, developed in an earlier cultural epoch to pick up knowledge in this field, has been that of apprenticeship. This method presupposes the availability of a master craftsman to take the seeker of knowledge under his care. But today the seekers far outnumber the masters. The masters are sufficient in number only to give demonstration. Further embellishments, of what can be picked up in the immediate presence of the master, have to be made by oneself. As an aid to this self-education, society has now begun to produce books on all kinds of Arts and Crafts. The scatter of subjects is immense. Books are now available even in tiny regions and corners of the applied field—

Calligraphy
Paper Making
Type Casting
Compositor's Job
Printing
Block Making
Ink Making
Typewriting
Book Binding
Book Selling
Cookery
Making of Special Dishes
Serving
Wool
Silk
Linen
Dress Making
Rug Making
Cane Work
Basket Making
Pottery
Furniture Making
Carving
Embroidery
Bead-work
Knitting
Household Work
Smithy
— for each of diverse metals —
Moulding
Carpentry
Glass Making
Glass Blowing
Carding
Spinning
Weaving
Dyeing
Textile Printing
—diverse Textile Materials like Cotton
Leather Work
Optician's Trade
Ceramics
Electric Wiring
Electronics
Work with Plastics
Framing
Dairying
Fishing
Poultry Keeping
Pet Birds and Animals
Bee keeping
Shellac

Lace-Making
Toy Making
Laundry Work
Varnishing
Tennis
Cricket
Rowing
Mountaineering
Card Play
Chess

and the unending series of other little subjects. Here again Book Selection should remember the fundamental saying "Diverse are the interests of men". Apart from these subjects of narrow extension there are the vast traditional fields of Applied Sciences, Engineering, Technology, and Agriculture. Book Selection should care for these too.

21 MESSAGE 72

The seventy-second message of the First Law to Book Selection is:

> *In view of the wide scatter of interest among people, book selection should give representation to every possible art and craft and sports.*

3 The Plight of India

Indian libraries of today are in a sad plight in regard to Book Selection in the above-mentioned group of subjects. It is during the last few centuries of India's sleep and exhaustion, change-over has taken place in other countries from dependence on apprenticeship to dependence on books in these subjects. It is again in the same period that the wants of people have been multiplied beyond recognition; with the result, that practically the whole nation — other than those engaged in administrative, educational, and other clean-collar jobs — is now turned on some art or craft. Moreover, it is during this period that science has harnessed hitherto unknown forms and sources of power which are transforming the techniques of the Arts and Crafts from year to year. It is these factors that have been responsible for the precipitation of books on Applied Sciences down to the minutest craft. During the period that this has been happening elsewhere India had been merely a market on which foreign goods, from aeroplane to the pin, had been dumped. Its man-power had been running to waste. Its languages had been paralysed, as they were not allowed to keep pace with the developments in Arts and Crafts. Therefore India possesses few books on these subjects which are intelligible to the common man. And yet since independence, the inhibiting forces have partially withdrawn. The innate urge to do, to construct, and to create has been released. Economic pressure is driving the masses to take to Arts and Craft with great avidity. They want to learn. They do not find books to help them. This is the plight of India today in regard to books on Applied Sciences including Arts and Crafts. In these circumstances, the Indian libraries have to adopt a transitory measure. They will have to select books in this field from among those written in foreign languages, particularly in English. They will have to select them not on the ground that they will be directly used by all those who are in need of their thought-content. They will have to be selected for the use of the bi-linguals who can read them and translate them to others — orally for immediate consumption and through books for the normal way in which knowledge is picked up through print. This special emphasis on foreign books may not be necessary in developed countries. This special emphasis is quite different from what was stated in Sec DP5 about the value of thought produced in one country being circulated in other countries on grounds of universal appeal and of promotion of international understanding and peace.

31 Message 73

The seventy-third message of the First Law to Book Selection is :

> *In a country such as India just recovering from cultural exhaustion, book selection should, as a transitory measure, include books in arts and crafts produced in a foreign language widely used in the country — for example, English in India or French in Algeria.*

4 Time-Factor

The rate of progress in Applied Sciences is now very great. Books in these subjects go out-of-date almost every year. It is certainly so in the case of their annual hand-books. Book Selection will have to keep itself abreast of the changes in practice. There is time-lag between the changes in practice and the appearance of books embodying them. This time-lag should be circumvented by

Book Selection by selecting the periodicals communicating nascent thought in regard to practices and by replacing every year the serials (annual hand-books) giving the latest data and specifications.

41 Message 74

The seventy-fourth message of the First Law to Book Selection is :

> *In the field of applied sciences, book selection should include the latest editions of the serial hand-books, giving data and specifications in their respective subjects, and getting published annually or at other intervals.*

CHAPTER DS

PURE SCIENCE

1 Eminent Domain of Intellect

Of the four spheres into which the universe of knowledge has been divided for purposes of this chapter, the Pure Sciences form the 'Eminent Domain' of intellect. Imagination and intuition have of course to act as starters. But once the start is made, the intellect carries forward with unbridled energy, circumventing crisis after crisis by adjustments made by itself. This it does until it gets itself caught up amidst a turbulence in the universe of knowledge, baffling and overpowering it. Even as Sugriva had to turn to Rama when overpowered and vanquished by Vali, intellect has then to turn to intuition and ask to be pulled out and re-started on a further lap of flight. The method of intellect is just the opposite of that of intuition. Intuition gets at the thing-in-itself directly unmediated by primary senses or by aids of any kind or by intellect. It seizes the thing-in-itself globally. The approach of the intellect on the other hand is mediated by the senses and by material aids increasing their capacity. It breaks down, analyses, atomises and gets at things only in tiny bits. Having endeavoured to understand each bit, it tries to piece them up in a patient and laborious way and thereby to get a picture of the original even as the blind men reconstructed the picture of the elephant in the *Aesop's fables*. This way of getting at things makes them in-comprehensible to the ordinary man. It becomes too abstract for him. The effect of this on Book Selection is that Pure Science figures comparatively little in the selection for a public library. It is at its maximum in the selection for an academic library — be it the library of a college or of a university or of an institution or of a learned body. This peculiarity, stemming from the high degree of abstraction reached in the Pure Sciences, is by no means of reflection on the importance of these subjects.

2 Quick Exploitation

On the other hand the importance of Pure Sciences is inestimable. They have transformed life at every level. They have transformed our nutrition, clothing, shelter, transport, communication, economics, industries, and every other activity and plane of existence. Indeed the progress in Pure Sciences has brought about a complete re-orientation of our view of the very nature and meaning of life. Even turns of expression have been transformed. An interesting investigation suggests itself in this regard. Random samples of imagery and phraseology used by poets during the last thousand years should be taken for each epoch. The progress of science as we know it will provisionally suggest the following epochs.

1 Century-intervals till 1600 ;
2 Half-century-intervals till 1850 ;
3 Quarter-century-intervals till 1900 ; and
4 Decade-intervals thereafter.

The samples pertaining to each epoch should be written on separate sheets of paper. There should be two copies for each epoch. One copy should have the year of the originals mentioned on it. This should form the control. The other copy should be without its mention. Let us call it the undated copy. Let us thoroughly shuffle all the undated copies. If any of them is picked out, the imagery and phraseology found on it will enable one to fix its date. My conjecture is that there will not be many mistakes in dating the copies. The number of scientific discoveries has been growing in geometric progression. The frequency with which changes take place in the sciences is increasing at a tremendous rate. The quickness with which advancement in Pure Sciences is brought down to the level of application and made to affect the common man is also increasing. All these factors have significance in Book Selection.

3 Academic Library

Book Selection in academic libraries will have to pay special attention to time factor. The rate of progress in Pure Sciences is now so great that it is usually too late when new results get embodied in books. Reference books are very costly to produce and the market for them is uneconomical in Pure Sciences. But the First Law insists on the latest ideas being brought into use. It therefore turns to periodical literature. It is thankful that the invention of printing and recent improvements therein have not only led to the invention of periodicals but has also multiplied them a thousand-fold so as to cover most of the subjects being currently investigated. According to the First Law, Book Selection is largely periodicals selection in Pure Sciences. It does not mean that books need not be selected. It only means that the proportion of periodicals selected to books selected — and in particular the proportion of the funds spent on them — will be the opposite of what it is in humanities. The front-line materials offering themselves for use in Pure Sciences are periodicals. The second-line materials, which Book Selection should build up, are the smaller monographs and bulletins. Generally speaking, treatises and books appear only in the third line. The replacement of books by later editions may not be needed in Pure Sciences as frequently as in Applied Sciences. Specialisation in Pure Sciences is now carried to such a fine degree that in the libraries for specialised workers it is only a limited sector of the field of science that has to be covered. This narrowness of sector for each library has been increased considerably by the enormous expansion of specialised research during and since the Second World War. Evaluation is usually easier in the case of science books and science periodicals than in the case of Humanities and Social Sciences. This is due partly to the almost total absence of emotion, imagination, and subjective element in the books in sciences. It is also due to the fact that, on account of limited market, there is a tendency for worthwhile books being more numerous than venturesome books of doubtful value. However, the situation is not so simple in regard to Book Selection for college libraries. At the text-book level there is a greater variety of books of varying values.

31 Message 75

The seventy-fifth message of the First Law to Book Selection is :

> *In a college library, book selection should allot more money to a variety of text-books and confine itself only to a few general periodicals and encyclopaedic treatises.*

32 Message 76

The seventy-sixth message of the First Law to Book Selection is:

> *In a research library including a university library, book selection should allot more money to periodicals, serials, encyclopaedic reference books, and advanced treatises, than to ordinary books.*

4 Public Library

In spite of the forbidding degree of abstraction which scientific work involves, we cannot conclude that books in Pure Sciences do not figure in Book Selection for public libraries. For, there is evidence of a rising tide of popular interest in what happens in the field of Pure Sciences. Some of the discoveries in Pure Sciences and perhaps some of their applications have attained even news-value. Moreover, during the last thousand years, culture has changed over from a defensive to an offensive phase so to speak. In the far off days every element in the environment was a source of fear to man. Even the very hills, the rivers, the open sky, the woods, and empty space itself appeared to be out to tease, if not to injure him. Does not the primitive man in us raise ever so many objections to the occupation of a house that is too large and had been unoccupied for a long time? The primitive man sought to protect himself from nature by charms, sacred formulae, propitiatory rituals, and all forms of sympathetic and ritualistic magic. But a reference to the four volumes entitled *A history of magic and science* by Lynn Thorndike will show that about the end of the fifteenth century the pendulum turned. A different understanding of the elements of the environment began to take shape. It induced in man a desire to bring them under subjection. The signal for the offensive given by Columbus was as follows:

> "Gold is a wonderful thing! Whoever owns it is the lord of all he wants. With gold it is even possible to open for soul a way to paradise."

Not merely metals but space itself is now attacked. The book on polar expedition and space vehicles are examples. Not merely expedition but the study of scientific phenomena in those bleak regions and high altitudes has now become well established. The depths of the ocean are now swept by science. The roof of the sky is being pierced through to beyond a hundred miles. The attack on matter *qua* matter is now occupying the thought of the foremost thinkers. In the fear that the solid, liquid, and gaseous fuel found from the bowels of earth may fail us, attempts are now being made to get inside the atom, in search of power, break its nucleus into fundamental particles, and study the life history of each of them. Even the mystery of life is not left alone. Mathematics, Physics, and Chemistry are used to attack the mystery of life itself. Ambition appears to be to create life! The way in which voice and pictures are carried round the earth in a trice rouses curiosity in the common man to ask "How"? Hiroshima, which will last in human memory eternally as a reminder of how progress in science through dry intellect without control by the spiritual in man can lead man to inhuman and shameful extremes, has made nuclear fission "News". The few sensitive souls are made to recall the verse in the *Bhagavad gita,* "There will be benign service, truly beneficient success, useful enrichment, and assured rectitude, if and only if the Arjuna Principle of intellection and action is sublimited and controlled by the Krishna Principle of global, eternal, spiritual insight" (Chap 18, Verse 78). This apart, there is a steadily widening general reading public for books in science. The new generation comes up with a clearer understanding of science. The very service of the library makes the common man eager and competent to have a general account of the happenings in the world of science. Many persons who are not accustomed to abstract thinking are nevertheless keen to know the results of abstract thinking on the part of specialists. Thus demand for popular books in Pure Sciences is growing. The supply too is coming forward to meet this demand. Front rank scientists occasionally step down to the popular level and produce books to meet this demand. Moreover, society is also throwing forth a set of interpreters of science. The publishing trade is able to discover such authors. There are also scientific periodicals which evaluate such popular expositions of Pure Sciences. Thus, Book Selection for public libraries in Pure Sciences is no longer like the proverbial lecture on snakes in Iceland. It is more like culling choice flowers from a small cultivated garden.

41 Message 77

The seventy-seventh message of the First Law to Book Selection is:

> *In a generalist library — be it a public library or a children's library — book selection should include a good assortment of popular books and periodicals on the latest thought in the different subjects in the natural sciences — both physical sciences and biological sciences — written with flair and with plenty of illustrations but free from jargon or technical details and yet without loss of accuracy.*

5 Biological Sciences

Pure Science is also called Natural Science. It falls into two groups, Biological Sciences and Physical Sciences taken along with Mathematics. Of these two groups, the former lends itself more than the latter to concrete treatment. Popular books in the Biological Sciences are therefore more in demand than those in the Physical Sciences. The demand for popular books in Mathematics is almost negligible. The vital element in the entities studied in Biology, their movement, their response to environment, and their more intimate relation to man stimulate imagination and curiosity. The result has been that we have popular books of various levels written with various degrees of imagination and in various degrees of correlation to man's life. It has even moved artists in prose to write books conveying biological information, which at the same time make a powerful emotional appeal even as literature. The volumes of W H Hudson are examples. Some even give a minute, thriller-like account of pets and plants in order to use it as the spring board to enter into the realm of philosophical reflections or for drawing morals. Maeterlinck's *Life of the bee* and *Life of the ant* are examples. Darwin's *Earth worm* is a fine work of art. It does everything to throw us into a mood of reflection. It is throughout argumentative and intellectual and yet readable. But it was by the discoverer himself. The *Science of life* by H G Wells is another example of the kind of book which Book Selection in Biological Sciences for public libraries should look for. In this book the balance of the concrete and the abstract is always maintained in favour of the non-specialist reader. Books on the human body — that is on Medicine — is much in demand for obvious reasons and there are popular books on it written with great vigour and clarity. Animal and plant books are popular with children. Book Selection should sweep the publication world for biological books of all these kinds to satisfy the craving in the common man to know about living bodies and their development.

6 Physical Sciences

Physical Sciences have of late come into popularity with the lay public. This is largely due perhaps to the family resemblance of Einsteinian fourth dimension and curved space to the eternal craving and speculation of man about the world beyond, levitation, and transcending of spatial barriers. Conceptions of an expanding and a contracting universe, the resemblance of quantum phenomena to magic, and the family resemblance of modern work on isotopes and radio-activity to the medieval transmutation of metal — all these are points of contact between the non-specialists and modern happenings in the world of Physics and Chemistry. As if to satisfy the curiosity of the common man and meet his demand, human society has thrown forth eminent scientists, who are equally eminent as masters of style, to supply such books. Whitehead, Russell, Eddington, Jeans, Gamow, and Einstein himself are examples. Astronomy has always evoked curiosity and interest in man. Apart from stellar physics, it is now lending itself to many interesting popular books in Astronomy. Even books on descriptive astronomy and astronomical atlases and almanacs are always in demand from the general public. The First Law assures Book Selection for public libraries that there is both supply and demand for books even in the extreme class of abstract sciences.

Part E

SECOND LAW OF LIBRARY SCIENCE AND BOOK SELECTION

CHAPTER EA

SECOND LAW

1 Enunciation

The Second Law of Library Science has two forms — "Books for all" and "Every reader his book".

2 Chorus

As given in my *Five laws of library science* (Ranganathan series in library science, 12), 1957, Sec 25, the chorus of the Second Law is :

There's room for all
Let not the mean
Or learned dean
Restrict the books
T' a favoured few.
We've Books for all.

Books for the rich
And Books for the poor
Books for the man
And Books for the dame.

Books for the sick
And Books for the fit
Books for the blind
And Books for the dumb.

Books for the bungler
And Books for the wrangler
Books for the burgher
And Books for the cotter.

Books for the lettered
And Books for the fettered
We've Books for all
For one and all.

Books for all ;
Books for the land ;
Books for the sea ;
Books for one and all.

3 Contrast with the First Law

The general trend of the First Law of Library Science in determining book selection policy is, so to speak, statistical. Its interest is to see that, generally speaking, all books that can be of use should be selected and that books, which may not be useful or may prove harmful, should be avoided. The Second Law on the other hand looks at the problem from the individual's point of view rather than *en masse*. It will disclose its implications for book selection more readily if we put it in the form "Every reader his book".

CHAPTER EB

INDIVIDUAL WANT

1 Difficulty in Estimation

From the point of view of the Second Law, Book Selection should be based on the wants of individual readers. It is not easy to determine these accurately. Firstly, because the work involved in contacting each person within the area of service of a library will be stupendous. Secondly, books are to satisfy intellectual wants. Intellectual wants are not compelling. Moreover they are fleeting. Perhaps for these two reasons and for other reasons, few persons are able to enunciate their wants in exact terms. Not even those in the uppermost quartile of the intellectual scale are able to state their wants correctly and fully. However, it may be possible to help persons to indicate their wants to some extent, if the books themselves or at least lists of them are displayed before them. The library is obviously unable to display before readers the books about whose selection they have to decide. The only possible course for them is to display or circulate lists of books.

11 Message 1

The first message of the Second Law to Book Selection is:

> *In a specialist library including a university library, prepare book selection cards for currently published books of the appropriate standard, group them under subject headings determined by the subject-field of specialisation of the experts, and circulate periodically each group of cards to the appropriate group of experts requesting each expert to express his selection or rejection in a specific place in the book selection card.*

2 Pedlar Method

One method of finding out individual wants is for a member of the book selection staff to make house to house visit with lists of current publications. (To make the discussion definite we shall consider only book selection in regard to current publications, for the time being.) He should show the list to every person within the jurisdiction of the library and note down all that interests him. The library representative may have to interpret the titles, explain their scope, standard, etc, and thus help the person to make up his mind about his wants. This method is seldom followed systematically although some house to house survey is made occasionally. Taking advantage of the Banaras Hindu University being essentially a residential one, I experimented with this method in 1946 with the teachers resident within the campus. I found this to be helpful. If this can be done, the Second Law will be satisfied in both of its forms — Books for All and Every Reader His Book.

21 Message 2

The second message of the Second Law to Book Selection is :

> *Play the pedlar by taking lists of currently published books to potential readers. This is essential in a specialist library. In a generalist library, approximate to this as much as possible.*

3 Shop-Keeper Method

What can be done easily and should be done is to ascertain the wants of every person visiting the library and base book selection on the wants of all such persons. This is done as follows. A copy of the weekly or monthly list of the National Bibliography is shown to the reader. He may ask for any of the titles entered there. The usual help is given to him to give shape to his wants. If any of the books wanted by any of the readers is not already in the library, it is selected and actually purchased without any delay. To the great joy of the Second Law, I found this practice in the Middlesex Libraries. I did not find any library catalogue in most of its branches. It was in discussing this daring experiment, that I learnt that they had decided to include in book selection every book that any reader might require. There was therefore no need to have a special library catalogue. All that was needed was a copy of the file of the weekly issues of the National Bibliography and their cumulations. I found that some of the Danish public libraries went a step further. They make a bulk-purchase of the monthly issues of the National Bibliography from the National Bibliography

Institute and either distribute them free among their readers or sell them at a nominal price. As a follow-up, any book which any reader asks for is procured. This method of Book Selection satisfies the Second Law in the form "Every Reader His Book".

31 MESSAGE 3

The third message of the Second Law to Book Selection is:

> *Play the shop-keeper by discussing the book needs of each reader coming to the library, by scanning with him the list of currently published books.*

4 Reference Librarian's Initiative

A still more restricted method for finding out individual wants to help Book Selection is in the hands of the reference librarians on floor duty. It is they that come into intimate contact with the readers. It is they that work with the readers both to find out their wants and to satisfy them. The wants that come to light in reference service can be taken to be true wants or wants of the first order. Whenever the wants go beyond the reading materials actually in the stock of the library, the reference librarian should note down the new books that should be procured. This method of finding individual wants is possible in every library which functions up in the faith of modern librarianship that library exists only at the moments when there is the triple contact of the reader, the librarian, and the reading material. This method of book selection also satisfies the Second Law in the form "Every Reader His Book".

41 MESSAGE 4

The fourth message of the Second Law to Book Selection is:

> *Get the help of the reference librarian. Ask him to note the books needed by readers but not in the collection of the library. Make use of his notes.*

5 Reader's Own Initiative

A still more restricted method of ascertaining the wants of an individual reader is a method in vogue in many libraries. It is the method of Suggestion Book. Each reader has the freedom to enter in the Suggestion Book the specification about his wants — say the title of each book he would like the library to procure. On the mechanical side, this Suggestion Book may be either a note-book or may consist of slips on the basis of one title one slip. If this method is to have any value at all, the Suggestion Book should be scanned every week for incorporation in the week's Book Selection. However, in many libraries the Suggestion Book turns out to be a mere ritual appendage. One of the reasons alleged for slighting the Suggestion Book is that the suggestions are often frivolous, irresponsible, and even fantastic. It is not fair to the readers, to neglect the Suggestion Book on this ground. The correct way of rescuing the Suggestion Book from such faults is for the library staff — preferably a reference librarian — to make personal contact with the few readers who shed their shyness and are daring enough to make suggestions on their own initiative. The contact is best made at the time the suggestion is written out by the reader. In the cases in which this has not been done, there should be contact at least when the acceptance or the rejection of the suggestion is decided. In one of these stages the reader is helped to enter his suggestion properly.

51 Message 5

The fifth message of the Second Law to Book Selection is:

> *Maintain a Suggestion Book. Help readers to understand the broad book selection policy of the library. Scan the Suggestion Book periodically and make the best possible use of it.*

CHAPTER EC

PAST WANTS

1 Frequency of Use

If Book Selection can be based on the present wants by ascertaining individual wants and integrating them, it would be ideal. But it is not easy. None of the methods suggested above is practicable to the extent of disclosing the wants in their entirety. A method which is more easily workable and is in actual use is to ascertain the past wants. A reliable picture of past wants is given by the issue register. This method would have given exact data about individual wants if the entries in the issue register mentioned the headings and titles of books, as they used to do before the introduction of the modern mechanised methods of issue. It is not possible now to reverse the hand of the clock and go back to the otherwise wasteful issue registers of the past. The present issue method can only give a statistical picture of past wants. But it is open to Book Selection to ask for such ways of maintenance of statistics as will be of particular use to it. Book Selection would like to know the frequency of the use of books based on Subject, Standard, and Language respectively.

2 The Three Scatters

In other words, Book Selection would like to know the

1 Subject-scatter ;
2 Standard-scatter ; and
3 Language-scatter

of the books used. The word "Scatter" will be explained in the succeeding chapters.

CHAPTER ED

SUBJECT-SCATTER

0 Two Kinds

There are two kinds of subject-scatter :

1 Subject-scatter of use ; and

2 Subject-scatter of accession.

1 Subject-Scatter of Use

Subject-Scatter of Use is the proportion in which various subjects are studied, as measured by the number of books issued for use. To provide information to Book Selection in regard to subject-scatter, it is now usual to maintain the daily statistics of use — consultation as well as loan — for each of the main classes of knowledge and in the case of certain main classes even for some of their subclasses. These daily statistics are cumulated weekly, monthly, and annually. The details of the mechanics and the methods of collecting these statistical data are described in Chapter 26 of my *Library administration* (1960). The scatter of subjects in book selection may be guided by their scatter in use. It is not meant that the two scatters should be the same. They cannot be the same for various reasons. In the first place the subject-scatter of the books available in the market must be taken into consideration. The impress of the subject-scatter of use on the subject-scatter of availability in the market will yield a subject-scatter for Book Selection which is different from either. With the strict understanding that the subject-scatter of past use is only a rough index to Book Selection it is worthwhile using this method of using a knowledge of the past wants. Here is a sample table of the subject-scatter of use, for the volumes used in the City of Madras in 1939. This table and the succeeding ones are taken from A Rajabhupati's *What Madras reads?* published in the *Memoirs* of the Madras Library Association, 1940, 73-84.

VOLUMES ISSUED IN THE CITY OF MADRAS
1939

Subject CC N	*Subject* Name	*Number of volumes issued*	*Per-centage*	*Rank*
	Generalia	6,410	1.7	17
B	Mathematics	13,502	3.7	8
C	Physics	9,498	2.6	14
D	Engineering	18,284	5.0	6
E	Chemistry	8,554	2.3	16
F	Technology	2,279	0.6	27
G	Natural Science	8,687	2.4	15
H	Geology	5,896	1.6	20
I	Botany	3,945	1.1	26
J	Agriculture	4,018	1.1	25
K	Zoology	5,970	1.6	10
L	Medicine	44,103	12.1	2
M	Useful Arts	4,212	1.2	22
Δ	Mysticism and Spiritual Experience	4,054	1.1	24
N	Fine Arts	4,117	1.1	23
O	Literature	59,972	16.8	1
P	Linguistics	6,329	1.7	18
Q	Religion	11,722	3.2	11
R	Philosophy	12,768	3.5	9
S	Psychology	5,828	1.6	21
T	Education	14,093	3.9	7
U	Geography	11,068	3.0	12
V	History	31,523	8.7	3
W	Political Science	10,637	2.9	13
X	Economics	20,088	5.5	5
Y	Sociology	11,895	3.3	10
Z	Law	24,288	6.7	4
	Total	3,63,740	100	—

2 Accession-Scatter

To get an idea of the correspondence of this subject-scatter to that of actual Book Selection the following table of Accession-Scatter is given.

ACCESSION IN THE CITY OF MADRAS
1939

Subject		Number of volumes accessioned	Percentage	Rank
CC N	*Name*			
	Generalia	166	3.4	8
B	Mathematics	319	6.6	4
C	Physics	159	3.2	9
D	Engineering	238	4.9	6
E	Chemistry	140	2.8	10
F	Technology	15	0.3	27
G	Natural Science	24	0.5	24
H	Geology	42	0.8	19
I	Botany	45	0.9	18
J	Agriculture	18	0.4	26
K	Zoology	90	1.8	13
L	Medicine	828	17.0	2
M	Useful Arts	21	0.4	25
△	Mysticism and Spiritual Experience	25	0.5	23
N	Fine Arts	56	1.1	16
O	Literature	1,331	27.0	1
P	Linguistics	112	2.2	12
Q	Religion	115	2.3	11
R	Philosophy	81	1.6	14
S	Psychology	39	0.8	21
T	Education	41	0.8	20
U	Geography	52	1.0	17
V	History	340	6.9	3
W	Political Science	39	0.8	22
X	Economics	305	6.2	5
Y	Sociology	64	1.3	15
Z	Law	221	4.5	7
	Total	4,926	100	—

3 Correlation

The correlation between the above two tables can be visualised by the following table.

ARRANGEMENT OF SUBJECTS BY THEIR RANK

Rank	Rank according to the number of		Rank
	Volumes Accessioned in	*Volumes Used in*	
1	Literature	Literature	1
2	Medicine	Medicine	2
3	History	History	3
4	Mathematics	Law	4
5	Economics	Economics	5
6	Engineering	Engineering	6
7	Law	Education	7
8	Generalia	Mathematics	8
9	Physics	Philosophy	9
10	Chemistry	Sociology	10
11	Religion	Religion	11
12	Linguistics	Geography	12
13	Zoology	Political Science	13
14	Philosophy	Physics	14
15	Sociology	Natural Science (General)	15
16	Fine Arts	Chemistry	16
17	Geography	Generalia	17
18	Botany	Linguistics	18
19	Geology	Zoology	19
20	Education	Geology	20
21	Psychology	Psychology	21
22	Political Science	Useful Arts	22
23	Spiritual Experience and Mysticism	Fine Arts	23
24	Natural Science (General)	Spiritual Experience and Mysticism	24
25	Useful Arts	Agriculture	25
26	Agriculture	Botany	26
27	Technology	Technology	27

4 Annotation

41 The appearance of Literature in the first rank in the accession-scatter as well as the use-scatter is perhaps in conformity with what happens in most centres. 27% of the books procured and 17% of the books used belong to the Main Class Literature.

42 The Position of History and its percentages are perhaps also normal and could have been expected.

43 But the appearance of Medicine at the second place both in accession and in use, and of Mathematics in the fourth place in accession and as high as the eighth place in use are peculiar. The dominant library in Madras was then the University Library.

44 The high position of Medicine is due to a non-recurrent fluke which happened in 1939. That library received a large gift of volumes on Homoeopathy. As a result of their arrival being publicised widely, the issue of Medicine went up that year far beyond its usual level.

45 With regard to Mathematics, however, the situation was a regular characteristic of Madras. The simultaneous appearance of the world-renowned Ramanujan and of two Smith's Prize men, the fact that the foundation of the Indian Mathematical Society was brought about by Madras, and the greater frequency of contributions from Madras to the *Journal* of the Indian Mathematical Society, are perhaps indexes of the mathematical awareness of Madras. If we add to this, what has already been said — viz that the University Library was the dominant library in Madras — the position of Mathematics in the accession-scatter and in the use-scatter can be understood.

46 An internal anomaly is the difference between the rank 20 of Education in the accession-scatter and its rank 7 in the use-scatter. The university question papers were classified in Education. These volumes were in constant use practically throughout the year. To base Book Selection on use-scatter, the figures should be corrected for this aberration.

47 If Book Selection is based on the use-scatter without careful correction like those mentioned above, it may not satisfy the Second Law to the necessary extent.

5 Librametry

Detailed instructions for making up library statistics will be found in Chap 26 of my *Library administration*, (Ranganathan series in library science, 3), 1960. Apart from the aid of common sense, it is desirable that librarians who have to make use of statistical data for Book Selection should familiarise themselves with the general principles of statistics, corrections for anomalies, the reliability of random samples, and so on. The new subject Librametry, which I had suggested elsewhere, should be developed to take care of this problem and to make the method of making useful inferences from past wants valid. It is only then that we can secure for the community the fullest value of the money that it votes for the libraries. It is only then that the library profession will be doing its duty by the community which maintains it. And it is only then that the library profession will be respected by the community and will be given facilities to become increasingly serviceable to society.

6 Generalist Library

The determination of the subject-scatter, to help Book Selection to the satisfaction of the Second Law, is important in any generalist library, be it a public or a school or a college or a university library.

61 MESSAGE 6

The sixth message of the Second Law to Book Selection is:

> *In a public library, a vocational survey of the locality and the study of the subject-scatter of the books used will jointly give much help in book selection.*

62 MESSAGE 7

The seventh message of the Second Law to Book Selection is:

> *In a school or a college library, the subjects prescribed for study and the subject-scatter of the books used will jointly give much help in book selection.*

63 MESSAGE 8

The eighth message of the Second Law to Book Selection is:

> *In a university library, the subjects of research and the subject-scatter of the books used will jointly give much help in book selection.*

7 Specialist Library

In a specialist library, the subject headings for the collection of the statistics of use should include several sub-divisions of the subject of specialisation and of the auxiliary subjects. If the library belongs to a learned body specialising in one subject, most of the subject headings for the statistical data of use will consist of the diverse sub-headings of the subject of the learned body. In an industrial library, the restriction to a single subject cannot be so severe among subject headings. The subject headings will really fall in an Apupa pattern (alien, umbral, penumbral, umbral, and alien subject headings). It is the umbral region that may have to be broken into several subject headings. This will also be true of government departmental libraries.

71 Message 9

The ninth message of the Second Law to Book Selection is :

> ***In a specialist library, work out the subject-scatter in the Apupa region of the subjects, of specialisation, with several sub-divisions for the umbral subject, as the basis for book selection.***

CHAPTER EE

STANDARD-SCATTTER

1 Ebucational Library

In a school or a college library, the Second Law will urge Book Selection to care as much for standard-scatter as for subject-scatter. The standard-scatter can be found jointly by the number of pupils or students belonging to the several standards and by the standard-scatter of use. As text-books are costly, the students will not be able to buy copies of text-books other than the ones prescribed as basic for detailed study. Therefore, several copies of the other text books should be procured.

11 Message 10

The tenth message of the Second Law to Book Selection is :

> *In a school or a college library, book selection should care for each of the standards at which pupils or students are found in the school or in the college respectively. Further, the proportion of the books of the different standards should be determined by the number of pupils or students found in the respective standards. Many copies of different text-books should be selected.*

2 Public Library

In a public library, Book Selection will have to depend mostly upon standard-scatter of use. For, there is no definite way of independently finding the standard-scatter among the readers. There may be a shift in standard-scatter from period to period. This may be brought about by the very service given by the library. If library service is conducted efficiently, this shift in the standard-scatter will be gradual and continuous. But changes in subject-scatter are usually caused by social or economic or political or other sociological changes. They may sometimes be sudden.

21 Message 11

The eleventh message of the Second Law to Book Selection is :

In a public library, find out the few standards in which readers are found and select books in each of the standards. The proportion of the books of the different standards should be determined by the number of readers found in the respective standards.

3 University or Research Library

In a University library and in the library of a learned body or of a research institution, the standard-scatter has very little standard deviation. It is only high standard that the Second Law would ask Book Selection to care for.

31 MESSAGE 12

The twelfth message of the Second Law to Book Selection is:

In a university or a research library, select only books of a high standard leaving books of low standard to the college library or the public library as the case may be.

32 MESSAGE 13

The thirteenth message of the Second Law to Book Selection is:

In a residential unitary university library, make book selection as for both a college library and a research library.

4 Business Library

In an industrial or commercial or other business library, books of a high standard in theory may require a smaller representation than those of a practical and know-how variety. Therefore trade lists, commercial catalogues, and statistical and descriptive publications will have to be acquired in large numbers in an industrial library, though their value may not be lasting.

41 MESSAGE 14

The fourteenth message of the Second Law to Book Selection is:

In an industrial or commercial, or other business library — a specialist library other than research library — select more books of application including trade lists, commercial catalogues, and statistical and descriptive publications than of books of high-theoretical standard, of which only a few representative books need to be selected.

CHAPTER EF

LANGUAGE-SCATTER

1 Public Library in a Uni-Lingual Locality

Language-scatter also plays an important part in Book Selection. In the public library of a uni-lingual area, books in languages other than the local one will be sought only by a comparatively few readers. Perhaps the classical language of the area will have some appreciable demand. As for the demand in foreign modern languages in a public library, the language-scatter needed for Book Selection is best ascertained by a study of the language-scatter in use. In India to-day, English is the dominant foreign language in use in almost every locality.

11 Message 15

The fifteenth message of the Second Law to Book Selection is :

> *In the public library of a uni-lingual locality, give the greatest representation to books in the language of the area. Select also some books in the classical language of the area and the one or two modern foreign languages, including, in countries, such as India, the languages of the other States in the measure of the language-scatter of the people of the locality.*

2 Public Library in a Polyglot Locality

The importance of language-scatter in book selection assumes great importance in a public library in a polyglot locality. Such a locality will have to choose between two alternatives. It may have a separate library for each language or it may have books in all the languages in each of the libraries of the locality. Which of these two courses is more suitable will depend upon the linguistic make-up of the locality. If each linguistic group lived within a zone of its own, the first method will be preferable. Due to cultural and other sociological reasons, such linguistic zones do get formed in some localities. The provision of the amenity of linguistic libraries may itself encourage the strengthening of linguistic zones, along with other conveniences such as linguistic schools, shop-keepers speaking the language, and so on. In the Public Library Act of Czechoslovakia of the period between the two World Wars, there was an explicit provision that wherever there was a certain minimum of population in a language other than the majority language of a locality, a separate library in the language of the minorities had to be maintained. During the British period, partly by chance and partly for political reasons, polyglot Constituent States had been formed. The result has been formation of cities such as Bangalore, Bombay, Calcutta, Delhi, Hyderabad, and Madras, which have a considerable linguistic heterogeneity. Rivalry between these linguistic groups had often been stimulated or at least exploited in resisting the movement for the use of the mother tongue as the medium of instruction in schools. The story of the cunning monkey and the foolish decadent catpair had been cleverly enacted to put down all the languages alike and uphold the continuation of English as the medium of instruction. The polyglot localities formed in that period naturally still persist. The acrimony among the linguistic groups also still persists. It is difficult to say that this problem of polyglotism in Book Selection will get minimised, if not eliminated, in such Indian cities. Book Selection will therefore have to face the language problem for a long time.

21 MESSAGE 16

The sixteenth message of the Second Law to Book Selection is:

> *In the public library of a polyglot locality, the representation, in book selection, of the different languages in use should be related to the language-scatter of the people of the locality. This applies not only to the public library system of a city as a whole but also severally to the branch library in each of its divisions or zones.*

3 Research Library

In a university library or in the library of a research institution, Book Selection will have to care for books in several languages forming the medium for current thought. Several European languages and Chinese and Japanese have now reached that stage.

Several of the universities therefore make competence in a few of these languages a desirable qualification for scholars. They also make provision for teaching them. But to buy books in each of the foreign languages on the same scale as in the language of the country will not be warranted. It is therefore wise to restrict the representation of the foreign languages to learned periodicals, reference books, classical works, and outstanding compendious treatises, such as the volumes of the series. Handbuck Der Physik, and Handbuck Der Experimental Physik. Even here the language-scatter will be a useful guide.

31 Message 17

The seventeenth message of the Second Law to Book Selection is:

> *In a university or other research library, book selection should also include important periodicals, reference books, classical works, and compendious treatises in the different foreign languages, in the measure of the importance of the communication in those languages and as indicated by the language-scatter of the users.*

4 Make-Up of Language

Apart from polyglotism, even with regard to a single language, Indian libraries will have to face for some time difficulty in Book Selection in regard to the kind of language used. This applies only to the modern languages of India. Should the language be of the severe, medieval, and ornate kind, or should it be modern and easily understandable by the common man? This fight is most visible among authors and scholars themselves. It also makes its appearance in Book Selection in libraries. This difficulty stems from the fact that the modern Indian languages are now recovering after a long period of paralysis. There is a considerable difference between its qualities in the pre-paralysis and in the post-paralysis forms. Moreover there is another problem in regard to Hindi. As it is spoken by more than a hundred million people, it has developed some pronounced local variants. The fact that the area in which Hindi-speaking people live is so extensive adds to the rigid crystallisation of these local variants. To add to this spatial factor, there is also a complicating temporal factor. Different varieties of Hindi get formed by the different proportion of the Persian and Sanskrit elements absorbed. It is too early for a standard Hindi to get established. It is so with a few of the other Indian languages too. It is hoped that the enormous facility for communication, the extension of the circulation of newspapers, and the adoption of the Indian languages by the administration, judiciary, and educational institutions as media for communication at all thought-levels, will facilitate the formation of standard language.

41 MESSAGE 18

For the time being the eighteenth message of the Second Law to Book Selection is:

> *Pay attention to the variant-scatter of the language of the library, as determined by the impression of reference librarian and by field survey.*

CHAPTER EG

POTENTIAL WANT

1 Obligation

The Second Law would like Book Selection to be based not only on expressed wants of everybody in the community — expressed now or in the past — but also on unexpressed or potential wants. The sensing of potential wants needs greater ability than the finding of expressed wants. It needs greater penetration into the springs of human thought and feeling. It needs a comprehensive understanding of the social factors and forces acting on the community. It needs also a realisation of the dependence of human progress on the quick and correct communication of information, news, and knowledge to the diverse intellectual and economic strata in the community. Above all the library profession should activate itself to the full discharge of the responsibility of the library as a social institution designed to cultivate the human resources by feeding them with information and knowledge.

11 MESSAGE 19

The nineteenth message of the Second Law to Book Selection is:

> *Do not stop with the expressed want as inferred from the subject-scatter of accession, the subject-scatter of circulation, and other indications of the wants of the past; but use your knowledge of the changing social needs, the intellectual possibility, and the changing emotional wants of the community and select books accordingly so as to serve and exploit such needs and possibilities.*

2 Change in Potential Want

The potential wants like actual wants cannot be taken to be permanent. They are bound to change. Various factors may change them. Change in the industrial set up of a locality or in residential re-adjustment or in shift in the location of the chief institutions may bring about a change in potential want. Apart from these changes due to external causes, the intellectual level of the community may change as a result of the educational facilities. Cultural interests may change as a result of social re-construction schemes. The potential changes may also happen globally in all kinds of libraries as a result of national or world trends. For example, during the last one generation the radio has been responsible for a considerable change in the potential reading-wants of the patrons of all kinds of libraries. An international war has always a tremendous effect on the potential want of a reader. The establishment of the United Nations and its Specialised Agencies has had a great influence on the reading interests not only of the general public but also of the student-world patronising school, college, and university libraries. There may be other similar causes which produce change in reading interests.

21 Message 20

The twentieth message of the Second Law to Book Selection is :

Keep yourself ever alert to re-assess the potential unexpressed wants of readers from time to time.

CHAPTER EH

ANTICIPATED WANT

O Introduction

Apart from actual and potential wants, Book Selection should also be guided by anticipated wants. The aids to anticipation of wants will vary with the kind of the library. We shall examine here some kinds of libraries by way of illustration.

1 School or College Library

In a school or a college library, for example, the courses of studies are usually prescribed one or more years in advance. The Second Law would ask for a perusal of the course of studies and select reading materials in anticipation to suit them. It will be a good policy for such a library to bring the members of the teaching faculty into consultation at the end of each academic year and determine Book Selection in time to put the new books into use when the new academic year begins.

11 MESSAGE 21

The twenty-first message of the Second Law to Book Selection is :

> *In a school or a college library, book selection should be done in consultation with the members of the teaching faculty at the end of each academic year, so as to put on the shelves from the beginning onwards of the next academic year, books necessary to meet the needs, of the curriculum -- not merely the prescribed books, but also the books needed for preparatory, parallel, and follow-up study.*

2 University Library

In a university library, the librarian should keep himself in intimate touch with the members of the faculty. He should closely watch the progress and research. He should himself be aware of any possible changes in the subjects of investigation. On this basis, he should make Book Selection move abreast of the progress and of the changes in research.

21 Message 22

The twenty-second message of the First Law to Book Selection is:

In a university or a research library, book selection should be done from time to time in consultation with the members of the faculty or the research body, so as to put on the shelves the books needed in the anticipated change in the research activities, in good time before the changes take place.

3 Government Departmental Library

Book Selection to meet anticipated want is of the very essence in the library of the legislature or of any ministry of a government. Government business, whether legislative or executive, has now become too involved to be done properly, either merely with the high order of flair or highly organised personalities, functioning as ministers and secretaries, or merely in the light of precedents or even with a combination of both of these. Educational, political, international, economic, social, and legal problems are now getting into a high rate of flux. The ideologies influencing them are getting much diversified. A considerable research is being made in the theory involved in all those problems. A knowledge of the latest development in theory and of the happenings in the other countries are now necessary to make decisions on policy-making as well as the methods of implementing policy. The traditional secretariat staff can only put up a precedent. It is the duty of the library of the Parliament or of the department concerned to feed the legislators, the policy makers, and the administrators with the thought in the wavefront of knowledge bearing on their work. This feeding will fail in its purpose unless it is done when any resolution or bill gets debated in Parliament or drafted in the secretariat. In other words, to serve its purpose, the library should inform itself quite in advance about the likely matters coming up for consideration and select and procure the necessary books and periodicals before the consideration is begun. For example, if the prohibition policy is likely to be taken up, the librarian should procure the necessary books on the theory of prohibition and the practice of prohibition in other countries before any deliberation takes place either in the secretariat or in the legislature. Similarly, if there is a proposal on Income Tax Act, the library should select books on the latest theories of income tax and its impact on the economic development of the country and on the current practices and on the relevant history of income tax in other countries so as to procure the necessary books even before the deliberation begins at any level whatever. It is easy to multiply examples.

31 MESSAGE 23

The twenty-third message of the Second Law to Book Selection is:

> *In a government departmental library including that of the legislature, contemplation of development schemes, legislative measures, and policy-making should be watched with vigilance. The department concerned should take the librarian into confidence and alert him in good time. Book selection should be done immediately in collaboration with the persons concerned in the department.*

4 Business Library

No enterprise can now be successfully managed by the mere flair of exceptional organisers. However much it is necessary, it is not sufficient by itself. Practically no enterprise is in reality an isolated one to day — whether it is a factory producing a commodity, or an organization giving a service, or a commercial house engaged in marketing a commodity, or a service. The library of an enterprise will not be doing its duty unless it anticipates the needs of a person all along the line — from the top management through the Design Department, the Production Department, the Purchase Department, the Marketing Department, the Personnel Department, the Finance and the Accounts Departments, and the Audit Department.

41 MESSAGE 24

The twenty-fourth message of the Second Law to Book Selection is:

> *In a business library, the librarian should keep himself informed of all anticipated developments in each of the departments and select the books necessary to make the decision in the action of the department concerned conform to the latest theory and practice in the matter.*

5 Public Library

In a public library, anticipatory Book Selection should be guided by the calendar of public events, so to speak. Local celebrations, national celebrations and events, and international occurrences should be anticipated and the reading materials bearing on them should be procured and kept ready so that when the actual demand arises every reader will get his reading material. When for example in 1946 the Indian Constituent Assembly began to function, libraries with faith in the Second Law acquired copies of proceedings of constituent assemblies in diverse countries such as the United States, Switzerland, Canada, and Australia. They also secured, in anticipation of demand, literature on the formation and the powers and duties of such constituent assemblies. Again, when the Ramakrishna Centenary was celebrated two decades ago, it was anticipated that there would be a great demand for the works on and sayings of Sri Ramakrishna and the works by and on Swami Vivekananda and other members of the Ramakrishna Order. This was to the satisfaction of the Second Law. When the partition of India was agreed upon in 1947, the Second Law made efficient librarians anticipate demand of books on successor governments, boundary problems, refugee problems, and a host of other subjects in which both the officials and the public were likely to look for reading materials. When the Suez Crisis developed in 1956, many libraries in the United Kingdom anticipated the demand and assembled materials on the Suez problem — its history, its politics, its economics, its sociology, and its laws. There was a stream of readers for them as anticipated.

51 Message 25

The twenty-fifth message of the Second Law to Book Selection is :

> *In a public library, book selection should be made in anticipation in the light of the forthcoming international, national, and local events and occurrences.*

CHAPTER EJ

REFERENCE BOOK

1 Externalised Memory

The Second Law urges Book Selection to remember that every reader is in need of information apart from knowledge. Nowhere in the world is it now sufficiently well known that a person is entitled to get his information from the library. He often goes to friends, specialists, the wise men, the mystery men, and so on, believed to be repositories of information. This habit was formed before the library-era of today began. In those days there was no other way for anybody to get his information. But in the present economic pressure on man-power, it is wasteful to the giver as well as to the taker of information to find common time and tempo for useful and timely exchange of information. It is as difficult to tap memories in other living persons as it is to hold everything wanted in one's own memory. It is these economic and psychological facts that have been responsible for the creation of a new species of books — reference books — which can act as externalised memory for anybody who is literate. The creation of reference books is a recent affair. The artificiality of their make-up is still acting as a barrier in their use. Libraries are yet to push their use amidst the public and make them media for self-help to the extent which is possible.

11 Message 26

The twenty-sixth message of the Second Law to Book Selection is:

> *In a public library, select a good assortment of reference books such as biographical dictionaries and serials, directories of the locality and of other important cities, travel aids such as, railway, shipping, and air guides, and tourist books, anthologies, linguistic dictionaries, and encyclopaedias of a general nature and in such of the subjects as are of local interest.*

12 Message 27

The twenty-seventh message of the Second Law to Book Selection is :

> *In a university or a research library, select as many as possible of authoritative reference books in each subject of study. These should include bibliographies, directories of the learned world, encyclopaedias, linguistic dictionaries — particularly technical ones — trend reports, patents, standards, and specifications.*

2 In India

While this is so even in developed countries, in India which is still undeveloped in library matters we are in an even more difficult situation. Except in six Indian languages, we have no Encyclopaedia. We have not yet got a separate comprehensive *Who's who*. We do not have directories for different branches of business. Each State has not got a general Directory. When even materials of such local interest are absent, one need not expect any reference book which presents the world to the readers from the Indian angle. "If so," Book Selection can say, "what part can I play here ? My work begins only when the books themselves are produced". The Second Law will plead with Book Selection and ask it to do some extension work, so to speak. It would say, "There is no denying that every citizen is in need of reference books in all these sectors of information. It may be expressed or it may not be expressed. But it is there all the same. In the past when life was very circumscribed and localised, few people felt the need for information along these lines. But today the forging of the different parts of India into a single whole, the economic pressure interlacing Indian interests with the interests of other countries, and the great inherent awareness spontaneously blossoming in many people as a part of the renascence precipitated by the phenomenal and intimate influence of Mahatma Gandhi and the political independence brought by his life to the country — all these have shaken the people out of their old narrow insular outlook." In my wanderings in the interior of Kerala, I was amazed at the desire for information evinced by some of the illiterate farmers and weavers. They wanted information exactly like what is usually found in Industrial and Trade Directories, in the various Consular Reports of the developed countries, and in gazetteers and atlases. As soon as they were told who I was, they pleaded with me, saying in effect, "Though we are illiterate, we do have one or two literates in our place. We meet here every night round this kerosene lantern. Our literate friend reads out to us from books and newspapers. The books are mostly of a religious or philosophical kind. We do want them. They do give us solace. The newspapers give largely political or some sensational information. We do want them. But we want also information touching on our daily life, about our potential markets in India and abroad, the changing fashions of the world likely to affect our vocation and about the political stresses and strains in various countries, likely to affect our market. It is true that newspapers give us some current information on the last-mentioned point; but we should like to have an unbiased background picture about the political framework of other lands and of our own. We do not have any books answering these questions facing us from day to day. When you visit the headquarters, can you not request the big publishers to bring out books giving current information of this sort?" The penetrating power of their questions and the simple way in which they expressed themselves filled my heart with joy from one angle and with sadness from another. Some years ago, our illiterate brethren in the villages did not have this awareness. I was happy to know that this awareness has dawned among the masses. At the same time I was sad to see their plight. I was sad to realise that no attempt was being made to satisfy this hunger for information among the masses. It is here that the Second Law asked for extension work on the part of Book Selection. It would ask Book Selection to include topical reference books of all sorts, published in English and prepared in other countries for their own purposes, so that they may serve as models for those who are responsible to produce similar materials for the use of our people. Incidentally, these books may also go a small way in satisfying the informational wants of our people either by their directly reading them or by their having them read out in case they are illiterates. I would regard the primary purpose of Book Selection of this kind to be that of serving as models.

21 Message 28

For the time being, the twenty-eighth message of the Second Law to Book Selection is :

> *Select reference books in English to supplement those in Indian languages. Further, create public opinion for the production of reference books of all kinds in each Indian language.*

CHAPTER EK

BOOK

1 Field Survey

In the pioneer period of library development in India, it will be difficult to base Book Selection on our experience in the past, even in the case of ordinary books. The reason is simple. We have had few libraries. Many of even these few libraries have been ritual appendages rather than live institutions. Those responsible for the maintenance of the libraries had never realised that books serve an intellectual want, that the intellectual want is not compelling, that it is fleeting, that it dies out unless it is satisfied immediately, and that it won't keep growing unless reading materials are brought to notice and served in a missionary spirit. The turn-out of our libraries is therefore meagre. It is truncated. It is not truly representative of the potential wants of the readers. A consequence of the situation is that the pioneer generation of librarians in India will have to depend not so much on statistical analysis of past circulation, as a field survey. Direct contact with the potential readers and even explaining to them at length the potentiality of the library to meet their potential wants will be necessary. It is only in that way that potential wants can be sensed.

11 Message 29

The twenty-ninth message of the Second Law to Book Selection is:

> *In a country such as India, recovering from cultural exhaustion and just developing thereafter, book selection will have to be based for some years not merely on statistics of issue but essentially on field survey of and personal contact with potential readers.*

2 Character and Integrity

The Second Law would plead with Book Selection that in the present transitional stage of India, it is not sufficient merely to imitate the methods of Book Selection current in the more developed countries. In particular, Book Selection should not be a matter of taking up the catalogues of some of the libraries of the developed countries or the catalogues of the scattered publishers of India in haphazard manner and ticking off *ex cathedra* items appealing to the librarian's personal fancies. This method of Book Selection without any attempt at relating it to the potential wants of the readers is almost equivalent to a fraud on the public. The Second Law would plead that the pioneer librarians should not take advantage of the fact that no public opinion has taken shape in this matter and therefore they could decide the matter in any way they liked behind closed doors. Nor is it helpful or honest to make Book Selection a means of propitiating the immediate superiors whose experience and personal prejudices are likely to be very unhelpful to the view of the Second Law on Book Selection.

21 MESSAGE 30

The thirtieth message of the Second Law to Book Selection is:

High character and integrity on the part of the library profession should be brought to bear on the discharge of its duties in regard to book selection along with an all-round attempt to assess the potential wants of the readers — free from any sneaking tendency to please the whims and fancies of the individual members of the Library Authorities.

CHAPTER EL

PERIODICAL

1 Potential Use

Practically all the remarks made about selection of books in Chapter EK are applicable to the selection of periodicals also. Potential use of general periodicals is always to be judged. Indeed, this fact is even utilised by enterprising libraries to attract readers to the library by providing a good assortment of general periodicals for use.

11 Message 31

The thirty-first message of the Second Law to Book Selection is:

In a public library, selection of periodicals should cover a few generalia periodicals of the popular variety and some specialised periodicals bearing on the chief vocations of the people of the locality as determined by field survey.

12 Message 32

The thirty-second message of the Second Law to Book Selection is :

In a school library, selection of periodicals should cover children's periodicals capable of entertaining and informing them on the one hand, and developing in them, on the other hand, the habit of perusing periodicals.

13 Message 33

The thirty-third message of the Second Law to Book Selection is:

In the library of a business organization, selection of periodical publications should cover the periodicals and the serials falling within the umbral region of interest of the parent body and also of a few of appropriate ones falling within the penumbral region of interest.

14 Message 34

The thirty-fourth message of the Second Law to Book Selection is :

In a university or a research library, selection should cover periodical publications falling within the purview of the subject of their specialization and also on the subjects auxiliary to them.

2 Continuity

A periodical publication — a periodical or a serial — is by its very nature intended to be continued indefinitely by its sponsor. The selection of a periodical publication therefore presents new problems not arising in the selection of books. The problems in answering the questions are :

1 Is a periodical publication, selected once, to be continued in all the succeeding years ?

2 Can the policy of the continuation or otherwise be the same in all kinds of libraries ?

The answer to these questions will differ as between a periodical and a serial. A serial is usually costly. Further, the changes in the facts presented by it may not differ significantly from the edition of one year to that of the next year. This factor should be taken into consideration.

21 MESSAGE 35

The thirty-fifth message of the Second Law to Book Selection is :

In a university or a research library, cutting down the subscription to a periodical in one year, restoring it in the next year, and cutting it down later will cause an inconvenient break in the set. Once the trial period is over and a decision is made to take the periodical, it should be continued until the standard of the periodical goes down abnormally.

22 MESSAGE 36

The thirty-sixth message of the Second Law to Book selection is:

In an industrial or other business library, the continuity or otherwise of a periodical publication is best determined from year to year by the needs of the work in progress in the parent body.

23 MESSAGE 37

The thirty-seventh message of the Second Law to Book Selection is :

In a generalist library, be it a public, or a college, or a school library, freedom may be taken in the policy of continuity or otherwise in the case of a periodical not to be bound and preserved, according to the policy of the library.

24 MESSAGE 38

The thirty-eighth message of the Second Law to Book Selection is:

In the case of a serial, other than a statistical one, it may be possible to subscribe for it at intervals, say every other year or once in three years.

3 Cumulative Index

In a research library where periodicals are continuously taken from year to year, the publication of their cumulative indexes should be carefully watched and these should be procured automatically without fail. These are materials for which there is always potential demand. They save the time of the reader. But they are produced only in a limited edition.

31 MESSAGE 39

The thirty-ninth message of the Second Law to Book Selection is:

In a library — such as a research or a university library — preserving a continuous set of volumes of a periodical, its successive cumulative indexes should be bought as and when published.

4 Newspaper

The selection of newspapers for libraries depends upon the nature of the library. In India today many so-called libraries are often nothing more than reading rooms for newspapers. Newspapers usually differ in their policies and outlook. They often belong to different schools of thought, for example in politics and in economics. A public library should therefore make a balanced selection so as to respect the Canon of Reticence — that is, library should not favour one school of thought or another in its newspaper selection. Local, State, and National Newspapers should be fully represented. It is also desirable to have representation of foreign newspapers. The potential demand for newspapers may be reasonably said to cover all these types. It is a moot point whether academic and business libraries should provide newspapers. Every reader of such libraries may be reasonably expected to have his own newspapers or to use the newspapers in the public library. The potential wants of the clientele of such institutional libraries should not be left to be determined by their personal predilections but by the wants as determined by the needs of the institutions themselves.

41 MESSAGE 40

The fortieth message of the Second Law to Book Selection is :

In a public library, make a balanced selection of newspapers — balanced in respect of their political, economic, and social leanings.

42 MESSAGE 41

The forty-first message of the Second Law to Book Selection is :

Avoid selecting common newspapers for a library other than a public library or a reading room.

CHAPTER EM

SUBNORMAL READER

O Kinds of Subnormal

The Second Law emphasizes that the "All" in "Books for All" includes not only normal persons but also subnormals. From the point of view of Book Selection we may recognise three kinds of subnormals

1 The blind ;
2 The cripple ; and
3 The neo-literate.

The first two are the physically handicapped. The third is taken to comprise only adults and not children. Their handicap is not physical but is one due to not having had the benefit of elementary education in their childhood.

1 The Blind

There are two classes of books to be cared for by Book Selection to satisfy the wants of the blind-braille books and sound records of books. In this case, the result of the Book Selection may not be as much for purchase as for production or borrowing. Progressive libraries keep themselves in touch with the blind people within their jurisdiction and produce braille books systematically to answer their needs. They also have sound recording equipment and take the honorary services of socially minded people to read out books for recording.

11 MESSAGE 42

The forty-second message of the Second Law to Book Selection is :

Bear in mind the humane responsibility to provide books in braille or in sound records for the blind.

2 The Cripple

Another class of reading material to which the Second Law

would turn the attention of Book Selection is on the so-called Ceiling Books. These are really books reproduced in films which can be projected on the ceiling. The equipment for the use of these books is such that the cripples who have to be in bed can manipulate it so that the pages of the book are successively projected on the ceiling. Supply of such books can give great relief to the cripple whose forced confinement to bed is rendered unbearable on account of boredom.

21 MESSAGE 43

The forty-third message of the Second Law to Book Selection is:

Bear in mind the humane responsibility to provide ceiling books for the cripple confined to bed.

3 Neo-Literates

Book Selection has also to care for neo-literate adults whether they are neo-literates in their mother tongue or in a foreign tongue. To meet the wants of such people the so-called sound-books are now being produced. These are books printed in bold type and carrying within pockets at their ends gramophone plates giving a reading of the book. The supply of these books with the necessary gramophone machine is a great boon to neo-literates. It provides opportunity at once to read a book and pronounce the sentences and the words correctly.

31 MESSAGE 44

The forty-fourth message of the Second Law to Book Selection is:

Select sound books for the neo-literates. If they are not already available, work for their production.

Part F

THIRD LAW OF LIBRARY SCIENCE AND BOOK SELECTION

CHAPTER FA

THIRD LAW

1 Enunciation

The Third Law of Library Science is, "Every book its reader". In a sense, the approach of this Law is in a direction opposite to that of the Second Law. That Law concerns itself with the actual requirement of each individual reader and with the actual total requirement of all the readers. Its message to Book Selection was thus from the angle of readers. The Third Law would approach Book Selection from the angle of the book. The Second Law is the result of considering the details of the First Law, arising out of emphasis on the reader — that is, the user. The Third Law, on the other hand, will have to consider the details arising out of emphasis on the book — that is the entity to be used.

2 Implications of the Third Law

The Third Law should work out the details for getting a reader for every book. Most of the details lie in the area of

1 Open access system ;
2 Shelf arrangement ;
3 Catalogue entries ;
4 Reference service ;
5 Public relation work ; and
6 Extension work.

Extension work may be of two kinds. In the first kind, the use of the premises of the library is allowed to learned bodies, hobby organisations, and cultural associations, in order thereby to increase the chances for the books to get their readers. In the second kind, the books themselves are voluntarily taken out of the library and displayed and distributed to those still without library-consciousness or without easy access to the library. All the same, the Third Law has some details to care for in the sphere of Book Selection.

CHAPTER FB

THIRD LAW AND SECOND LAW

1 Common Ground with the Second Law

The Third Law will accept every book selected by the Second Law. Because, the Second Law will bring into the library only books for which there already exist an assured group of readers. For, it first thinks of the readers and then only of the books. Therefore, Book Selection made out of deference to the Second Law may be automatically taken to be Book Selection made out of deference to the Third Law.

2 Basis for Book Selection

The Second Law bases Book Selection on the certitude of demand. The Third Law, on the other hand, bases Book Selection on the probability for demand. For this purpose, the Third Law would seek information about the reading taste, the intellectual attainment, the vocational interest, the general interest, and the overall requirements of the potential readers falling within the sphere of the service of the library. It would act in the belief that the probability for the use of the books will be appreciable if the following sources are used for getting the above-mentioned information.

1 The suggestions received directly from the readers;

2 The suggestions recorded by the assistants at the Ready Reference Desk;

3 The notes made from day to day by the Reference Staff on the floor duty;

4 The main vocations of the Local Public;

5 The prospective events of national or local importance;

6 The impressions gained in interviews with the leading members of the local community and so on.

The sources used by the Third Law to infer probability for use are virtually the same as those used by the Second Law to infer certainity of use.

3 The Forty-four Messages

Thus, all the forty-four messages of the Second Law to Book Selection can also be deemed to be messages of the Third Law to Book Selection. There is no need to repeat them here. Apart from these joint messages of the Second and the Third Laws, the Third Law has some messages of its own. The sources used by the Third Law to infer probability for use are virtually the same as those used by the Second Law to infer certainty of use.

CHAPTER FC

THE NEW HELPING THE OLD

1 Lure-Effect

Experience and psychology suggest to the Third Law that of the method of increasing the chance for an old neglected book to get its reader is to procure a new book on the same subject. A new book often acts as a bait to lure a hitherto reluctant reader to pull out some of the old books on the same subject, and therefore lying near to the new book on the shelves, and peruse them. I have experienced something similar to this in regard to my own books. Every time a new book of mine comes out, it stimulates a fresh instalment of demand for the older ones.

11 Message 1

The first message of the Third Law to Book Selection is:

> *Remember to include in the book selection list new and attractive books likely to lure their readers towards some of the books of the library failing in their appeal to readers, and thereby to increase the probability for such old books to be put back into circulation.*

2 To Enhance Lure-Effect

The chance for this lure-effect will increase with the extensiveness of the bibliographical references in the new book selected. The bibliography added to a book is in effect equivalent to the author of the book telling his readers "I have perused these books with profit. It may be worthwhile for you to look out for these books in your library and read them. It may perhaps even be that you understand and appreciate my book with greater facility if you read the old books I have cited. At any rate those books will give you some additional information or arguments not repeated in my book."

21 Message 2

The second message of the Third Law to Book Selection is:

> *To enhance the lure-effect of a new book on the old books, select such a new book as has a good bibliography.*

CHAPTER FD

MUTUAL HELP

1 Associated Books

Apart from depending on the arrival of a new book in a specific subject increasing the probability for the older books in that subject finding their readers, the Third Law would also like to exploit relations between books other than old and new. These relations are more compelling than the relation between the old and the new. It may even be that the reading of a book becomes difficult, if not impossible, unless another related book is also read.

2 Examples

The selection and purchase of a new book containing a commentary on a classic may get readers for the copy of the classic already in the library. Reciprocally, the selection and purchase of a new edition of the classic may get readers to the commentaries already in the library.

Similarly, the selection and purchase of a new book containing the translation of a work may get readers for the original work already in the library. Reciprocally, the selection and purchase of the original work of a translation already in the library may get readers for the translation itself. Books on theory and those on application have a similar reciprocal relation to the satisfaction of the Third Law. So also is the case with a treatise on law and a book of case studies. In many subjects treatises and source books have similar reciprocal relations which the Third Law would ask Book Selection to exploit. A still another example of such a reciprocal relation of value in Book Selection is found between a book embodying an original work and another embodying an evaluation of it. Books belonging to a good publisher's series often help one another in finding their respective readers. Again there is another pair of related books peculiar to a school library. Each such pair is made of a book for the taught and an associated handbook for the teacher.

21 MESSAGE 3

The third message of the Third Law to Book Selection is :

Select books so as to exploit the mutual dependence of books in cases, such as, a (an)

1 *Classic and the hierarchy of its commentaries* ;
2 *Original and its translations* ;
3 *Book on a theory and its application* ;
4 *Expository book and the related laboratory handbooks* ;
5 *Law book and case studies on the law concerned* ;
6 *Source books and treatises* ;
7 *Original and its evaluations* ; *and*
8 *Books belonging to a publisher's series.*

22 MESSAGE 4

The fourth message of the Third Law to Book Selection is :

In a school library, select books so as to exploit the mutual dependence of pupil's books and the related teacher's handbook.

CHAPTER FE

SOME DON'TS

1 Language

The language forming the medium of expression is an essential element in a book, as viewed from the angle of the reader. To get a reader for a book among the clientele of the library there should be persons with capacity to read its language. This is no doubt an absolute truism. And yet, there are cases in which this truism has been overlooked. For example, some years ago, the Department of Physics of an Indian University had as its head a professor with capacity to read Russian. He was the only person in that university with a knowledge of that language and yet he insisted on much of the book fund of the department being spent on Russian books. He even went to the extent of using his influence to give trouble to the librarian because his request was not accepted. Here the librarian had to choose between loyalty to the Third Law and smooth sailing with the influential professor. In another university library in India, the librarian was beginning to learn German. It was not a language taught in the university. A few professors, however, could read German. It was legitimate, therefore, to select some advance treatise in German in the subjects of those professors. The books in German could certainly, find a few real readers to the satisfaction of the Third Law. But the librarian spent a good slice of the book fund left to his own discretion in buying German books of the school standard in some subjects. These could find hardly any reader in the university. The curse of the Third Law necessarily descended on the head of that librarian.

11 Message 5

The fifth message of Third Law to Book Selection is :

Do not select books in a language not understood by the readers of the library.

2 Standard

All books on a subject are not in the same standard. Some are super-advanced ; and some are advanced. Some are elementary ; and some are ultra-elementary. Some strike the medium. Standard forms a continuous spectrum, so to speak. No sharp line exists to demarcate the different standards. And yet it is helpful to recognise four distinct standards. These four standards had been marked out in Indian tradition — each with its own name. These have been already described in Sec DG1 to DG5 of this book.

21 MESSAGE 6

The sixth message of the Third Law to Book Selection is :

Do not select any book of a standard which has few readers among the clientele of the library.

3 Subject

Subjects are getting more and more diversified. The range of subjects is so far too vast to enable a library to find readers to all the subjects. Further, subjects are also subjected to the action of fate, as it were. They have their own ups and downs. Kierkergaard expounded his existential philosophy a century ago. At that time the subject of his books was too new to find any reader. Evidently, about a century later, humanity seems to have developed interest in his subject. There was then a sudden demand for his books. Indeed, they even came to be translated into several languages. In medieval Europe, mystics — such as St Francis of Assisi and St Paul — were respected. The subject of their work attracted readers. But from about the fourteenth century mysticism fell into evil days in Europe. The works of mystics could find few readers. After the shocking experience of World War I, some rethinking began. The scale of values got changed. The biographies, the sayings, and the works of mystics began to find readers. Sir C V Raman once said about one of his books that in all probability that book had only two readers — himself and the proof-reader — because of the novelty and obtrusiveness of the subject. To take another instance Linear Programming and Cybernetics may find readers in a specialist library but not in a generalist library. A N Whitehead's *Process and reality* covered a subject which could hardly find a reader in the public library of many a town. Same was the case in the subject of Shri Aurobindo's *Life divine*.

31 MESSAGE 7

The seventh message of the Third Law to Book Selection is:

> *In a specialist library, do not select books in subjects not falling within the field of study of the library, including its fringe area.*

32 MESSAGE 8

The eighth message of the Third Law to Book Selection is:

> *In a generalist library, do not select books in a subject not likely to be of interest to any reader, either for intensive study or even for general acquaintance.*

4 Misleading Title

The titles of some books are mischievous and misleading. For example, forty years ago a book with the title *Life of Johnson* was announced. At that time, it was the practice in a university to prescribe Samuel Johnson's book for detailed study. Therefore, the Board of Studies of that University selected that book for the university library. When the book arrived it turned out to be a trivial book on the pet dog of the person who wrote the book and who evidently had the necessary money to print it. Unfortunately, it was not fashionable in that university area to include dogs among pet animals. The result was that the library never found any reader other than the classifier who had to read it as a part of his duty. Naturally the Third Law was enraged. The Board of Studies in Mathematics was captivated by the term "Calculus" in the title *Calculus of variants* by W W Grigg. The book was selected and acquired. It turned out to be a book on manuscriptology — the method of reconstructing the original text of a work represented by several differing manuscripts. At that time there was nobody within a radius of 500 miles of the library either engaged in or interested in manuscriptology. The book never got any reader.

41 Message 9

The ninth message of the Third Law to Book Selection is:

Avoid selecting a book by the title alone without examining either the book itself, or a review of it, or an annotation on it, lest its subject should be outside the purview of the library or without any interest to any reader.

CHAPTER FF

RESPONSIBILITY FOR BOOK SELECTION

1 Public Library

From the early years of the public libraries right up to World War II the Library Committee took it to be its statutory duty for itself to make Book Selection. In those conditions it often happened that a book was selected because some member of the Committee had interest in its subject. Sometimes a book was selected because it existed. Little weight was given to the demand of the Third Law. The probability for the book selected to get its reader in the library was seldom assessed. An extreme case was an amusing incident. While visiting a borough library 40 years ago, I happened to meet several members of the Library committee when one of them told me in perfect innocence, "I have recently become a member of the borough council. The council put me on the Library Committee. Evidently because they know that in my professional career I had never read books and that, therefore, I shall be impartial in selecting books for the library." The Librarian's experience about the probability about the use of a book was seldom used. However, after a century of experience in working the Public Library Act, several Local Library Authorities have begun to realise that this practice sins against the Third Law. They now confine themselves to the framing of some general principles of policy and leave the actual Book Selection to the librarian who alone has knowledge and experience to estimate the probability for the book selected to get its readers. Even a further step is being taken in large libraries. The librarian finds his time too much taken up with the managerial and administrative problems to determine this probability by himself. Whenever this sensible view is gaining ground, Book Selection is usually made the responsibility of the reference staff. For, they alone spend most of their time in the book-reader context. Such has been the gradual shift in the locus of responsibility of Book Selection. As a measure of caution the Library Committee sets up a panel of experts who may be consulted in cases of doubt. Such a wisdom is yet to dawn in the minds of Library Committee or Library Authority. In public libraries, recently established in newly developing countries such as India, the sooner they slough of and transfer the responsibility for Book Selection to the librarian, the better will be the result to the satisfaction of the Third Law.

11 MESSAGE 10

The tenth message of the Third Law to Book Selection is:

In a public library, the responsibility for book selection should be vested in the library staff who alone can have the experience necessary to assess the probability for a book to find its readers.

2 Academic and Specialist Libraries

About 40 years ago, the Madras University Library had no professional librarian. At that time, Book Selection in diverse subject fields was left to the care of a few members of the faculty of teaching in the respective subject fields. They had neither the tools for Book Selection nor the experience of the book-reader context in the library. To add to this, request for selection would come once in a year marked urgent with a red label. Usually the chief of the faculty would call his junior most assistant and say, "Go to the different colleges and make a list of the newly bought books. If the total does not add up to the amount sanctioned, duplicate the necessary number of books". Poor Third Law. Even today, in spite of their being professional librarians in charge of academic libraries, the members of the teaching faculty often take Book Selection to be a prestige affair and keep it as their own close preserve. This should end.

21 MESSAGE 11

The eleventh message of the Third Law to Book Selection is:

In an academic library — be it a university, a college, or a school library — book selection should be the joint responsibility of the library staff and the teaching staff; they should be guided by the probability of getting readers for the book selected.

22 MESSAGE 12

The twelfth message of the Third Law to Book Selection is:

In a business library — such as industrial, commercial, and government departmental library — book selection should be the joint responsibility of the library and the representatives of the different divisions of the parent body.

3 Patronage Motive

About 30 years ago, a university library used to get books in French and German in scientific subjects. In order to meet the actual demand for them from the teachers and the advanced students, a Britisher in the administration became allergic to the export of money into Germany and France. He therefore, tried to put a spoke in the wheel of Book Selection. Fortunately, however, the authorities of the university satisfied themselves about the certainty of readers for these books and ruled that Book Selection should not be determined on grounds of patronage. But unfortunately, the authorities of many libraries are viewing Book Selection largely from the angle of patronage. They go to the extent of prescribing in what proportion the book fund should be distributed — among the publishers and book sellers without any consideration of the probability for readers for the book so got. The public library system of one state allows an influential group of authors and publishers to confine the Book Selection of all the libraries to their own publications. This implies scant respect to the Third Law. This should not happen in the present age.

31 MESSAGE 13

The thirteenth message of the Third Law to Book Selection is:

Book selection in any library should be based on the probability for readers, and should never be vitiated by considerations of patronage.

CHAPTER FG

AUDIT BOGEY

1 Distant Book Market

A large percentage of the books needed for use in India continues to be in the English language. A big percentage of the English books needed is published in UK and USA. Thus the chief book markets are thousands of miles away. This results in the time interval between the selection of a book and its arrival in an Indian library between three and six months. This time factor leads to a considerable violation of the Third Law. This violation has become acute today.

2 Book Sellers in India

In recent years, some Indian book sellers show a considerable enterprise. They take the risk of stocking some foreign books in anticipation of sale. They have often to look out for some opportunity to clear their stock. This predicament of the book sellers contributes to the violation of the Third Law.

3 Mode of Violation

During the last ten years, India — this often means the governments in India — rightly provides annually large grants to libraries for book purchase. The authorities communicating the grant are not sensitive to the factors mentioned in the two preceding sections. They communicate to a library, information about the grant often after November along with the usual rider that the grant will lapse, if not spent before the succeeding 31 March. The Library Authority is also insensitive to the factors mentioned in the two preceding sections. It delays the signal to the librarian for the appropriation of the grant often by a few weeks. "To use the grant somehow or to surrender part of it." That becomes the crucial question. It goes against prestige not to grasp the grant given. The librarian is permitted to go to two or three book centres such as Bombay, Calcutta, Delhi, and Madras and bring books to cover the last pie of the grant. This makes impossible for Book Selection — it is really book purchase — to assess the probability for each to get its readers.

4 Result

Whatever book is available with the book seller is selected and bought on the spot at one stroke. Often copies of even the books already in the library, without getting any reader, have to be bought to spend the grant. It is no wonder that this puts the Third Law into a rage.

5 Remedy

There are only two remedies for this disaster.

1 The rider attached to the announcement of grant should be "You may take seventeen months to spend the grants to the satisfaction to the Laws of Library Science — particularly the Third Law. As the main book market is thousands of miles away, the average time needed between one instalment of Book Selection and the receipt of books selected is five months. You cannot select books for the entire amount in one instalment. You must spread the work over a whole year. We have been advised about this difficulty. The audit has instructions to replace the absolute date 31 March for lapse of grant by the relative date '17 months from now'. The Third Law should be fully respected."

2 The account and financial rules should be so amended as to admit of the automatic inclusion in the next year's budget of the unspent balance of the book fund of a year, subject to conditions prescribed to prevent indolence in the expeditious utilisation of the budget amount. This was the finding of the Library Committee of the University Grants Commission of India chaired by me five years ago. These should be applicable not only to university and college libraries but to every library to the extent to which its book fund has to be spent on foreign books. The seminar on public libraries conducted by me for the government of Andhra Pradesh in March 1962, whole-heartedly approved these findings.

51 MESSAGE 14

The fourteenth message of the Third Law to Book Selection is:

In the utilisation of the fund of a library, set apart for books to be purchased from foreign countries, do not make a fetish of the absolute 31 March fixed by audit or budget. Work on the basis of the relative time-limit of seventeen months after the sanction of the book fund.

CHAPTER FH

EGOCENTRICITY

1 Necessary but not Sufficient

The Second and the Third Laws may jointly succeed in making a Library Authority vest in the librarian the responsibility for Book Selection. The Third Law may further succeed in changing the audit and budget rules. All this is no doubt necessary. But it is not sufficient.

2 Seeking After the Favour of Superiors

These by themselves will not ensure satisfaction to the Third Law. The satisfaction has to depend on the way in which the librarian discharges the responsibility for Book Selection vested in him. Unfortunately, responsibility is taken by some to be in power and the power is abused. One kind of temptation for abuse may spring from a combination of the narrow, personal interest of the librarian and equally the narrow proneness of his authorities to succumb to flattery in the form of special personal service. For example, a Secretary of a Government Department had some children of his house-hold studying in colleges. The librarian of the department was enterprising enough to find out that among the children taken together, about half a dozen plays of Shakespeare were in frequent demand. He promptly bought several editions of each of these plays for the departmental library and lent them out to the children. The children conveyed to the Secretary their appreciation of the timely service of the librarian. The Secretary told them, "Yes, I do have an excellent librarian in my ministry". But the Third Law protested saying, "Your children do not form the legitimate clientele of your ministry's library. You should remember that these editions of Shakespere will not find any reader from among the staff of your ministry. Your librarian sins against me by abusing the power of Book Selection vested in him ; you also sin against me by looking upon the abuses of power as a virtue. And thereby ranking him as an able, dutiful librarian." This method of seeking favour of the superiors should be put down.

3 Slavery to Passion

Another kind of temptation to abuse of the power of Book Selection is illustrated by an unusual occurence in a big library. The librarian was extremely envious of the reputation of a person known to him. It happened that an ignorant hit-below-the-belt, polemical book decrying the achievements of that person came to be published. The librarian immediately bought a dozen copies of the book, and made a forced conversion of his subordinates to become readers of the copies of these books. His envy was thus propitiated. But the Third Law protested saying, "The term 'Reader' in 'Every Book its Reader' denotes a Reader drawn from the clientele of the library. No person of your reading public will ever become a reader of this frothy, venomous book. Do not imagine that you are propitiating me by forcing your staff to read this unwanted book. You are only propitiating your own passion. You are really abusing the responsibility for Book Selection vested in you."

4 Sacred Trust

Several other kinds of similar abuse, by librarians, of the power can be cited. It is after a century of trial and error that the world is recognising that the person most competent to know the probability of any new book selected to find its reader is the reference librarian. Members of the Library Authority have now realised that they have no opportunity to assess this probability. The librarian should not abuse the result of the realisation of these facts. He should not abuse it to serve his own egocentric, private purposes.

41 Message 15

The fifteenth message of the Third Law to Book Selection is :

> *A librarian should regard the responsibility for book selection vested in him as a sacred trust to be discharged in the best interest of the legitimate clientele of his library.*

Part G

FOURTH LAW OF LIBRARY SCIENCE AND BOOK SELECTION

CHAPTER GA

FOURTH LAW

1 Enunciation

The Fourth Law of Library Science is "Save the time of the reader". The first three laws concerned themselves with the reader-book relation. In the enunciation of the Second and the Third Laws, the reader as well as the book gets mentioned explicitly. In the First Law, the reader is implied and not expressed. The term "Reader" is suggested by the term "Use". To balance these, as it were, in the Fourth Law book is implied and not expressed. The term "Book" is suggested by the term "Time". For, there can be no Law of Library Science without bringing together implicitly or explicitly the terms "Reader" and "Book". Moreover, a Law of Library Science cannot interest itself in the time of the reader, except in so far as it is involved in his expressing his book need, his getting his book, and his using the book. The Fourth Law has implications in every activity of the library, leading to the saving of the time of the reader. In this book, we are concerned only with the work of Book Selection.

2 Two Kinds of Time

The Fourth Law would ask us to remember that relatively to a reader — in fact relatively to any person — two kinds of time should be recognised. One kind is common to all readers. It is public time. It is objective time. It is at bottom measured by the sun and the stars. It is also measured by the clock. The time interval is the same whoever is the reader. On the other hand, relative to each reader in a particular context, there is also a private time. It is subjective time. A minute of subjective time may have the value of as much as an hour of public time in the mind of a reader who is in an acute state of expectancy. Conversely, an hour of subjective time may have the value of only one minute of public time in the mind of a reader who is in an acute state of ecstasy and deep delight. William Blake, described this kind of time with the words, "There is a moment in life which contains eternity". Book Selection should take note of both these kinds of time in making inferences for its own regulation.

3 Corollary to Fourth Law

In Sec GA1 it was stated that the staff has to do many things to save the time of the reader. One of them is reference service. Everything else done will not get fulfilled unless the time of the reader is saved by reference service at the very moment of his seeking his documents. Therefore, as many man-hours of the library staff as possible should be released for reference service. In its turn this implies that the time of the staff spent on the other activities of the library as well as the time of the reference staff itself needed for searching for documents should be saved as much as possible. Thus, "Save the time of the staff" is an important corollary of the Fourth Law. Book Selection should take note of this corollary.

CHAPTER GB

RHYTHM OF BOOK SELECTION

1 Reduction of Time Lag

The time lag between the release of a book by the publisher and the availability of the same to a reader in a library should be reduced to a minimum. For this purpose, every item of work in a library — Book Selection, Book Procurement, Book Classification, Book Cataloguing, Book Processing, and everything else — and the whole sequence of work should be streamlined. The work flow in the library in making a book pass from the hands of the publisher to the hands of the reader should have the maximum speed. We are here concerned with the work of Book Selection. Book Selection should not contribute even a day to time lag.

2 Wrong Leisurely Rhythm

A bad habit in many a library is to make a year the period of the Rhythm for Book Selection. To reduce it to six months or even three months is not sufficiently good. In a large library the period of Rhythm should not be more than one week. In no library should it be more than one month. A single annual Book Selection sins not only against the Fourth Law, but leads to sinning against the other Laws also. So it is with periods of Rhythm larger than a week or a month ; for, when the period is long, inevitably, even the reference service staff, not to speak of the other staff, are ordered to suspend their normal service to readers and to work on Book Selection. The right thing is to make Book Selection keep close to the heels of the announcement of the release of the books by the publishers. In UK and USA — our chief markets — a weekly consolidated list of books released is regularly published. There is every hope that India too will soon reach that standard. Apart from this, a library known to be alert and active usually gets, every week, lists of books published from individual publishers. "Procrastination" may argue, "How can you make the selection for utilising the book fund of a year before you know all the books published during the year?" The answer of Book Selection to this is, "I shall first allot the annual book fund to the different subject fields in the light of experience. I shall break the annual allotment for each subject field into weekly or monthly quanta. I know from experience that I can safely appropriate a certain percentage of the weekly or monthly quantum, in the week or month itself. I can make Book Selection promptly out of the books produced every week or month without any time lag, and meet exceptional cases from out of the percentage of the quantum left unappropriated in its own period."

21 MESSAGE 1

The first message of the Fourth Law to Book Selection is :

> *Do not adopt the long leisurely rhythm of one year, six months, or even three months. Adopt the weekly rhythm, and in exceptional cases, the monthly rhythm.*

3 Elimination of Time Lag

Some publishers make advance announcement of the books being printed by them. They usually come in bunches such as, spring announcements, summer announcements, and so on. Time lag can be almost eliminated in the case of such books, if Book Selection utilises such announcements. Part D has explained the safeguards to be used in judging the values of such still unpublished books, on the basis of the author, the publisher, and the series. There is also the chance that some of the books announced may be abandoned by the publisher. But this does not create any risk in Book Selection. Basing Book Selection on such advance announcements will satisfy the Fourth Law, particularly in terms of "Subjective time" in the case of specialist readers. The satisfaction of the tempo of such readers will add to the reputation of such a library as being supreme in respecting the Fourth Law. Even in a generalist library, the elimination of time lag by this method in the case of much-sought-for books in certain periods, will give satisfaction to the tempo of the readers. Some examples of books which are known to be good, to be topical, and to be best-sellers are Churchill's *War memoirs*, Mahadev Desai's *Life of Mahatma Gandhi*, Bhandarkar's Oriental Research Institute's edition of the *Mahabharata*

31 Message 2

The second message of the Fourth Law to Book Selection is :

To eliminate time lag, book selection may, with due circumspection, base itself on the advance announcements of books by publishers of repute.

CHAPTER GC

BIBLIOGRAPHY

1 Macro Document

One of the ways in which the time of a reader is wasted within the library is in searching for reading materials. If a reader wants a particular book by a particular author, the library catalogue enables him to locate the book without any loss of time. In other words, for author and title approach the catalogue of the library is sufficient to satisfy the Fourth Law. But it is a matter of experience in libraries that the subject approach is more frequent among readers than author and title approach. Literature and particularly fiction may be an exception to this. But in this case, the author is made a class by himself — a Quasi-Class. In other popular classes of books such as biographies and travels, it is more the subject approach than the author approach that is common. "Biographee" denotes the subject of the biography. In a biography, it is the name of the "Biographee" rather than the name of the "Biographer" that is more often brought up by the reader in searching for his book. This amounts to saying that in biographies the subject approach is more common. More people ask for "Life of Mahatma Gandhi", "Rt Hon'ble V S Srinivasa Sastriar's letters", "Life of Ramakrishna", "Queen Victoria's letters", "Life of Napoleon", and so on. It is true that occasionally the reader wants Mahadeva Desai's *Life of Mahatma Gandhi* or Ludwig's *Napoleon*. But, this author approach is comparatively rare. All that has been said about biography applies equally to travels. It is the country and the period of travel that are more commonly remembered by readers than the authors. In other subjects belonging to Social Sciences, Useful Arts, and Pure Sciences, subject approach is even more common than in Humanities. This is particularly so in public libraries and with generalist readers. Here again, the library catalogue will meet the situation with its Class Index Entries, if it is of the Classified kind or with its Specific Subject and *See also* Entries if it is of the Dictionary kind. All this is about whole books or macro document.

2 Micro Document

But the position is quite different when what is wanted is not so much a whole book or macro thought, as an article in a periodical or a section of a book — in other words, micro thought. In this case the subject approach is decidedly dominant. In fact, it often happens that the author's name is not known at the time of enquiry. It is not a knowledge of the name of the author that brings the reader to his material. It is the name of the subject that does it. It is only after locating the reading material that the name of the author is discovered. This applies widely in regard to articles in periodicals and occasionally to even parts of books. The same thing applies also even if micro thought is embodied independently in a pamphlet. In other words, pamphlet literature too is more often approached through the name of the subject rather than the name of the author or title. These experiences in libraries go to show that the time taken by a reader to locate his reading material can be saved only if the catalogue is unsparing in making Subject Analytical Entries. But hardly any library is able to be fully analytical in its catalogue. From the national point of view, each library being profuse in analytical entries will amount to an avoidable waste. I have stressed in my *Heading and canons* (1955) that even for ordinary library catalogue without analytical entries, it is wasteful for each library to prepare its own catalogue. Indeed, I have advocated Pre-Natal Centralised Cataloguing — that is,

1 Books should be catalogued by the National Central Library, or State Central Library in the case of books in the language of the State, even when they are at proof stage;

2 Catalogue cards should be printed for supply to libraries, by the publisher or by the National Central Library or State Central Library, as the case may be; and

3 Printed catalogue cards relating to a book should be given along with the book to every library buying it.

With regard to macro thought or books, a nation or a state forms the most economical unit for Centralised Cataloguing.

3 International Documentation Periodical

But with regard to micro thought or articles in periodicals, even a nation is too uneconomical a unit for centralised work. It has been shown in my *Public library provision and documentation problems* (Indian Library Association, English series, 2), 1951, that the subject bibliographies are best built by international co-operation. Today, we do have plenty of bibliographies, more or less international in scope, on many subjects. The Fourth Law would urge Book Selection to be aware of this and to select bibliographies relating to all sectors of knowledge coming within the purview of the library.

31 Message 3

The third message of the Fourth Law to Book Selection is :

> *Select up-to-date bibliographies of the subjects covered by the library.*

CHAPTER GD

ARRANGEMENT OF ENTRIES IN BIBLIOGRAPHY

1 Mode

The extent to which a bibliography satisfies the Fourth Law is determined by the way in which its entries are arranged. Five outstanding modes of arrangements are in vogue :

1 Alphabetically by the names of authors ;

2 Chronologically by the dates of publications ;

3 Alphabetically by the names of authors and the names of subjects — Dictionary Arrangement ;

4 Grouping broadly by subjects and in each subject group alphabetically by the names of authors or chronologically by the dates of publications ; and

5 Minutely classified by subjects and fitted with an alphabetical index for names of authors and subjects — Classified or Bipartite Arrangement.

11 Message 4

The fourth message of the Fourth Law to Book Selection is :

Select that form of the bibliography available, which comes latest in the following list :

1 *Author List* ;

2 *Chronological List* ;

3 *Dictionary List by the names of authors and subjects* ;

4 *Subjects list with broad subject heading* ;

5 *Minutely classified list.*

CHAPTER GE

ANNOTATED BIBLIOGRAPHY

1 Pre-Open Access Days

All books are not of equal standard. Nor all books are of equal authenticity and authority. Books differ also in readability. Before open access days, a reader had to select his book merely from the catalogue entry. It was virtually a blind choice. Quite often the book used to disappoint him in respect of standard, authority, and readability, when it reached his hands. He had again to spend time over the catalogue to call for some other book in the hope of it being suitable to him. In this process of hit or miss, a reader had often to waste much of his time. This meant a violation of the Fourth Law. Therefore, a library used to add an annotation in the main entry of a book indicating its qualities mentioned above. But an annotated main entry takes a little more than double the time of a bare entry. Each library had to spend this extra time on one and the same book. This went against national economy. It also went against the corollary of the Fourth Law — Save the time of the staff — in order to provide for maximum reference service. This called for the publication of an annotated bibliography by a national agency.

2 After Open Access

Open access came into being widely during the present century. This allowed a reader to browse amidst books and select the book with qualities suitable to his needs. This naturally made the library to save the time of the staff needed for annotation. Therefore, annotation was generally dropped. However, the dropping of the annotation led to the violation of the Fourth Law in another sense. A reader does not often find time to dip into several books to choose the one with the qualities needed by him. This happens particularly in the case of specialist readers usually fully preoccupied with their own work. Apart from this, a generalist reader in a public library or in a school or a college library has often to be helped by the reference librarian in the choice of the book appropriate to him. In discharging this essential function, the reference librarian has himself to spend time in judging the qualities of the book on the spot in the absence of annotation in the library catalogue. This fact again brings up the necessity for the production of an annotated bibliography by a national agency.

3 Examples

National agencies for the production of annotated bibliographies do function in some countries. The National Book League of UK, and the Library of Congress of USA are examples. No doubt some publishers' catalogues give annotation. But national agencies are necessary to bring together in one bibliography books by all the publishers. Again, as part of public relation work, an individual library may publish annotated bibliographies on topical subjects. But these carry a considerable local colour and are for local consumption only. Therefore, production of annotated bibliography in diverse subjects by a national agency is desirable. Wherever such bibliographies exist, Book Selection should include them in respect of the subject fields in demand among the clientele of the library. The following is a short illustrated list of annotated bibliography.

31 Illustrative List

Note.

1 This is a short illustrative list.

2 The entries are made according to the *Classified catalogue code*, Ed 5 (1964).

3 The entries are arranged by Colon Classification Numbers.

k Encyclopaedia

ka'N7 Encyclopaedia, Bibliography, 1970s

1 N60 Undernick (Robert L). About encyclopaedias : Annotated bibliography. 1960. Jackgonville. Illinois.

J Agriculture

J,08; 4a'N7 Agriculture, Seed, Disease, Bibliography, 1970s

2 N58 Noble (J de Tempe) and Neergaard (Paul). Annotated

list of seed-borne disease. 1958. Commonwealth Mycological Institute. Kew. England.

L Medicine

***La*'N7 Medicine, Bibliography, 1970s**

3 N61 INSTITUTE FOR ADVANCEMENT OF MEDICAL COMMUNICATION. Annotated bibliography of studies on the flow of medical information to practitioners. 1961.

Q Religion

***Qa*'N7 Religion, Bibliography, 1970s**

4 N56 DIEHAL (K S). Religions, mythologies, folk uses : Annotated bibliography. 1956. Scarescrew Press. New Brunswick.

S Psychology

***Sa*'N7 Psychology, Bibliography, 1970s**

5 N51 BRITISH PSYCHOLOGICAL SOCIETY (London). Psychology: Selected list of books compiled for the National Book League. 1951. Cambridge University Press.

T Education

T4. 73*a*'N7 Education, University, USA, Bibliography, 1970s

6 N60 EELSS (Walter Crosby) and HOLLIS (Ernest V). Administration of higher education : Annotated bibliography. 1960.

V History

V ; 19*a*'N7 History, Foreign policy, Bibliography 1970s

7 N58 CONOVER (Helen F). Guide to bibliographic tools for research in foreign affairs, Ed 2 with supplement. 1958. Library of Congress. Washington.

X Economics

X : 958. 73*a*'N60←N35 Economics, Social Security, USA, Bibliography, 1935-1960

8 N60 UNITED STATES OF AMERICA, HEALTH, EDUCATION, AND WELFARE (Department of—). Basic readings in social security, 1935-1960. 1960.

32 MESSAGE 5

The fifth message of the Fourth Law to Book Selection is :

Select annotated bibliographies of books in all the subjects covered by the library.

33 Message 6

The sixth message of the Fourth Law to Book Selection is :

The annotated bibliographies selected for a library, primarily to save the time of the readers, will serve also the secondary purpose of saving the time of the staff engaged in book selection.

CHAPTER GF

VARIETIES OF DOCUMENTATION LIST

1 Documentation List

To distinguish a bibliography of whole books or macro documents from that of parts of books and articles in periodicals or micro documents, it is convenient to denote the former by the old term, "Bibliography" and the latter by the new term "Documentation List". A documentation list is usually on a specific subject rather than on the whole universe of knowledge. To emphasise this aspect, a documentation list is called a "Subject Bibliography".

2 Closed or Open

A documentation list may be a retrospective one covering a specific period of time. There may be no intention to bring it periodically up-to-date. Such an isolated documentation list is said to be a "Closed" one. A documentation list may also appear as a regular periodical. It is said to be an "Open" one. It may be called a "Documentation Periodical". The coverage of each of its volumes is usually one year. The volume may be brought out in weekly or monthly instalments or issues, or annual issues or on the basis of some other period. The coverage of each such issue will be its period. Consequently, a documentation periodical will cover only current documents embodying current or nascent thought. There is a tendency now to bring out a documentation periodical giving an advance list of documents getting printed in their respective host-periodicals. It may be called "Advance Documentation Periodical"

3 Documentation Periodical

Three varieties of documentation periodicals exist today — viz,

1 Indexing periodical ;
2 Abstracting periodical ; and
3 Trend report.

CHAPTER GG

CLOSED BIBLIOGRAPHY

1 Saving of Time

As the learned periodicals are today, it takes a considerable amount of time for a reader interested in a particular topic to pick out exhaustively all the articles contained in the volumes of all the periodicals carrying articles on his topic. This would lead to the violation of the Fourth Law. Even for the reference librarian of each library picking them out exhaustively by himself will be a violation of the corollary of the Fourth Law — Save the time of the staff. It will be a violation of this corollary even for each country to prepare such a retrospective documentation list. The Fourth Law would therefore recommend its preparation being entrusted to a regional organisation for each linguistic region or even an international organisation.

2 Saving of National Time

Such an advanced and economical international organisation has not come into being for closed documentation lists. However, such lists are published now and again in certain countries only. The following is a short illustrative list.

21 LIST OF CLOSED BIBLIOGRAPHIES

Note.

1 This is a short illustrative list.

2 The entries are arranged by Colon Classification Numbers.

3 The entries are made according to the *Classified catalogue code*, Ed 5 (1964).

***w*73—1*a*'N7 Biography, USA, Autobiography, Bibliography, 1970s**

1 N61 KAPLAN (Louis). Bibliography of American autobiographies. 1961. University of Wisconsin Press. New York.

***z*2*a*'N7 Indology, Bibliography, 1970s**

2 N60 KANTIKAR (J M) etc. Bibliography of indology. V 1. Indian anthropology. 1960. National Library. Calcutta.

zM Malaviya

zMa'N7 Malaviya, Bibliography, 1970s

3 N62 BANARAS HINDU UNIVERSITY (Varanasi). Malaviyana: Bibliography of Pandit Madan Mohan Malaviya. Ed by P N Kaula. Comp by M M Job and I B Singh. 1962. Banaras Hindu University. Varanasi.

31,(A)a'N7 Authorial Art, Natural Sciences, Bibliography 1970s

4 N61 SHANK (Russell), *Ed.* Bibliography of technical writing. Ed 3. Rev by Society of Technical Writers and Publishers. 1961.

Aa'N5 Natural Sciences, Bibliography, 1950s

5 N54 SHANK (Russell). Bibliography of technical reference literature and sources of information. 1954.

6 N58 JOHNSON (I). Selected books and journals in science and engineering. 1958. MIT Press. Massachusetts.

7 N59 GOLDMAN (S). Guide to the literature of engineering, mathematics, and the physical sciences. 1959. Johns Hopkins University.

Aa, z73'N5 Natural Sciences, Bibliography, USA, 1950s

8 N58 HAWKINS (R R). Scientific, medical, and technical books pubiished in the USA. Ed 2. 1958. Bowker. New York.

Aka'N7 Natural Sciences, Encyclopaedia, Bibliography, 1970s

9 N61 UNESCO. Bibliography of interlingual scientific and technical dictionaries. Ed 4. 1961. Paris.

A. 2a'N7 Natural Sciences, India, Bibliography, 1970s

10 N60 NATIONAL LIBRARY (Calcutta). Indian scientific and technical publications; Exhibition 1960. Council of Scientific and Industrial Research. New Delhi.

AZa'N5 Mathematical Sciences, Bibliography, 1950s

11 N58 PARKE (Nathan G) (III). Guide to the literature of mathematics and physics. Ed 2. 1958. Dover.

B951a'N5 Meteor, Bibliography, 1950s

12 N58 BROWN (H S). Bibliography on meteorites. 1958. University of Chicago Press. Chicago.

C9B2a'N5 Physics, Nuclear, Bibliography, 1950s

13 N55 MICHIGAN UNIVERSITY LIBRARY. Bibliography of current materials dealing with atomic power and related atomic energy subjects for non-specialists. 1955.

Da,(CW12)'N5 Engineering, Bibliography, Abstracting periodical, 1950s

14 N55 SPECIAL LIBRARIES ASSOCIATION (New York). Bibliography of engineering abstracting services. 1955. (SLA bibliography, 1).

D4A.58a'N5 Engineering, Airway, Soviet Russia, Bibliography, 1950s

15 N55 LIBRARY OF CONGRESS (Washington), Reference (—Department). Aeronautical sciences and aviation in the Soviet Union: Bibliography. Comp by Bertha Kucherov. 1955. Washington.

D6a'N5 Electrical Engineering, Bibliography, 1950s

16 N59 ASLIB (London). Handlist of basic reference material in electrical and electronic engineering. 1959.

E4a'N5 Chemistry, Salt, Bibliography, 1950s

17 N58 JONZ (George J). Bibliography on molten salts. 1958. Rensselaer Polytechnic Institute. Troy. N Y.

F191a'N7 Metallurgy, Bibliography, 1970s

18 N61 SPECIAL LIBRARIES ASSOCIATION (New York). Guide to metallurgical information. 1961. (SLA bibliography, 3).

F53a'N56←N36 Technology, Food, Bibliography, 1936 to 1956

19 N58 BIBLIOGRAPHY OF FOOD: Select international bibliography of nutrition, food, and beverage technology and distribution. 1936-56. 1958. Academic Press.

G12a'N50←M84 Biology, Tissue, Bibliography, 1884 to 1950

20 N53 MURRAY (M R) and KEPECH (C). Bibliography of the research in tissue culture, 1884-1950. 1953. Academic Press.

Ha, (CM)-3T4-z7'N5 Geology, Bibliography, Thesis, University, America, 1950s

21 N58 CHRONIC (John) and CHRONIC (Halka) and PETROLEUM RESEARCH CORPORATION. Bibliograpy of thesis written for advanced degrees in geology and related sciences at universities and colleges in the United States and Canada through 1957. 1958. Pruett Press. Boulder. Colorado.

Ha,(CM)-3T-z73'N5 Geology, Bibliography, Thesis, Educational Institution, USA, 1950s

22 N54 TURNER (D S). Bibliography of geology thesis, colleges and universities of the U S. 1954. Denver.

H1163a'N7 Mineralogy, Selenium, Bibliography, 1970s

23 N59 LUTTRELL (W). Annotated bibliography on the geology of selenium. 1959. US Geological Survey. Washington D C. (Bulletin 1019-M).

H9Ca'N5 Geophysics, Bibliography, 1950s

24 N57 NATIONAL SCIENCE FOUNDATION (Washington). Bibliography for the international geophysical year. 1957. Washington.

I22a'N5 Algae, Bibliography, 1950s

25 N58 NOVA SCOTIA RESEARCH FOUNDATION (Halifax). Selected bibliography on algae. 1958. Halifax.

Ja,(CF1)'N5 Agriculture, Bibliography, Bibliographies, 1950s

26 N57 LAUCHE (Rudolf), Ed. World bibliography of bibliographies. 1957. Bayerischer Landwirtschaftsverlag. Munich.

J16a'N00<—L00 Floriculture, Bibliography, 1700 to 1900

27 N56 SITWILL (S) and BLUNT (W). Great Flower books, 1700-1900: Bibliographical record of two centuries of finely illustrated flower books. 1956. Collins. N Y.

Ka'N5 Zoology, Bibliography, 1950s

28 N58 SMITH (R C). Guide to the literature of the zoological sciences. Ed 5. 1958.

K96a'N46<—N39 Ornithology, Bibliography, 1939-46

29 N47 STRONG (R M). Bibliography of birds. 3 V. 1939-46. Field Museum Nation History. 1947.

La'N5 Medicine, Bibliography, 1950s

30 N54 MORTON (L T). Garrison and Morton's medical bibliography. 1954. Grafton. London.

La-z7'N7 Medicine, Bibliography, America, 1970s

31 N61 GUERRA (F). American medical bibliography. 1961. Harper.

L : 42a'N5 Medicine, Infection, Bibliography, 1950s

32 N58 BLOOMFIELD (Arthur L). Bibliography of internal medicine: Communicable diseases. 1958. University of Chicago Press. Chicago.

L9T*a*'N5 Medicine, Aviation, Bibliography, 1950s

33 N58 NATIONAL LIBRARY OF MEDICINE (Washington). Bibliography of space medicine. 1958. (US Public health service publications. 617.)

L9V, 72 : 4 : ϕ91*a*'N58<–N52 Medicine, War, Psychiatry, Bibliography, 1952 to 1958

34 N59 NATIONAL LIBRARY OF MEDICINE (Washington), Reference (Division of —). Bibliography of military psychiatry, 1952-58. Comp by Charles Roos and Jeanettee Barry. 1959. US Department of Health, Education, and Welfare. Washington.

M*a*'N5 Useful Arts, Bibliography, 1950s

35 N54 KINGERY (R E). How-to-do-it books. Ed 2. 1954. Bowker.

36 N57 SMITH (F S). Know-how books. 1957. Bowker.

M31*a*'M60<–L42 Cooking, Bibliography, 1742 to 1860

37 N54 LINCON (W). American cookery books, 1742-1860. 1954. American Antiquarian Society. Worchester. Massachusetts.

NR*a*,3 W'L20<–K65 Music, Bibliography, Publisher Walsh, 1655 to 1720

38 N48 SMITH (W C). Bibliography of the musical works published by John Walsh during the years 1655- 1720. 1948. Bibliographical Society. London.

O111, 1MO8*a*'N5 Literature, English, Chaucer, Bibliography, 1950s

39 N58 GRIFFITH (D D). Bibliography of Chaucer 1908-53. 1958. University of Washington Press. Seattle.

O111, 2J64*a*'N58<–N36 Shakespeare, Bibliography, 1936 to 1958

40 N63 SMITH (Gordon Ross). Classified Shakespeare bibliography, 1936-1958. 1963. Pennsylvania University.

O11173, 3N2<–L5 : *ga*'N59<–NOO Literature, American, Fiction, (Authors of 1750s to 1920s), Evaluation, Bibliography, 1900 to 1959

41 N61 GERSTENBERGER (Donna) and HENDRICK (George). American novel 1789-1959: Checklist of twentieth century criticism. 1961. Denver.

O11173, 3M76*a*'N5 Sherwood Anderson, Bibliography, 1950s

42 N60 SHEEHY (Eugene) and LOHF (Kenneth A). Sherwood Anderson : Bibliography. 1960. Talisman Press. California.

R*a*'N7 Philosophy, Bibliography, 1970s

43 N56 VARET (G). Manuel de bibliographie philosophique. 1956. 2 V. Presses Universitaires de France. Paris. V1 : Les philosophies classiques. V 2 : Les sciences philosophiques.

S*a*'N7 Psychology, Bibliography, 1970s

44 N55 HARVARD UNIVERSITY, PSYCHOLOGY AND SOCIAL RELATIONS (Department of —). Harvard list of books in Psychology. 1955. Harvard University Press. Massachusetts.

SZ*a*,(CM)-3T4. 1 'N50<—N40 Social sciences, Bibliography, Theses, University, 1940 to 1950

45 N52 UNESCO. Thesis in the social sciences : International analytical catalogue of unpublished doctorate thesis, 1940-50. 1952. Unesco. Paris.

V*a*-*z*1-3'N45<—N40 History, Bibliography, British Empire, 1940 to 1945

46 N47 FREWER (L B). Bibliography of historical writings published in Great Britain and the empire, 1940-45. 1947. Blackwells. Oxford.

V3*a*'K03<—H85 History, Great Britain, Bibliography, 1485 to 1603

47 N59 READ (Conveyors). Bibliography of British history. Tudor period, 1485-1603. Ed 2. 1959.

V42*a*'N5 History, Japan, Bibliography, 1950s

48 N54 BORTON (Hugh) etc. Selected list of books and articles on Japan in English, French and German. 1954. Harvard University Press. Cambridge. Massachusetts.

X6*a*'N7 Economics, Credit, Bibliography, 1970s

49 N64 DONALDSON (G) and STUBBS (C), Comp. Corporate and business finance : Classified bibliography of recent literature. 1964.

X8(A).1(Y:494) *a*'N5 Economics, Industry, Undeveloped countries, Bibliography, 1950s

50 N56 UNITED NATION LIBRARY (Geneva). Bibliography on industrialization in under-developed countries. 1956. New York.

Y: 5. 73*sa*'N5 Sociology, Demography, USA, Statistics, Bibliography, 1950s

51 N54 UNITED NATIONS, STATISTICAL (Office). Bibliography of recent official demographic statistics. 1954. (Statistical papers, series M, 18).

Z*a*'N5 Law, Bibliography, 1950s

52 N55 SZLADITS (C). Bibliography on foreign and comparative law : Books and articles in English. 1955. Oceana publications. New York.

Z*a*'N58<–N57 Law, Bibliography, 1957 to 1958

53 N58 INDIA, LAW (Ministry of —), LIBRARY. Legal literature: Select bibliography, 1957-1958. 1958.

22 MESSAGE 7

The seventh message of the Fourth Law to Book Selection is :

> *In a generalist library, such as a public, or a college, or a school library, select documentation lists giving a list of general and popular articles on the subjects covered by the library.*

23 MESSAGE 8

The eighth message of the Fourth Law to Book Selection is :

> *In a specialist library and in a university library, select as exhaustively as possible closed documentation lists on the subjects of specialisation.*

CHAPTER GH

INDEXING PERIODICAL

1 Heterogeneity in Periodicals

The number of periodicals current today is very large. Moreover, hardly any periodical confines itself strictly to a single well defined subject-area. In other words, heterogeneity prevails in learned periodicals instead of homogeneity in respect of the subjects covered.

2 Interlaced Roots

The first cause for heterogeneity is intrinsic to the universe of knowledge itself. It does not admit of dissection into clean cut, absolutely mutually exclusive subject-areas, though two subject areas may appear to be mutually exclusive on the surface. The roots of the subjects are often found interlaced. When we pull out any one subject-area to its very roots, the other interlaced roots are also drawn out along with the other related subject-areas visible on the surface. For example, the modern investigation of the sub-atomic particles depends largely on the use of photographic plates. The Atomic Physicist often works out the necessary photographic film by himself or with the help of a Chemist. The paper on Elementary Particle will necessarily contain an account of the preparation of the photographic plate. But strictly speaking it belongs to the subject field Photography or more strictly to Photographic Chemistry. The criss-crossing of the subject fields Virology, Bacteriology, Pathology, Immunology, Pharmacology, and Biochemistry particularly Enzyme Chemistry is well-known.

3 Seepage

The second cause for heterogeneity is intrinsic to the business of publication. The publication of a learned periodical is not a profit making business. At present most of the work connected with it — all work except physical production, that is, writing out the articles, editing them for the press, providing them summaries, compiling the bibliography, part of the proof-reading and indexing

— is now done as work of love without remuneration. If we take into consideration the total cost of all such honorary work, the production of a learned periodical is certainly a losing business. Even confining ourselves to the cost of physical production one has to be extremely careful to avoid loss. There is also the urge to make the appearance of the issue conform to the intended period and to make the number of pages in each issue the same. These factors also make a learned periodical accept articles on subjects lying only in the fringe of its core subject area. Sometimes it even becomes necessary to go further away from the core into alien subject. The result is either Scatter or Seepage. When the core subject of a learned periodical is totally alien to the subject of the document, there is Seepage. When alienness is not total, but there is some degree of filiation, it is called Scatter. It is not easy to distinguish between Seepage and Scatter. In this connection *see* Chapter B6 "Why of Documentation" by S R Ranganathan in *Documentation and its facets* (1963), ed by S R Ranganathan. *See also* the papers "Seepage, Multifocalness, and Slant in a Document", "Scatter, and Seepage of Documents" by S R Ranganathan, 'Scatter and Seepage in Radio Engineering" by D Gundu Rao, and "Seepage of Documents in Medical Electronics" by A Neelameghan and M V Ranga Rau in *Documentation periodicals: Coverage, arrangement, scatter, seepage, and compilation*, ed by S R Ranganathan and A Neelameghan. (DRTC Seminar, 1) (1963).

4 Loss of Time

The inevitable scatter and seepage currently incident in learned periodicals leads to the violation of the Fourth Law if each reader is obliged to turn through the pages of all the current issues of the learned periodicals in order to locate, pin-pointedly, and exhaustively just the documents of interest to him at the moment. Here is an estimate of the measure of the time to be spent by the reader. The following assumptions are made :

1 Number of learned periodicals current = 50,000

2 Average number of articles published each week in these periodicals = 50,000

3 Average number of pages of an article = 10

Then,

the number of pages to be turned through by the reader each week in the original periodical to locate the few documents of interest to him at the moment will be = 500,000

5 Saving of Time by an Alphabetical Indexing Periodical

The following assumption is made :

1 Average number of index entries in a page of an alphabetical indexing periodical = 50

Then,

1 Number of pages in a weekly issue of it to cover 50,000 articles = 1,000

2 Number of pages to be turned through by the reader each week in the alphabetical indexing periodical to locate the few documents of interest to him at the moment will be = 1,000

3 The reduction ratio for the time for location will be = 1/500

6 Saving of Time by a Classified Indexing Periodical

The following assumptions are made :

1 Average number of index entries in a page of a classified indexing periodical = 25

2 The number of articles of interest to the reader at the moment = 50

Then,

1 The number of pages in a weekly issue of a classified indexing periodical to cover the 50,000 articles will be = 2,000

2 The minimum number of pages to be turned through by the reader each week in a classified indexing periodical to locate the 50 documents of interest to him at the moment will be = 2

3 If there are adequate and profuse cross reference entries to articles indirectly of interest to the subject of the reader, the maximum number of pages to be turned through by the reader each week in the classified

indexing periodical to locate the documents of interest to him at the moment will be = 5

4 The reduction ratio for time of location will be between $\frac{1}{10,000}$ and $\frac{1}{25,000}$

7 Illustrative List

An omnibus indexing periodical covering all the current learned periodicals does not exist. Nor will it be economical, nor can it be produced without loss of time. There are indexing periodicals only in different subject areas. The following is a short illustrative list of subjects having indexing periodicals.

2	Library Science	L	Medicine
A	Natural Sciences	M	Useful arts
B	Mathematics	N	Fine arts
C	Physics	O	Literature
D	Engineering	S	Psychology
E	Chemistry	T	Education
F	Technology	U	Geography
G	Biology	V	History
H	Geology	W	Political Science
I	Botany	X	Economics
J	Agriculture	Y	Sociology
K	Zoology	Z	Law
KX	Animal Husbandry		

71 Message 9

The ninth message of the Fourth Law to Book Selection is :

In a generalist library, such as, a public, or a college, or a school library, select indexing periodicals giving a list of general and popular articles on the subjects covered by the library.

72 **Message 10**

The tenth message of the Fourth Law to Book Selection is :

> *In a specialist library and in a university library, select as exhaustively as possible indexing periodicals on the subjects of specialisation.*

8 National Indexing Periodical

The time lag between the publication of an issue of an international indexing periodical covering current issues of all the learned periodicals in a subject field will be great. It may be between one to three months. To this extent the Fourth Law will be dissatisfied. This time lag can be eliminated by being selective in the learned periodicals covered by the international indexing periodical. Such a selective coverage is not possible at the international level. But it is possible in an indexing periodical produced at the national level for the National Indexing Periodical need not include every article published. It can restrict itself to articles bearing on the subjects actually engaging the attention of the specialists in the country. Of course, this list of subjects will have to be revised from time to time by the National Documentation Centre. Secondly, a National Indexing Periodical can be further restricted to cover only such periodicals as are currently taken within the country. In the field restricted in these two ways, the National Documentation Centre can procure, by airmail post, microfilm copies of the contents page of the periodicals covered, and on their basis it can produce the National Indexing Periodical. Each issue of such an Indexing Periodical can reach the service library in the country and the work tables of the specialist either a few days earlier or simultaneously with the current issues of learned periodicals covered by it. Then the Fourth Law will be satisfied to the maximum possible extent. From 1950 onwards, I had been working for the establishment of the Indian National Scientific Documentation Centre in order to satisfy the Fourth Law in full measure. The Insdoc was eventually established in 1952. It inaugurated the fortnightly *Insdoc list* in 1954. I am now living in the hope that it will rapidly outgrow the rickety stage and will soon grow as fully as similar national documentation lists started in other countries such as, Yugoslavia and the USSR nearly at the same time.

81 MESSAGE 11

The eleventh message of the Fourth Law to Book Selection is:

In a specialist library and in a university library, select the National Documentation List without fail.

CHAPTER GJ

ABSTRACTING PERIODICAL

1 Difference from Indexing Periodical

We saw in Sec GH6 that the reduction ratio for the time of location of articles of the interest to reader in a classified indexing periodical would be between $\frac{1}{10,000}$ and $\frac{1}{25,000}$. But in an abstracting periodical it cannot be as low as that, for, an abstract added to an entry occupies a considerable space. Therefore, the space occupied by an entry in an abstracting periodical will be nearly ten times the one occupied by an indexing periodical. Therefore, the average number of entries in a page of an abstracting periodical will have to be taken as 2.5 instead of the 25 in the indexing periodical.

2 Saving of Time by a Classified Abstracting Periodical

The following assumptions are made :

1 Average number of index entries in a page of a classified abstracting periodical	=	2.5
2 The number of articles of interest to the reader at the moment	=	50

Then,

1 The number of pages in a weekly issue of the classified abstracting periodical to cover the 50,000 articles will be	=	20,000
2 The minimum number of pages to be turned through by the reader each week in a classified abstracting periodical	=	20

3 If there are adequate and profuse cross reference entries to articles indirectly of interest to the subject of the reader, the maximum number of pages to be turned through by the reader each week in

the classified abstracting periodical to locate the document of interest to him at the moment will be = 50

4 The reduction ratio for the time of location will be between

$$\frac{1}{1{,}000} \text{ and } \frac{1}{2{,}500}$$

3 Time Lag in an Abstracting Periodical

An abstracting periodical cannot be produced as promptly as an indexing periodical. For, each article has to be read through and abstracted. In the past, the time lag, between the appearance of an issue of an abstracting periodical and of the appearance of an issue of a learned periodical abstracted, used to be about a year. After World War II, the tendency is to reduce the time lag. It has been reduced to three months. The Unesco has played no small part in this reduction.

4 National Level

Time lag is unavoidable, whether the abstracting is done at the national level or at the international level. Therefore, a National Documentation Centre will not bring any benefit by taking up abstracting service. Wisdom lies in its confining itself to the indexing periodical in the manner described in Sec in GH8. This is, however, apart from its share of the abstracting work for international abstracting periodicals.

5 Local Level

Till the international abstracting periodical arrives, a local service library will have to do some asbstracting work. It need not abstract every article in every periodical received by it. An economical plan will be

1 To circulate the indexing periodical to each member of the clientele ;

2 To send to the library a list of the articles for each of which they would like to have an abstract; and

3 For the library to prepare abstracts only on such requisition.

6 Advantage of Abstracts

There is a positive advantage in supplying abstracts to the specialist. The first advantage is the saving of time in the general browsing of the articles in the measure of $\frac{1}{1,000}$ to $\frac{1}{2,500}$ as shown in Sec GJ2. Secondly, the abstract will help the specialist to decide which article he should read in the original and for which article he should ask for a translation.

7 Illustrative List of Subjects Having Abstracting Periodical

An omnibus abstracting periodical covering all the current learned periodicals does not exist. Nor will it be economical, nor can it be produced without loss of time. There are abstracting periodicals only in different subject areas. The following is a short illustrative list of subjects having abstracting periodical.

8 List of Subjects Having Abstracting Periodicals

1	2	Library science	27	D66	Electrical engineering
2	2: 97	Documentation	28	D67	Nuclear engineering
3	A	Natural sciences	29	D8	Sanitary engineering
4	B	Mathematics	30	D854	Water supply engineering
5	B28	Statistics			
6	B9	Astronomy	31	D9	Instruments
7	C	Physics	32	E	Chemistry
8	C2 : 2	Rheology	33	E : 3	Analytical chemistry
9	C21	Solid state physics	34	E5	Organic chemistry
10	C5 : 3	Spectroscopy	35	E97	Vitamin
11	C6	Electricity	36	E9G	Biochemistry
12	C9B3	Nuclear science	37	F	Technology
13	C9D1	Cryoscopy	38	F191	Metallurgy
14	D	Engineering	39	F191 : 94	Corrosion
15	D : 1	Applied mechanics	40	F5	Chemicals
16	D2	Building engineering	41	F51	Rubber
17	D411	Highway engineering	42	F52	Plastics
18	D415	Railway engineering	43	F53	Food science
19	D42	Marine engineering	44	F54	Beverage
20	D43	Aeronautics	45	F55	Fuel technology
21	D513	Automobile	46	F555	Petroleum
22	D541	Missiles and rockets	47	F5895	Paint
23	D6	Power engineering	48	G	Biology
24	D6386	Vacuum engineering	49	H1	Mineralogy
25	D65	Electronics	50	H9C	Geophysics
26	D65,8(B)	Computer	51	I	Botany

52	J	Agriculture
53	J1	Horticulture
54	J1 : 1	Soil
55	J142	Agricultural entomology
56	J251	Herbage culture
57	J452	Tobacco culture
58	J781	Cotton growing
59	J97 : 6	Plant breeding
60	JX	Forestry
61	KX	Veterinary science
62	KX311	Dairy science
63	KX332	Fisheries
64	L	Medicine
65	L : 17	Anesthesiology
66	L : 42	Medical entomology
67	L : 43	Medical mycology
68	L : 4 : 7	Surgery
69	L : 57	Hygiene
70	L : 573	Nutrition
71	L183	Otology
72	L185	Opthalmology
73	L2	Gastroenterology
74	L214	Dentistry
75	L293:46	Diabetes
76	L4:4241	Influenza
77	L51	Urology
78	L7	Neurology
79	L71:423	Poliomyelites
80	L9B	Embryology
81	L9C	Pediatrics
82	L9C : 7	Child development
83	L9F : 3	Obstetrics
84	L9T	Aviation medicine
85	L9X	Industrial medicine
86	LX3	Pharmacology
87	M14	Printing
88	M31	Baking
89	M6	Glass technology
90	M7	Textile technology
91	M95	Photography
92	M98	Packaging
93	MA	Home economics
94	MY25	Angling
95	O	Literature
96	O111	English literature
97	P	Linguistics
98	Q	Religion
99	S	Psychology
100	T	Education
101	U28	Meteorology
102	V	History
103	V1 :19	International relations
104	V7	Archaeology
105	X	Economics
106	X:51	Marketing
107	X:8D	Finance
108	X:8H	Accountancy
109	X:9	Personnel management
110	X:97D	Labour union
111	X8(H91)	Diamond industry
112	X8(J)	Agricultural industry
113	X8(J311)	Sugar industry
114	X8(M5)	Furniture industry
115	XX	Management
116	Y	Sociology
117	Y:411	Alchoholism
118	Z	Law

81 Message 12

The twelfth message of the Fourth Law to Book Selection is :

In a specialist library and in a university library, select as exhaustively as possible, abstracting periodicals on the subjects of specialisation.

CHAPTER GK

TREND REPORT PERIODICAL

1 Distinctive Feature

An indexing or abstracting periodical may be said to give an atomised view of the wavefront in the universe of knowledge in the week or in the month or in any other period covered by it. This is no doubt necessary as a help in the day to day work of a specialist. But it is not sufficient. On the other hand, a specialist should also have an integral view of the happenings in his area of the universe of knowledge during the year taken as a whole. The reporting periodical serves this purpose. This is necessary for various reasons.

2 Help Given to a Specialist

A reporting periodical helps the specialist to know the

1 Fallow regions of knowledge to be cultivated in the subject area falling within his purview ;

2 Areas in which there is unintended and unnecessary duplication of effort in the country or in the world taken as a whole ;

3 The names of peers or of the specialists working in different countries in order to facilitate his getting into personal touch with them ;

4 The density of the world effort during the year in the different sub-areas of his subject field ; and

5 World activities in the fringe subject fields and the regions of overlap between his own subject field and that of the others.

3 Illustrative List

An omnibus reporting periodical covering the progress in all subject does not exist. It is neither economical nor can it be produced without loss of time. There are reporting periodicals in several subject areas in which there are abstracting periodicals (*See* Sec GJ71).

From its very nature it can be seen that international economy requires that the agency for the production of a reporting periodical is an International Body.

31 Message 13

The thirteenth message of the Fourth Law to Book Selection is:

In a specialist library and in a university library, select as exhaustively as possible reporting periodicals on the subjects of specialisation.

4 "Short Communication" Periodicals

It is now well accepted not only by research workers and librarians but also by publishers of periodicals, that new ideas should be disseminated as early as possible in order to minimise the chances of duplication of research work. In respect of the publication of periodicals this has led to

1 Priority assignment to papers to be published in a periodical; and

2 Provision of sections such as "Preliminary Communications" and "Shortnotes" to accommodate a number of short articles expounding ideas being newly created. *Nature* (London), *Current science* (Bangalore), are examples of periodicals of this kind.

The basis of the latter practice is that it involves less of editing and more of them could be accommodated in an issue of a periodical. However, when longer papers and "short communications" are included in one and the same issue of a periodical, the delay in publication will normally depend on the editing time etc spent on the longer papers. Thus, there is no significant gain in speeding up the dissemination of new ideas through such a periodical.

Therefore, in the last few years, periodicals containing "short commuications" alone have began to appear. This new medium is intended to provide an opportunity for "rapid publication of timely and significant observations in the form of short but *well documented communications*".

41 Illustrative List

The following is an illustrative list of "Short Communication" Periodicals:

1 *Physical review letters.* F. 1958.
2 *Tetrahedron letters.* F. 1959.
3 *Biochemical and biophysical research communications.* M. 1958.

42 Message 14

The fourteenth message of the Fourth Law to Book Selection is :

> *In a specialist library and in a university library, select as exhaustively as possible "Short Communication" periodicals on the subjects of specialisation.*

5 "Pre-view" Periodicals

Another method adopted by a periodical to provide advance information about the articles to be published in it, is to publish an associate periodical of the "pre-view" type. An issue of such a periodical contains summaries of the articles to be published four to five months later in the parent periodical publishing the full papers. A summary gives advance information about the scope, the contents, and the conclusions reached in the paper.

An example of this kind of periodical is *Biochimica et biophysica acta previews*, published as an associate periodical to *Biochimica biophysica acta.* It is noteworthy that subscribers to *Biochimica biophysica acta* receive the "pre-view" periodical free of cost.

51 Message 15

The fifteenth message of the Fourth Law to Book Selection is :

> *In a specialist library and in a university library, select as exhaustively as possible "Pre-View" periodicals on the subjects of specialisation.*

CHAPTER GL

REFERENCE BOOKS

1 Need

Apart from the need for documentation lists and periodicals useful in locating reading materials in any given subject, there is need also for reference books giving information and facts without loss of time. These reference books may be Encyclopaedias, Tables, Directories, Year Books, Dictionaries, and Gazetteers. These may cover subjects of varying degrees of extension. To cull information on any particular topic from various treatises will be a laborious process. Very often a reader may not have the patience or the tempo to read through general books and collect the information he wants.

11 Message 16

The sixteenth message of the Fourth Law to Book Selection is:

Select as many reference books as possible in all the subjects of interest to the clientele of the library.

CHAPTER GM

DUPLICATION

1 Book of Topical Interest

The Fourth Law wants not only that the tempo of the reader be saved and his interest be exploited before it evaporates, when he comes into the library for any specific information, but also even when he is outside the library in certain circumstances. Very often certain books become centres of public interest. This may be due to the author's reputation or the topical nature of the subject matter or any other equally important cause. In these situations several persons are likely to be eager to read such books. But unless the books are made available within a reasonable time the urge to read them may die. For example, in 1948, I saw many libraries in the United Kingdom having selected, purchased in advance, and kept ready several copies of the volumes of Churchill on World War II, for release to the public on the day fixed by the publisher. The Fourth Law would plead for duplication in such cases. It would even ask for several copies.

2 Text Book

In an academic library such as a school or a college library, need for multiplication of copies may arise because a book has been prescribed for study. In their case, the study may have to be completed before a prescribed date. There is then no way of giving opportunity for every student to study it unless the copies are multiplied to the necessary extent. In fact, the high cost of text books today puts it beyond the capacity of individual students. Therefore, many libraries now build a Text Book Collection with several copies of many text books.

21 Message 17

The seventeenth message of the Fourth Law to Book Selection is:

Select a reasonable number of copies of books of topical interest in any library and of text books in an academic library.

CHAPTER GN

ANTHOLOGY

1 General Anthology

It often happens in literature that a reader is interested in the profound sayings of great poets, dramatists, and other men of letters and of authors of reputation, on some theme or topic. The time taken to cull all such excerpts will be very great. Not only it will be a waste of time for a particular reader, but also for each of the several readers interested in the same topic. From the national point of view the wastage then becomes enormous. Not only time is wasted but very often the tempo of the reader may fail before he makes a satisfactory search. To eliminate losses like this a great variety of anthologies have been published. Anthologies exist for many languages and for different forms of literature. We have, **for example :**

z4'xk Orientalia, Collection, Dictionary

1 FIELD (C H A). Dictionary of oriental quotations.

O111xk Literature, English, Collection, Dictionary

2 BARTLETT's Familiar Quotations.
3 CASSELL's classified quotations.

O11,6 Literature, English, Prose

O111,6xk Literature, English, Prose, Collection, Dictionary

4 ALLIBONE. Prose quotations from Socrates to Macaulay.

O15,1x Literature, Sanskrit, Poetry, Collection

5 JALIHALA. Ratna samuchchaya.
6 PARAB. Subhshita ratna bhandagaram.
7 SUNDARAM IYER (N). Subhashita ratnamala.
8 THOMAS (F W). Kavindravacana samuccaya.
9 VALLABHADEVA. Subhashitavali.

O164,1xk Literature, Persian, Poetry, Collection, Dictionary

10 MUHAMMAD ABDUL GHANI KHAN. Armaghan.

2 Anthology with Slant

Anthologies are now available with bias towards diverse subjects giving Book Selection ample scope to satisfy the Fourth Law in the case of readers with diverse interests.

O111,1x (G) Literature, English, Poetry, Collection, Biology

1 KNIGHT (A M). Nature: Anthology.

Q111,1x (J1) Literature, English, Poetry, Collection, Horticulture

2 LYNDALL (G O E). Anthology of gardens and flowers.

Q111,1x (K96) Literature, English, Poetry, Collection, Birds

3 MARLOW. Bird lover's anthology.

O111,1x (KX541) Literature, English, Poetry, Collection, Dog

4 MENZIES (L). First friend: Anthology of man and dog.

O111,1x (MV45) Literature, English, Poetry, Collection, Naval Science

5 FIELD (C). Old times afloat, a naval anthology.

O111,1x(MY6) Literature, English, Poetry, Collection, Hunting

6 LEWIS (P). Fox hunter's anthology.

O111,1x(△) Literature, English, Poetry, Collection, Mysticism

7 NICHOLSON and LEE. Oxford book of English mystical verse.

O111,1x (R437) Literature, English, Poetry, Collection, Friendship

8 MARLOWE (J). Anthology of friendship.

O111,1x (R46) Literature, English, Poetry, Collection, Ethics of leisure

9 MARLOWE (J). Anthology of leisure.

O111,1x (U.;56. L) Literature, English, Poetry, Collection, London

10 JAME (Brett). London anthology.

O111x (U. 563. E) Literature, English, Poetry, Collection, Edinburgh

11 CHALER (A). Edinburgh's charm. [An anthology in prose and verse with local bias].

O111x(V55) Literature, English, Poetry, Collection, History, Germany

12 BRECHTEL WAKE. Germany in story and song.

O15,1x (R4) Literature, Sanskrit, Poetry, Collection, Ethics

13 HEMACHANDRA. Aryadharmanithi [Moral verse].
14 WIJAYA SINHA. Pethyavakya or Nitisara.
15 KUPPUSWAMI SASTRI (T S). Nithimanjari.

21 MESSAGE 18

The eigthteenth message of the Fourth Law to Book Selection is:

Select a sumptuous assortment of anthologies to meet all interests.

3 Reading and Source Books

It is not merely in literature that we have anthologies. In other subjects similar excerpts which will save the time of a reader wanting statements on particular themes, will be found under titles "Readings" and "Source Materials". There are many such helps published in recent years on several subjects.

31 ILLUSTRATIVE LIST

w Biography

1 LOOMIS (R S) and CLARK (D L). Readings in biography and exposition.

2 Library Science

2 JANZOW (L M), *Ed.* Library without walls. (Classics of American librarianship. Ed by A E Bostwick.) 1927.
3 MOODY (K T), *Ed.* Library within the walls. (Classics of American librarianship. Ed by a A E Bostwick.) 1929.

A. 51 Natural Sciences, Greece

4 COHEN (M R) and DRABKIN (I E). Source book in Greek science.

B Mathematics

5 SMITH (David Eugene). Source book in mathematics.

B9 Astronomy

6 SHAPLEY (Harlow) and HOWRATH (Helen E). Source book in astronomy.

C Physics

7 MAGIE (W F). Source book in physics.

H Geology

8 MATHER (Kittery F) and **MASON (Shirley). Source book in** geology.

J : (E) Agriculture, Chemistry

9 BROWNE (C A). Source book of agricultural chemistry.

K Zoology

10 HALL (T S). Source book in animal biology.

L*v* Medicine, History

11 CLENDENING (L). Source book of medical history.

△7 Mysticism, Islam

12 SMITH (M). Readings from the mystics of islam.

NR*v* Music, History

13 STRUNK (W O). Source readings in music history.

O111,2J64, H Literature, English, Drama, Shakespeare, Hamlet

14 WILLIAMSON (C C H). Readings on the character of Hamlet, 1661-1947.

Q Religion

15 CHAMPION (S G) and SHORT (D D). Readings from world religions.

R Philosophy

16 RANDALL (J H) etc. Readings in philosophy.

S*v* Psychology, History

17 DENNIS (W). Readings in the history of psychology.

†. 73 Education, USA

18 COLUMBIA UNIVERSITY, TEACHERS, COLLEGE (New York). Readings in the foundations of education. 2 V.

V58 History, Russia

19 WALSH (S B). Readings in Russian history.

W Political Science

20 COCKER (F W). Readings in political philosophy.

X.44 Economics, India

21 SAXENA (S S) and MATHUR (P N). Readings in Indian economics. 2 V.

X8 (NF) Economics, Industry, Coins

22 SOURCE BOOK of coin machine industry.

Y : 1v Sociology, Civilisation, History

23 KIMBER (H H) and NULLE (S H). Readings in the history of civilization. V 1.

Y3 Sociology, Rural

24 SAYANA (V V). Readings in rural problems.

Z Law

25 HALL (J). Readings in jurisprudence.

32 MESSAGE 19

The nineteenth message of the Fourth Law to Book Selection is :

Select a sumptuous assortment of source books to meet all interests.

CHAPTER GP

CLASSICS

1 Edition with Many Commentaries

In Indian classics, there is a tradition of adding a hierarchy of commentaries — commentary on a text, commentary, on the first commentary, commentary on the second commentary, and so on. Moreover, on the same text there are diverse commentaries. Some of these texts are too condensed and economical to yield all their contents unless read together with commentaries and their hierarchies. There are editions containing single commentaries. There are also editions containing a complete chain of related commentaries. Again, there are editions containing diverse co-ordinate commentaries. It will indeed be a waste of time for a reader to look up dozens of volumes to get an insight into the text with the aid of all available commentaries. To obviate this, editions have been produced for certain texts, giving in a properly arranged and subordinated manner a variety of commentaries and hierarchies of commentaries. For example, the Gujarath Printing Press edition of the *Ramayana* gives five well known commentaries. Ananthakrishna Sastri's edition of Madhusudana Sarasvati's *Advaita Siddhi* gives Brahmananda Saraswati's commentary along with Vithalasopadhyaya's commentary on the above, Balabhadra's *Advaita siddhi vakya* and the editor's own *Chatur granthi*. Similarly, the Vanivilas edition of Sankara's *Brahmasutra bhashya* contains Vachaspati Misra's *Bhamati* which is a commentary on the *Bashya*, Amalananda's *Kalpataru* which is a commentary on *Bhamati*, and Appayyadikshita's *Parimala* which is a commentary of *Kalpataru*.

11 Message 20

The twentieth message of the Fourth Law to Book Selection is :

Select all multi-commentary editions.

2 Variorum Editions

In the case of modern western authors a similar help to save the time of the reader wishing to make an exhaustive study will be found in the variorum editions. For example, we have such editions for several of the plays of Shakespeare and for the works of Spencer.

21 MESSAGE 21

The twenty-first message of the Fourth Law to Book Selection is:

Select variorum editions of the works of diverse authors.

Part H

FIFTH LAW OF LIBRARY SCIENCE AND BOOK SELECTION

CHAPTER HA

FIFTH LAW

1 Enunciation

The Fifth Law of Library Science is "A Library is a growir organism". A library is a trinity of reading materials, humans, and building and equipment. Among these, humans again form a trinity of management, staff, and readers. In Book Selection we are concerned with the growth of reading materials, readers, and stack room.

11 Two Kinds of Growth

Two kinds of growth should be recognised. They may be represented by the terms "child growth" and "adult growth". Child growth is characterised by an overall continuous increase in size. On the other hand, adult growth is characterised by absence of overall growth ; it consists of addition and weeding out, more or less balancing each other.

12 Reading Materials

In regard to growth in reading materials, according to the principles of library organisation, the National Central Library or each State Central Library (of a constituent State) of a country will be allowed to have "Child Growth" for ever. Practically every other library — Local Service Library as we may call it — will ultimately be allowed to have only "Adult Growth".

13 Stack Room

As a consequence, a similar thing will happen in regard to the stack room.

14 Readers

In regard to readers, all libraries including the National and State Central Libraries will ultimately have only adult growth.

15 Basis for Principles

These facts help us in getting at the Principles of Book Selection arising out of the Fifth Law as implied in the :

1 Growth of reading materials in a National or a State Central Library;

2 Growth of stack room in a National or a State Central Library;

3 Growth of reading materials in a Local Service Library;

4 Growth of stack room in a Local Service Library; and

5 Growth of readers.

We should search for Principles of Book Selection in regard to each of the above categories and for each of them from the angle of the physical body, subtle body, and soul of books.

CHAPTER HB

PHYSIQUE OF BOOKS

1 Repository Library

We may consider together the effect of the growth of reading materials and of the stack room. According to the concepts developed in library organisation a National Central Library should be a repository of recorded thought produced in or on the country and by or on the nationals, in the past, present, and future. A similar statement holds good for a State Central Library also. This implies that there can be no weeding out. This also implies that there can be no rejection of any book. Till now the ideal of most countries in developing the National or a State Central Library has been like this.

2 Dormitory Library

However, the Fifth Law has begun to have its effect. The effect was first felt in regard to bound volumes of newspapers. The stack room space for them has to grow at a tremendous rate. A National or a State Central Library has for various reasons to be housed respectively in the metropolis of the country or of the state. We cannot possibly escape from this; and we cannot go into the reasons for this in this book. Therefore, the pressure of the Fifth Law on space soon becomes acute and crosses the limit of capacity. This pressure of the Fifth Law was first met by the segregation of the bound volumes of periodicals from the stack room in the metropolis and housing them in a dormitory quite outside the city but within reasonable reach. The invention of this idea, which arose out of necessity, is leading National Central Libraries to transfer to distant dormitories old books either outmoded in thought or worn out in their physical make-up and therefore only in occasional demand. This is what the National Central Library of France has done. Its dormitory for the overflow is at Versailles. UK is also doing it.

3 Micro Reprography

A second method of meeting the pressure has begun to develop today. This is to reduce bulky and not frequently wanted items to micro-films or micro fiche or micro cards — micro reprographs in one word. Here we are really annihilating the original physique and embodying the thought in a new physique. This is not book selection. This is book transformation. However, we have to consider it in relation to Book Selection for a very important reason. The above experience of meeting the pressure of the Fifth Law on stack room space is leading the producers of newspapers certainly and even of some books and periodicals — at any rate it will soon happen — to produce them with two physical embodiments the conventional book form for immediate and temporary use and the micro reprograph form, for enabling a National or a State Central Library to discharge its repository function. In a federal country like India, there can well be a division of function between the National Central Library and the State Central Libraries.

31 Message 1

The first message of the Fifth Law to Book Selection is:

A National Central Library and a State Central Library should select the micro reprograph form for preservation and the conventional form for current use.

4 Local Service Library

According to the principles of organisation of a National Library System, a Local Service Library should weed out periodically outmoded books and outmoded editions of classics. Some even weed out back volumes of learned periodicals earlier than a year to be fixed for each periodical. They are expected to draw copies of such weeded out publications, from the National or State Central Library, when wanted occasionally. Thus, there is no pressure of the Fifth Law on Book Selection in a Local Service Library as viewed from the angle of the physique of books. But, it does have a message in respect of micro reprograph form of publications.

41 MESSAGE 2

The second message of the Fifth Law to Book Selection is:

In a Local Service Library, book selection should resort to the selection of micro reprograph form of a publication only on grounds of:

1 Non-availability of a copy of the original publication in actual demand—either for purchase or for inter-library loan; or

2 The cost being cheaper than that of the original publication if needed only very sparingly by specialist readers.

5 Growth in Readers

The Fifth Law would urge the library to beware of increase in the number of readers. The very efficiency of library service will contribute to this social change and lead many young men to seek higher education. This will increase the number of student readers in the early stage. This is now happening to a pronounced degree in the UK and USA.

The pressure of the simultaneous demand for a particular text book by several students is creating an acute problem. In England, for example, the University Grants Commission has set up a committee to consider this problem. This effect of the Fifth Law affects not only academic libraries but also public libraries. Therefore, the library associations of UK and USA and the individual public library authorities in those countries are now attempting to find ways and means to meet this new problem about text books, created by the Fifth Law. A deferred consequence will be a similar demand for even general books from the adults themselves in the next few years. If we think only of the moment, this may be looked upon as a problem created by the Second Law. But the hand of the Fifth Law will not be missed if we take a perspective view.

51 MESSAGE 3

The third message of the Fifth Law to Book Selection is:

Book selection should be prepared to progressively change over to an increasing number of copies being selected in the case of an increasing number of books to meet simultaneous demand, by the readers.

52 MESSAGE 4

The fourth message of the Fifth Law to Book Selection is :

> *Even if the increase of readers leads, not to simultaneous demand for the same book, but only to stagger demand, book selection will have to take extra copies of the book for replacing the copy worn-out by use, if rebinding will not be cheaper.*

CHAPTER HC

NEW EDITION

1 Classics

The Fifth Law emphasises the replacement of readers from generation to generation. In other words, readers are mortals whereas the library is immortal. The library has therefore to serve successive generations of readers without end. From the point of view of the Fifth Law and the physique of books, the library has a special problem in regard to works that are themselves immortal — the classics as they have been called in my *Colon classification*, *Prolegomena to library classification*, *Reference service and bibliography*, *Library classification : fundamentals and procedure*, and *Library catalogue : fundamentals and procedure*. Whatever be the age of a classic, there is demand for it through succeeding generations.

2 New Editions

1 When we say that a classic is immortal, we really mean that the thought-content of it is immortal. But its physique cannot be. It is sure to perish and before it perishes out-right, it is sure to be so faded that it ceases to be attractive and perhaps even begin to be repulsive. Therefore, it is quite common for new editions of a classic — that is, new physical printed embodiments to be brought out from time to time. Here are some examples of classics several centuries old which are continuously printed.

The sacred books of religion, the various recessions of the vedas and the associated works, the puranas, the kalpasutras, the tantras, the agamas of Hinduism — Vedic and Post Vedic — the angas, the upangas, the prakirnas, the cheda-sutras, and the moola sutras of Jainism, the vinayapitaka, the suptapitakas, the abhidhamma pitakas, and the sud-dhama-pundarika and the other associated works of Buddhism, the Talmud of Judaism, the Bible of Christianity, and the Yi Ching, and other works of Confucianism ;

2 The philosophical work of Aristotle, Plato, the New-platonists of ancient Europe ; the Vaisesika works of Kanada, Vallabhacharya and their commentaries;

3 The Nyaya works of Gautama, Bhasarvajna, Udayana, Viswanatha, Varadaraja, Kesava-misra, Annam-bhatta, Jayanta, and their commentaries;

4 The Sankhya works of Isvara-krsna, Kapila, and their commentaries;

5 The Yoga works of Patanjali, Bhoja-deva, Vignana-bhikse, and their commentaries;

6 The Mimamsa works of Jaimini, Kumarila Bhatta, Mandanamishra, Prabhakara, and others with their commentaries;

7 The Advaita works of Sankara, Mandana-misra, Suresvaracarya, Vimuktatman, Sarvajnatman, Ananda-bodha, Sriharsha, Cit-sukhracarya, Madhu-sudana, Vidyaranya, Appaya Diksita, and others with their commentaries;

8 The Praty-abhijna works of Somananda, Utpala, and Abhinava-gupta, and their commentaries;

9 The Visistadvaita works of Yamuna, Ramanuja, Vedanta-desika, and others with their commentaries;

10 The Saiva Siddhanta works of Srikantha Sivacarya, Uyyavanda, Mey-kanda, Arunandi, Uma-pati, and others with their commentaries;

11 The Dvaita works of Madhava, Jaya-tirtha, and others with their commentaries;

12 The Bheda-Bheda works of Bhaskara, Bala-deva, and others with their commentaries;

13 The Dvaitadvaita works of Nimbarka and Kseva-kasmirin;

14 The Suddhadvaita works of Vallabha and their commentaries;

15 The Jain philosophical works of Umasvati, Kunda-kunda, Malli-sena, Amrta-candra, Nemi-candra, and their commentaries;

16 The Buddhistic philosophical works of Vasu-bandhu, Anuruddha, Maitreya-natha, Assanga, and their commentaries;

17 The Madhyamika works of Nagarjuna, Arya-deva, Dinnaga, Dharma-kirti, and their commentaries;

18 The Medical works of Caraka, Vag-bhatta, Aruna-datta, Sarnga-dhara, Cakra-pani-datta, Susruta, and others with their commentaries;

19 The publications of repeated new editions of the poets, the dramatists, and novelists in the different languages are well known; and

20 The linguistic works of Saunaka, Yaska, Katyana, Panini, Candra-gomin, Saka-tayana, Hema-candra, Sarva-varman, Narendra, Vopa-deva, Nagesa Bhatta, Amara-simha, Vara-ruci, Tolkappianar, Iraiyanar, Naga-varma, Nannaya, and others.

21 MESSAGE 5

The fifth message of the Fifth Law to Book Selection is:

Select new editions of classics from time to time.

CHAPTER HD

SUBTLE BODY : LANGUAGE

1 Translation in the Language of the Library

As a library lives through several generations, partly as a result of its own service and partly by a gradual extension in the outlook and field of interest down the succeeding generations of readers and particularly their gradual widening of cultural outlook, the Fifth Law would ask Book Selection to note that sooner or later there will be demand for the outstanding books produced in other languages. To meet this demand may not always mean procuring books in other languages ; for, people may not read many of the foreign languages.

11 MESSAGE 6

The sixth message of the Fifth Law to Book Selection is :

> *Select translations, into the language of the library, of works in other languages — foreign as well as classical — to the extent available.*

12 MESSAGE 7

The seventh message of the Fifth Law to Book Selection is :

> *Select translations, into the language of the library, of a work in a classical language even though the original is in the library.*

2 Translation According to the Scale of Languages

Perhaps books for which there are no translations in the language of the library may be treated in another way. The library should have a scale of languages in which the language of the library occupies the first place and the other languages follow in the decreasing sequence of the number of persons among its clientele who can read them.

21 MESSAGE 8

The eighth message of the Fifth Law to Book Selection is :

> *For works in foreign languages, without any translations in the language of the library, select translations into the*

language coming earliest in the scale of languages of the library.

3 Specialist Library

A specialist reader generally may be able to peruse and pick out the essence of a document even when it is in one or the other of a few foreign languages. The few foreign languages are easily determined by each local service library by experience. As library service continues through several generations the range of the few languages will increase. It may even happen that some of the ranges of the several specialist readers cover many languages. This is an effect to be normally expected as a consequence of a generation of specialist readers being replaced by successive generations in a developing community. Therefore, the Fifth Law would alert specialist libraries not to close down book selection against books in foreign languages in general and periodicals in foreign languages in particular.

31 Message 9

The ninth message of the Fifth Law to Book Selection is:

In a specialist library, make a liberal selection of books in foreign languages bearing on the subject of its specialisation.

32 Message 10

The tenth message of the Fifth Law to Book Selection is:

In a specialist library, make as complete a selection as possible of periodicals in foreign languages bearing on the subject of its specialisation.

4 Translations of Periodicals

After World War II, a new trend is developing in respect of learned periodicals. USSR began publishing Russian translation of whole periodicals. USA and UK have begun publishing English translations of whole periodicals in Russian. Some countries also may fall in line with this practice. The bearing of this practice on copyright law is not our concern here. Book Selection has to recognise the existence of translation of whole periodicals.

41 Message 11

The eleventh message of the Fifth Law to Book Selection is:

In a specialist library, select translations, into the language of the library, of periodicals in foreign languages, wherever available and financially viable.

42 Message 12

The twelfth message of the Fifth Law to Book Selection is :

In a specialist library, selection of a periodical in a foreign language is not obligatory if a translation of it into the language of the library is selected.

5 Bilingual Edition

Occasionally, bilingual editions of books appear giving a work in its original language as well as its translation in another language. It will be helpful to readers if such books are made available by the library. The volumes of the series of the Loeb Classical Library, form an excellent example of bilingual books for Greek and Latin classics. The verso pages give the text in the original language. The recto pages give its translation of the text into the English language. A recent example of a bilingual book is the *Commemoration bibliography of the first 1,008 books published by the South India Saiva Siddanta Publishing Society* by S R Ranganathan and R Muthukumaraswamy. The verso pages of the book give the text of the work in English, the recto pages give its translation into Tamil. Here is an example of a multilingual book :

British Standards Institution. Universal decimal classification: Trilingual abridged edition. (B S 1000B : 1958).

51 Message 13

The thirteenth message of the Fifth Law to Book Selection is :

Select bilingual and multilingual editions of works with the language of the library as one of the languages of the edition, wherever available.

CHAPTER HE

SOUL

1 Incomprehensibility

As the library ages, the intellectual standard of its clientele will increase in scatter. While there will always be immature minds among the clientele — say, children and the lowest quartile — the intellectual standard will be extended at the further end of the upper quartile. From the point of view of Book Selection this means that even though certain books might be of too high a standard to find a reader in the present generation, according to the Fifth Law the general improvement of the standard of the front-rank people will be such that difficult books of that nature come eventually within the comprehension of some readers. For example, Ramanujan's *Collected works* were not within easy comprehension when it was published in 1928. But today, the number of specialist readers feeling at home with this book is not only appreciable but is also increasing. Riemann's works were incomprehensible in his own days. Because they were acquired in certain libraries, two generations later they were made available by the library to Einstein, with what wonderful result we all know. Something similar had happened with regard to the fundamental work of Mendel. Some of the works of William Blake form another example. In the sphere of Philosophy the works of Soren Kierkegaard would have been lost to the world if under the urge of the Fifth Law some of the Danish libraries had not procured and preserved copies of them. We know today, the extensive way in which his works are sought and are even translated into diverse languages. The deferred appeal of the works of Karl Marx is well known. Few of the people of the middle of the nineteenth century were ever able to penetrate into the full potentiality of his works. But the present generation has begun to understand its seminal nature.

11 Message 14

The fourteenth message of the Fifth Law to Book Selection is:

Do not reject a book because it is difficult. It may be difficult for the present generation but it may become comprehensible for a later generation. Include them in book selection.

2 Intangibility

Even more elusive than incomprehensibility is the intangibility of a work. Intangibility is a supreme quality of first rate writings. The intangibility really acts as a cover to the endless layers of message conveyed by the writing. As the capacity of understanding gradually increases through generation after generation — it is the upper-most quartile that acts as the apical bud and develops the greatest sensitiveness possible in a generation — layer after layer of the intangible writing lays itself bare. The common standard of value may rise to a sufficiently high level in the next generation to find value in such a writing of the present generation. This may happen in later generations at least if not in the very next generation. A well-known tradition which is current is that copies of the first quarto of Shakespeare's play were rejected as unworthy of the library of the University of Oxford in the days of Shakespeare himself. But centuries later the level of value had arisen to such a high pitch that a considerable value was recognised in Shakespeare's quartos and considerable sums of money had to be spent in procuring them second hand. According to the Fifth Law, a library grows through time. It will get readers of greater sensitiveness in course of time. It asks Book Selection to provide for them.

21 MESSAGE 15

The fifteenth message of the Fifth Law to Book Selection is :

Judge not hastily or light-heartedly. Reject not easily. Err on the side of selection rather than rejection. Beware of intangible qualities in writings of the highest kind.

PART J

CONFLICT OF LAWS OF LIBRARY SCIENCE

CHAPTER JA

CIVIL WAR AMONG THE LAWS

1 Introduction

In Parts D to H, we worked out the implications respectively of each of the Five Laws of Library Science independently of one another. We should also consider whether all the Laws speak in unison and in one voice or whether they speak in different voices and pull in different directions. In other words, we should examine whether there is a Conflict of Laws.

2 First Law and Second Law

There can be conflict between the First Law and the Second Law. For example, the First Law may amplify the term "Use" into the term "Socially Benificent Use". If this be allowed, it would amount to Book Selection being influenced by considerations of Censorship. But against this, the Second Law may argue, "If a reader wants a book, it is the duty of the library to provide it. Consideration of censorship should not weigh with Book Selection. The faith of the Librarian today should be that censorship is not his function. The Government alone can have the duty and the power of censorship. Once a book has been allowed to be published and released for use or to be imported, the demand of the reader to have it is paramount." The First Law may argue, "No doubt the Librarian should not take up the responsibility for censorship. At the same time, the librarian should remember that the public library in his charge is a social institution for the betterment of the society. The Government censor may supress only books of immediate social danger or political disruption. But books with sinister anti-social suggestions set in a minor key and capable only of long term effect, may escape the censors. The librarian, though not a super-censor, has the duty to abstain from selecting books of such subtle anti-social nature." (*See* Sec DP13). The conflict is apparently irresolvable.

3 Second Law and Third Law

According to the Second Law, the term "Every Reader" in it denotes not merely "Every Reader" of the present generation but also "Every Reader" of all future generations. In other words, the Second Law would think in terms of eternity. It would ask for many books — not at all in current demand — to be selected in the hope that one day or other — even if it be at a very distant future — there might be demand for them. The Third Law would argue against this. It would say, "This is exactly like falling a prey to 'Maxwell's Devil of probability'. The position taken by the Second Law is not different from that of a person in a state of fright because there is some infinitesimal probability for his dying of asphyxia because of the infinitesimal probability for all the molecules of air deserting the spot where he is, for a sufficiently long time. Let us be realistic. Let us not fly far into the future. Let us confine the term 'Every Reader' to denote every reader in the present generation, otherwise my curse for not getting a reader for every book will descend upon the librarian, in the case of a book for which he may not find a reader in his life time." This conflict is apparently irresolvable.

4 Third Law and Fourth Law

To save the time and the tempo of the readers with their minds simultaneously fixed upon a current best seller, the Fourth Law would ask Book Selection to go in for a number of copies of a best seller. The Third Law would ask, "What will happen when the craze for the best seller subsides. How will it be possible for the librarian to find a reader for each of the copies thereafter, in order to escape my curse." This conflict is apparently irresolvable.

5 Third Party

These are examples of the kinds of civil war likely to arise among the Laws themselves. Many other such conflicts may arise from time to time. Each Law would like to fight to the finish with the Law coming into conflict with it. When there is a division in a camp like this, when there is civil war within the country like this, when bilateral reconciliations among the conflicting parties within the same group becomes difficult if not impossible, it is a third party that is brought in to decide the issue. The result may be disastrous to the conflicting parties within the same group, and yet it is on the third party they seek to depend. The fable of the two cats fighting over making an exactly equal division of the cake, their invoking the aid of the monkey as the third party to resolve the conflict, and the monkey's action leaving hardly anything for the cats, is well known. This fable carries a profound truth on how things develop in the world not infrequently. Let us then examine what third parties can be brought into the picture in order to resolve the conflict among the Five Laws of Library Science, without any selfish motive of their own. Possible third parties are capacity, finance, administration, organisation, social values, and scientific method.

CHAPTER JB

CAPACITY OF SHELF AND STAFF

1 Introduction

We can perhaps bring the mutually fighting Laws of Library Science to a reasonable mood of compromise by introducing the concept of Capacity. Capacity of a library may be determined in relation to shelf-capacity — in other words, stack room capacity — and size-of-staff capacity.

2 Shelf-capacity

If the shelf-capacity of the library is limited, as it is so in most cases, a time will come sooner or later when the shelves get to be choked. This purely physical factor would give Book Selection a severe pull up. There are instances where the Laws of Library Science had been trampled under foot by this physical factor. Further acquisition of books had been slowed down steadily. There are also instances when further acquisition of books had been totally stopped. In the latter case, there would have been no Book Selection. In the former case, there would have been only a nominal Book Selection satisfying none of the Five Laws fighting with one another. I remember cases when the demand for additional book shelves to house newly selected and acquired books led to the liquidation of departmental libraries altogether in a University. I remember a State Government having sent out directions to all its departments and institutions that no new books should be selected or purchased, if it would involve the purchase of extra shelving. The mentioning of these instances should not be taken to mean that such an attitude on the part of library authorities had been right. They are mentioned only to show that in the real world as it is found, shelf space and stack room space do loom large now and again. They take law in their own hands. Then the conflict among the Laws get quenched; the Laws of Library Science have to smoothen the conflict among themselves and make a combined appeal to the library authorities to view the situation in the proper perspective. This they have to do because the members of the library authorities are often far removed from the libraries managed by them, and also are often without any reading habit or urge for reading. If the Laws are to succeed in their appeal, they should offer the solution through the principles and methods of organisation.

21 MESSAGE 1

The first joint compromise message of the Laws and Finance to Book Selection is :

> *Book selection should go on without hindrance in all libraries. In a local service-library, space will be found by the weeding out of no-longer-wanted and worn-out books as its growth is adult-growth. In a National Central Library, space will be increased to the necessary extent as its growth is child-growth.*

3 Size-of-the-Staff Capacity

31 SELECTION NEEDS STAFF

Another factor often overlooked is the staff time involved in the selection, acquisition, and organisation of books for use. Large sums of money are given for the purchase of books without any thought whatever about the man-power needed to spend the money usefully. This has happened almost to an epidemic point among the university libraries in India for a few years. The University Grants Commission began to give liberal grants to universities for library purpose. The grant was accepted with satisfaction. But neither the University Grants Commission nor the university authorities had known what it was to spend large sums of money on the purchase of books. The announcement of the grant would reach the university authorities only two or three months before the end of the financial year by which time the grant should be spent out. University librarians could not produce any beneficial influence on the authorities in this matter. When this happened, I had ceased to have care of a library for nearly 15 years. In spite of it, a few pathetic letters used to come to me from a few university librarians who were more conscious than others. They used to ask me to send them within a week a Book Selection list for about a 100,000 rupees. Not only did the authorities fail to realise that our chief book market was five thousand miles away, but they also failed to realise that it requires a considerable staff time to select books in relation to the need and the demand on the one side and the existing stock on the other. The pathetic letters of the few librarians showed further that the librarians themselves had not realised these points. In these circumstances Book Selection naturally became futile. It became even more futile because there was no staff to place the order, to receive the books, to accession them, to classify them, to catalogue them, to put them in the proper places among the older books, and to bring these books to active use through adequate reference service.

32 Pathology of Unexpected Grants

The futility of Book Selection can be seen from the fact that librarians were sent out to the few cities in the country with bookshops and buy whatever was available; and if a sufficient variety of books were not available, to buy several copies of one and the same book. This has also happened in some of the big public libraries on whom the grants were showered by the Union Ministry of Education. When the books were brought to the library and came to be processed months later, it was often found that copies of some of those books were already in the library. But this unconscious and unintended duplication formed only a small fraction of deliberate purchase of several copies of some books in order to spend the grant to the last pie before the end of the financial year. Why was it done in that way? There were two reasons. The librarian could be branded as inefficient if he did not spend the money. University authorities felt that their prestige would be lost if the entire sum was not spent on time.

33 Help from UGC

Perhaps there was also a third reason — reason of fear — that the grant will be reduced in the next year if the full grant is not spent within the year. Whatever be the reason, there was in reality no Book Selection *qua* Book Selection. Thus, the size-of-the-staff capacity of a library nullifies Book Selection at one extreme. At the other extreme, if the librarian and the library authorities are keen and have the conscience to do Book Selection properly, there would naturally be a great restriction in Book Selection. In

1959, to examine this anamalous position Dr C D Deshmukh, the then Chairman of the University Grants Commission appointed a Library Committee to go into all such problems and to propose ways and means to secure that the library grant was properly and fully transformed into the needed and useful book service. I was invited to chair that Committee. The Committee exposed the pathology of the position. The Committee made two proposals by way of remedy. Firstly, that 20 per cent of the grant should be allowed to be utilised for Selection, Acquisition, Accession, Classification, and Cataloguing. Secondly, seventeen months should be allowed to spend the grant completely. This was approved by the University Grants Commission. These recommendations of the Commission have given due consideration to the possibility of the Size-of-the-Staff Capacity becoming a factor in making Book Selection futile. But this danger may arise at any time.

34 Message 2

The second joint message of the Laws and Finance to Book Selection is :

> *Insist on a fraction of the fund — say, twenty per cent — to be set apart for the staff — viz for selection, acquisition accessioning, classifying, and cataloguing.*

CHAPTER JC

FINANCE AND ITS EFFECT

1 Indirect Effect

In reality, all such factors as stack-room capacity and size-of-the-staff capacity working against proper Book Selection are ultimately traceable to finance. For, if there is adequate finance, shelf-space can be increased indefinitely. It need not restrict Book Selection. Again, the staff can be increased indefinitely. It need not make Book Selection futile.

2 Direct Effect

Apart from these indirect effects, finance controls book selection directly. If there is unlimited money, all published materials can be acquired. That is, there need not be any rejection. This means, there is no need for Selection. All that Book Selection would mean, would amount to knowing what is the supply position in the book market. Similarly, if there is unlimited money, any reading material, that is demanded by anybody at any time even if it be for use on a single occasion, can be selected. The only negativing factor will be absence of supply. Here again, selection would amount merely to verifying if there is any reading material answering the demand. With ultimated finance the conflict among the Laws of Library Science in relation to Book Selection will be eliminated to a large extent. Perhaps, the Third Law may be told, "You will be fulfilled if there is at least one reader per book at some time or other. There will be at least a bibliophillic reader, or a reader interested in the history of books who will be glad to have access to every book ever published."

3 Limited Finance

But money is limited — severely limited. It is a matter of experience that the first victim of the axe, when the slightest financial stringency takes shape, is the library. Within the library it is the book-fund that has first to face the axe, as staff-salary cannot be so light-heartedly pinched. Apart from such a crisis, even normally, hardly any library in the world can say that it ever gets all the money it needs to fulfil all the Laws of Library Science. We often look upon the libraries of the United States with a envious eye and imagine that they have access to unlimited finance. But we have only to speak with librarians of that country to know how restricted they feel. Again it must be repeated that the financial capacity of a library for book acquisition can only be a fraction of its total budget. We have to set apart a big slice of the budget for the cost of selecting, acquiring, and preparing a book, for use, and putting them on the shelves, the cost of the shelf space itself, the service charges such as lighting, sanitation, and housing, and the cost of putting the book to use without which book selection would serve no purpose. Experience shows that it is unwise and uneconomical to take credit for more than 40 per cent of the library budget for the purchase of books. This means a tightening of the financial belt. This should not be overlooked by library authorities. Finance is a determining factor in Book Selection. In fact, much of the weight in the conflict among the Laws of Library Science is taken away by the limitation of finance. The conflict between the Laws of Library Science taken together on one side and of finance on the other is more serious and damaging to Book Selection than the conflict among the Laws themselves.

4 Economy Measure

Finance is inexorable. It is relentless. It is man's own creation: and yet it enslaves him. It forces his hands to do many things against his own wish. And even against this benefit, it drives man from post to pillar. It leaves him no option except to make the best out of the limited finance available by administrative and organisational adjustments. So it is in the library world. Economy measures have to be devised in library service. Some of these are within a single library. These are of an administrative nature. Some economy measures embrace a group of libraries. These are at bottom of an organisational nature. The group may consist of the libraries within a city, a district, a constituent state, a country, a group of countries, or even the whole world. The library profession is forging such economy measures both at the administrative and the organisational level in order to reduce the havoc of the ruthlessness of finance on the ideals of book selection set by the Laws of Library Science. These measures manipulate other sectors of library work in order to take away the edge from the restriction put on book selection by limited finance.

CHAPTER JD

ADMINISTRATIVE EXPEDIENCY AND ITS EFFECT

1 Minimising Duplication

We saw in Chapter GM that the Fourth Law recommended free multiplication of copies of books to meet pressing demand. The first step in yielding to the pressure of finance is for the Fourth Law to make a compromise on this recommendation. It agrees to the compromise on the assurance of the administration that every effort would be made to meet the rush on a book by:

1 The use of be-speaking system;

2 The reduction of the period of loan; and if necessary even;

3 The conversion of the book to the status of a reference book — reserve book, as it is called — so that it may be kept actively used all the hours when the library is kept open;

4 Allowing such reserve books to go out on overnight loan so as to add to the number of hours it is kept used during a day; and

5 Restricting the duration of the use of a book even within the library suitably so as to make the readers realise the great demand for it and use it intensively in the time allowed.

To effect the last-mentioned measure, special book cards are made with provision for marking the hour at which the book must be passed on to the next reader. The readers themselves are informed of their position in the queue so that they may claim the book at the proper time without letting the book lie idle even for a minute. This is rationing carried to a fine degree. I saw it being done in the Yale University Library and some other libraries in USA. With the assurance of such an administrative measure, the Fourth Law is persuaded to relax its claim for duplication or multiplication of copies of books.

11 Message 3

The third joint compromise message of the Laws and Finance to Book Selection is:

Minimise multiplication of copies to the extent to which the rationing of the time of use — say, by days and if necessary, by hours — can be effected by administration.

2 Discontinuity of the Serial

The Laws of Library Science are next asked to yield in some measure in regard to Directories, Who's Whos, and other Year Books and Serials which have to be acquired to ensure for every reader his information. Instead of acquiring every issue of each serial, administration employs the economy measure of buying only, say, alternate issues or every third, fourth, or fifth issue, according to the rapidity with which the information contained in it goes out-of-date and also the extent to which the data or the information vary from year to year. As reference books are usually costly, this device of tolerating discontinuity in their run thus gives some financial relief to Book Selection and enables it to spread itself a little more freely in other directions.

21 Message 4

The fourth joint compromise message of the Laws and Finance to Book Selection is ·

In a service-library, as distinct from a dormitory library, a serial, may be acquired at suitable intervals instead of each year, if the information in it does not vary substantially from year to year.

3 Exploiting Abstracting Periodicals

Another economy measure, which may be resorted to when too hard pressed for finance, concerns the acquisition of periodicals. Careful investigation is made about the periodicals which can be discontinued by relying upon the abstracting periodicals taken. There is no doubt that one of the weakest and costly forms (in one sense) of literature are periodicals. In fact, periodicals present an apparently insoluble problem. Finance thwarts periodicals both where they are produced and where they are consumed. The more learned a periodical is, the smaller is its circulation. Indeed, the number of readers for any single article in a periodical will be so uneconomically small that nobody would dare to publish the article separately. That is the reason for stringing together quite a number of unrelated articles and publishing them under one cover as a single periodical. The result is that anybody wanting a particular article has to take the whole periodical. To give relief to the financial difficulty involved in production, recourse is virtually had in this method to a forced selling of unwanted articles. This forced thing will, of course, be in its worst form in relation to individuals. But even when the public share a periodical — that is, when a single copy of the periodical is acquired and served to all possible users within the jurisidiction of a library as a public project — there is still forced sale; for, there may be articles which are not wanted by any of the readers. Moreover, so much new thought is being created today and at such a high rate, by team work in research, that the number of periodicals needed to communicate them while, still in a nascent stage is very great. Even within one subject, the number of periodicals is too large for most libraries to take them all exhaustively. Here the administrative measure is for a library to take the abstracting periodicals in the fields of interest to the clientele. When a reader scans through an abstracting periodical, if he locates an article which interests him, it often happens that the very abstract is sufficient. He is satisfied. The Second Law is satisfied. If he feels the need for the full article, then either the particular issue in which it occurred is acquired or, if it will be cheaper, a reprograph is acquired. Thus, without undue violence to the Second Law, the financial obstacle is overcome. No doubt, there is a slight violation to the Fourth Law. Because the reader will have to wait for the order and receipt of the issue of the periodical or for its reprograph to be put through and the material produced for his use. Recently-developed-reprograph methods make this economy measure feasible. Bernal has gone into this question of economy in the supply of micro thought very elaborately. But the world seems to be lagging so much behind him in this forward thought of his. In the meantime, Rider's micro cards are making good progress and it is for the future to show how the injury caused by insufficient finance to the Laws of Library Science in respect of Book Selection—and particularly selection of periodicals—can be minimised or eliminated by them.

31 Message 5

The fifth joint compromise message of the Laws and Finance to Book Selection is :

Restrict the acquisition of periodicals to those in which all the articles are in sufficient demand. For those only in occasional demand, depend on abstracting periodicals and if necessary, on the acquisition of individual issues or of reprographs of the stray articles needed by the clientele.

CHAPTER JE

ORGANISATIONAL MEASURES AND RESOLUTION OF CONFLICT

1 Regional Co-operation

The threat of finance on the one side and the importunities of the Laws of Library Science on the other, have already made library organisation devote thought to the concept of "Viable Unit" for library service. This idea has been examined in detail in my *Library development plan: Thirty-year programme for India with draft library bills for the Union and the Constituent States* (1950), (University of Delhi, library science series, 2), and in my *Library development plan with a draft library bill for Kerala* (1960), (Government press, Trivandrum). A recent version of this will be found in the quarterly *Library Science* vol 1, 1965. By implementing the concept of "Viable Unit", the book-fund is kept at a level which can satisfy the Laws of Library Science to a greater degree than it would be possible, if areas smaller than that of a Viable Unit had their own independent libraries. Library organisation thus pools together and centralises library fund but it takes care to decentralise library service. It allows books to be served in branches or in delivery stations in all the divisions of a city and in all the villages and hamlets of a district (=county). Thus, without any violence to the Laws of Library Science in the matter of service, the Principle of Viable Unit places more funds at the disposal of book selection which is thereby able to satisfy the Laws of Library Science more than it could otherwise do. The developed countries arrived at this organisational economy measure after considerable wastage by the method of trial and error. A prize, which India should take for having been kept behind by world forces in releasing her library personality into growth, should be to take full advantage of such organisational lessons from the experience of the already developed countries. In the Viable Unit System, the reading materials are not allowed to stick to the shelves of any particular constituent library. They are moved from division to division, from town to town, from village to village, and from hamlet to hamlet, systematically so that the money spent on books gives the maximum possible return.

11 MESSAGE 6

The sixth joint compromise message of the Laws and Finance in respect of Book Selection to Library Organisation is:

> *Give up the old idea of having small independent libraries everywhere. But consolidate them into large Viable Unit Systems. Centralise and co-ordinate book selection and decentralise book-service.*

2 Co-operation within State

In a vast federal country, such as India, there should be a second tier of co-ordination at the level of each Constituent State. In each city or district — that is, in each regional unit — book selection should be primarily done according to local wants. But people outside the local area should have access to its resources, however far away they may be living. To make the book move about in this manner, certain organisational understanding is necessary. All the libraries in the State should agree to the principle of inter-library loan. To make inter-library-loan possible there should be a technical tool—viz. Union Catalogue or a substitute for it. Under the pressure of inadequate finance, the Laws of Library Science are driving library organisation to provide for this organisational economy measure by legislative action instead of leaving it to voluntary action on the part of participating libraries. Half a century ago, when the Second Law had not succeeded in extending the library privilege beyond a select few, the situtation was met by bilateral agreement among libraries or even made contingent on mere courtesy loans. But as the Second Law won its way more and more extensively, Great Britain, for example, started its National Central Library for students. This library acted as a medium for voluntary multilateral agreement for inter-library loan among a set of participating libraries. This set up even persuaded the so-called Outlier Libraries to lend out specialised books though there was very little chance for these to get any return service. The further extension in the success of the Second Law is finding the restriction of finance too powerful to be overcome by such voluntary participation among the libraries of the nation. A newly developing country such as India, whose library-personality is just taking shape, will therefore do well to make such inter-library co-operation statutory. That is what is provided in my Draft Library Bill, copies of which have been freely distributed to the members of the legislature in all the Constituent States of India in the hope that some member, if not the government itself, may feel interested in the matter and bring about its enactment. The clauses in the Draft Bill provide for co-ordination in book selection and co-operation in book service. The Public Libraries Bill, drafted in 1963, by a Committee with me as Chairman incorporating this organisational resolution of the conflict between the Second Law and Finance, has now become an Act. The earlier enactments by Madras and Andhra Pradesh, though based on my draft bill, had omitted this organisational provision from the Act, leaving it, as the Minister told me, to be taken care of, by the Rules framed under the Act. But no such Rules have yet been framed though the Act came into force in 1950.

21 Message 7

The seventh joint compromise message of the Laws and Finance in respect of Book Selection to Library Organisation is :

> *Federate the library systems in a Constituent State and make the State Central Library co-ordinate book selection and bring about inter-library loan for less frequently wanted books.*

3 National Co-operation

In countries of small extent such as many of the countries in Europe, the second tier of co-operation will be the country itself. But in vast countries such as, Australia, China, India, USA, and USSR, the second tier can only consist of the Constituent States. The country will form the third tier. All that has been said in regard to co-operation within a Constituent State will be applicable to co-operation within the country. Reading materials, which are likely to be too infrequently in demand even among all the libraries of a State taken together, may be got by inter-library loan from other States. Recourse may have to be had to this method of satisfying the Second Law very often in regard to books needed by a citizen who is obliged to live in an area whose language is different from his own. Linguistic specialisation can be made by each State in the confidence that the material in other languages wanted occasionally by people within its area can be had from other States on loan. This method of inter-State co-ordination in book selection can be extended also on subject basis in regard to the reading materials to be acquired by a country in languages which are foreign to it. A kind of modified Farmington Plan is indicated. An account of the Farmington Plan will be found in my *Library developement plan*, (1950), Sec 211. In the Farmington Plan it was a case of individual libraries voluntarily taking responsibility to acquire exhaustive collections from other countries. Instead of that, the sharing of responsibility may be between States rather than individual libraries. Each State might re-distribute its responsibility among select libraries within its area. The sharing of responsibility among States may be on the basis of the foreign languages or of subjects. In the former case, a State will get all books published in a particular language whatever be the subject; in the latter case, a State will procure all books in a particular subject whatever be the language. Co-ordinating book selection on this basis is indeed flouting finance! This degree of organisational economy measure would, indeed, mark the triumph of the Five Laws over the obstinate finance. The Farmington Plan is perhaps too much in advance of what is practicable in India today. However, for reasons stated in Sec JE2 the normal co-ordination in book selection and co-operation in service should not be left, in this late day, to the off-chance of voluntary agreement among the Constituent States. I have, therefore, made statutory provision for this organisational economy measure in the Draft Library Bill for the Union Government. A similar provision has also been made in the draft model State Library Bill. The Mysore Public Libraries Act (1965) has incorporated this provision.

31 Message 8

The eighth joint compromise message of the Laws and Finance in respect of Book Selection to Library Organisation is:

In a large country with many Constituent States, make the National Central Library and the State Central Libraries collaborate with the ultimate Library Systems. Bring about a Co-ordinated Book Selection Plan so that books and periodicals published in foreign countries may be secured for the country as a whole in as full a measure as possible. Bring about also Inter-State Library Loan both in respect of foreign books and periodicals and in respect of the books and periodicals in the languages of the different Constituent States.

4 Central Library

My Draft Library Bills invest the State Central Libraries and the National Central Library with another function to minimise the conflict between the Laws of Library Science and Finance. In fact, these are all multi-purpose institutions. One of the purposes is to function as a reservior library for the Constituent State or the Nation, as the case may be, to supplement the resources of local libraries with materials too infrequently in demand. A clause in the Bills secures copyright privileges to these libraries. A measure of a possible co-ordination, in regard to this, among the Central Libraries in the nation has already been indicated in Sec JE21. Taking advantage of the experience of other countries and implementing the measures of co-ordination implied in the Draft Library Bills, will release Book Selection from the strangling hold of Finance and satisfy the Five Laws to a remarkable degree.

5 National Documentation Centre

The further measure of economy is the establishment of a National Documentation Centre. This was advocated in my *Public library provision and documentation problems* (1951). This suggestion was realised in India in 1952. The Centre is called **Insdoc** — The Indian National Scientific Documentation Centre. It is situated in New Delhi. I was a member of the Committee that originated it and developed it till 1963. At the time of its foundation, I pleaded for its scope not being restricted to the Natural Sciences alone. Instead of **Insdoc**, I suggested **Indoc** — Indian National Documentation Centre. But the other members of the Committee had the conservatism of scientists and refused to accept the proposal. From 1960 onwards, the scholars in Social Sciences have been asking for a similar centre for their field. This is only an aside. The chief point is that the idea of a National Documentation Centre has been implemented in India. It has also been implemented in several newly developing countries. Unesco has been actively promoting their establishment. A detailed account of their development is given in my *Documentation and its facets* (1963), Parts B to D, M, and N.

51 Inter-Library Loan of Periodicals

One of the functions of a National Documentation Centre should be to manage inter-library loan of periodicals within the country. For this purpose, it should maintain a Union Catalogue of the learned periodicals in the libraries of the country. It is best kept current and perpetual in card form. It may be useful to publish the Union Catalogue as a book at suitable intervals. Such a provision will release the selection of periodicals from the strangling hold of finance and satisfy the Five Laws of Library Science to a remarkable degree. Co-ordination in the selection of periodicals backed by co-operation in service will circumvent the restrictions of Finance to the relief of the research workers in the nation, if the academic and industrial libraries pool together their funds for periodicals by mutual agreement.

52 Reprograph Service

A second function of a National Documentation Centre should be the supply of reprographs of any micro document needed by a reader. The economy effected by the system of supplying reprographs has been already indicated in Sec JD3. If the host periodical is available in the library of the National Documentation Centre or in some other library situated in the same locality as itself, the reprograph can be made by the National Documentation Centre itself. If it is found only in a library in some other locality, one of two things may be done. Firstly, if there are facilities in the locality of a library for making reprograph, the library itself may make and supply the reprograph to the readers, otherwise, the National Documentation Centre may take the volume of the periodical on inter-library-loan to make the reprograph.

53 Message 9

The ninth joint compromise message of the Laws and Finance in respect of Book Selection to Library Organisation is :

Each country should have a National Documentation Centre to have charge of inter-library-loan of learned periodicals and the supply of reprographs of micro documents whenever needed.

6 Internationl Co-operation

My Union Library Bill authorises the National Central Library to participate in international co-operation to give relief to Book Selection from the strangling pressure of Finance. If all the nations co-operate in this manner, the relief to Book Selection and the satisfaction to the Five Laws will be very great. Promotion of this international co-operation is no doubt one of the primary objectives of Unesco. If Unesco succeeds in it and if the United Nations too succeeds to become a true World State with power to outlaw war, perhaps the Farmington Plan will prove to be an unnecessarily ambitious scheme. It was possible only for USA in the financial vantage position it occupies today in the world, to think of such a plan. But even USA is not finding it easy to implement it fully. Other countries which are not equally rich cannot dream of such world-coverage. While each country should have in its National Central Library, the really fundamental, seminal, and informative books of all countries, the benefits of world-coverage should be derived really by each nation building up its own national collection without any flaw in intake and without any leakage in its storage and agreeing to participate in a scheme of international inter-library-loan of books and periodicals in very occasional demand

61 Message 10

The tenth joint compromise message of the Laws and Finance in respect of Book Selection to Library Organisation is :

Unesco should promote International Library Loan of books and periodicals only in occasional demand in the borrowing country. It should promote also International Reprograph Service.

CHAPTER JF

AUSTERITY MEASURES

1 Introduction

Even such a pyramidal system of economy measures as the one described in Chapter JE may not give the necessary relief to Book Selection and protect the Five Laws against the onslaught of Finance. It will be wise for the Five Laws themselves to practice some austerity and agree to certain austerity measures though they may restrain their full objective to some extent. These austerity measures are necessary now and may continue to be so, for many years — that is, till war is outlawed, the nations learn and agree to practise peaceful co-existence, and a World-State becomes a near-fact. Such austerity measures may centre round materials for entertainment, materials for mass communication, and discrimination between classes of readers. In an institutional library, such as an academic or a business library, the clientele is more limited, intimately known, and homogeneous than in a public library. Their wants are determinable by the work of the institution. The Third Law is at once with the Second Law, as every reader is sure to ask for exactly what he wants and the fulfilment of the institution makes it obligatory to care for all the members equally. An austerity measure will be not to acquire books for relaxation and entertainment. For such books, the clientele should be asked to look to public libraries. Beyond this measure, inadequate finance must result in inadequate book selection and incomplete service. The administrative and organisational economy measures described in Chapter JE are the only measures that can give relief to Book Selection. Hardly, any austerity measure can alleviate the immediate harshness of inadequate finance. However, it is not so in public libraries. Austerity measures may be possible in their case.

2 Sobering the Third Law

When Finance refuses to keep pace with the demands of the Second Law, the Third Law's voice may be heard by the Second

Law. The Third Law dips its divining rod, as it were, into the public mind. It says, "Let us be realistic. Let us make sure who want to read and what they want to read. Let us begin with now, and look into the future if there is still means left." The Third Law is at once with the Second Law in keeping the library door open to every person in the community. But it contends that this does not mean that everybody will enter. When finance fails, it is wise to reject reading materials for which there is no near prospect of readers. For example, the specialist reader will go to his academic or business library to find the treatises he wants. He will not go to a public library for them. Indeed, he should be discouraged from going to a public library for them. The Third Law will, therefore, suggest the Book Selection in a public library rejecting such treatises, in order to get more books of the "Know-How" kind for the non-specialist worker, likely to look to the public library for his practical books. In other words, according to the Third Law, when axe has to fall on the book-fund of a public library, the policy should be to make it fall first on books primarily helping research and last on those helping wide dissemination of knowledge. But with a warning. The austerity measure should not be used as a convenient tool to make the axe fall first on dissemination books of a heterodox kind pushed by power-groups for propagating their own views — the unsafe books! Closely associated with this is the question of the acceptance and retention of such propaganda books even when they are offered free. This really takes us to censorship. The Third Law's emphatic ruling on this is "No censorship please. Every book has its right to reach its readers. This is in the Bill of Rights of Books. It also occurs in the Bill of Rights of Libraries. The Committee on Intellectual Freedom is for these Bills of Rights." It holds that the battle of ideologies is best fought in men's minds and in discussion. Book-Selection-Policy, according to the Third Law, should be ever neutral in this matter. When finance forces libraries to reject books, it can only be on grounds which keep clear of the degree of orthodoxy or heterodoxy of the ideologies presented in them. With this warning, the Third Law will allow the axe to fall in the following sequence :

1 Books of remote use only, arranged among themselves in the sequence of degree of remoteness ;

2 Books of research value, arranged among themselves in the sequence of remove from dissemination value ; and

3 Books in demand from the richer classes only, so long as inequality in the distribution of wealth continues.

21 Message 11

The eleventh joint compromise message of the Laws and Finance in representing Book Selection is :

> *Do not allow the policy of Book Rejection, forced by finance, to be coloured or influenced by considerations of the orthodoxy or the heterodoxy of the ideologies presented in the book and by even the remotest propensity for censorship.*

3 Materials for Entertainment

It is in fiction, more than in any other class that the policy of austerity in Book Selection, difficult to frame and even more difficult to implement. In other classes, where information or inspiration is the criterion of selection, the number of claimants is comparatively small and they can easily be arranged in the sequence of their intrinsic worth or suitability to the class of readers to be served. The arrangement can be done objectively. The only danger in the case of such classes is mistaking personal prejudice for library's policy — a danger such as, "I do not like music"; "The committee is dead against religion"; "The chairman is keen about philosophy"; "Its ideology is subversive"; and so on. If this danger is avoided, the method of survey — of present, past, potential, and anticipated wants — will enable Book Selection to give reliable weightage to the subjects themselves and to particular books in them so that Book Selection can be equitably cut according to finance. But in fiction, this objective and democratic method — for the method of survey virtually amounts to taking the vote of readers — is in the wrong place. For it is blind feeling and not discriminating intellect that determines voting ; it is the moment's craze and not the lasting want that dominates. As in other spheres, the momentary impulsive force of passion usually elbows out the weak, though steady, force of intellect. Therefore, the selection of fiction must be guided by a definite policy determining the proportion of the book-fund beyond which fiction should not go in normal times; and the equal or unequal proportion of the distribution of the cut in book-fund among fiction and non-fiction, in case the axe has to be applied. While each library should determine these items of policy in relation to the "individuating particularities" of its clientele, it is possible to lay down some norms for general guidance.

31 Other Agencies for Entertainment

Two generations ago, it was difficult to keep out trashy fiction without a disturbing sense that we were thereby denying the unfortunates in the lower quartiles — as measured by capacity to derive joy from intellectual entertainment as distinct from emotional entertainment — the only harmless way in which they could spend their leisure-time, escape boredom, and perhaps forget their misery. But today, many other media for mass-entertainment (at the emotional level) have come into existence — radio, television, talkies, art-gallaries, museums, and so on. About 90 per cent of the people are said to listen to the radio every day. Some of these are free public projects. Some are commercial. There are also commercial circulating libraries. These commercial projects bring themselves within the reach of very low income-levels. This is so in the developed countries. For example, about 50 per cent of the people in such countries witness at least one cinema show in a week. This section is drawn liberally from the lower income-groups. In India, the lower income-groups have no surplus fund to go to commercial entertainments. This is true. But, nor are they literate enough to read fiction. Therefore, the question of cutting out trashy fiction, from the few libraries we have, does not give any trouble. But this question of policy will need positive consideration perhaps in another twenty years, if not earlier.

311 Message 12

The twelfth joint austerity message of the Laws and Finance to Book Selection is :

> *As a first economy measure in a public library, reject low-level fiction devoid of elevating literary merit.*

32 Not a Permanent Measure

But the rejection of trashy fiction should not be a permanent policy measure. This should be resorted to only in times of financial inadequacy. At other times, supply of such reading materials should be used as a means of attracting to the library the class of people under consideration. When so attracted, the public library can accustom them to a higher level of enjoyment and to an appreciation of their art collection and musical scores. It may even be able to make them change over gradually to the habit of deriving joy from books which make an emotional appeal of a higher order and in some cases even from books with some intellectual contents or bias.

4 Material for Mass Communication

Another group of materials, on which the financial axe may have to be allowed to fall earlier than on others, is that intended for communication of news.

41 Newspaper

Newspapers, for example, carry away a good slice of the book-fund of a public library. If money can be spared for them without prejudice to other reading materials, it is good to have them. For, it is well-known that the newspaper room is a good place where the librarian can meet persons in need of being helped to turn their minds to more lasting, elevating, and informing reading. But in times of scarcity of funds, this piece of service may be curtailed. As in the case of trashy fiction, this policy measure during periods of financial stringency will fall heavily on the lower income levels. But here also there is, today, a new factor taking away a good deal from the harshness of such a policy measure. The radio carries news over the air several times in the day. Even those depending on the reading of newspapers hitherto now prefer to turn the radios on or listen to the public installation of radios at the hours of news announcement. This mode of communication reaches 90 per cent to the people — much larger than what the newspapers in a public library can reach. It is true that newspapers carry more than news. They carry views too. In this respect, they are more like magazines. We shall consider this aspect along with magazines.

411 Message 13

The thirteenth joint austerity message of the Laws and Finance to Book Selection is :

> *Minimise, if not omit, selection of newspapers where community radio service is available, in case the book fund does not prove sufficient to take newspapers.*

42 Magazine

When the axe is unsatiated by victimising the newspapers in a public library, it may be shown the magazine room ; and in that room it may be shown those that are more of propaganda than of educative or informing intent. The portions of a newspaper other than the news columns, most eagerly sought, are also of the same kind as this class of magazines. A public library, keen about placing before its clientele a full diet of propaganda stuff, naturally selects newspapers and magazines of all schools of thought and ideologies. By cutting them out totally or partially so as not to disturb the balanced nature of the surviving ones, the public library will not now be doing much wrong either to the consumers or to the producers of such stuff. This is due to a new factor. The new factor is the presence of many other media for mass-communication. These are more widespread and more appealing than the newspaper or magazine room of a public library. All schools of ideology vie with one another in reaching the public mind through audio-visual media, needing less of intellectual effort for absorption than printed stuff. Advantage should be taken of this.

421 Message 14

The fourteenth joint austerity message of the Laws and Finance to Book Selection is :

> *Minimise selection of non-literary, non-scientific, non-craft-centred, low standard, propaganda magazines, without jeopardy to the balance among all schools of thought, if the book fund does not prove sufficient, to buy such magazines.*

43 Propaganda Book

All that has been said about magazines apply equally to books and pamphlets now being produced for mass-communication by diverse pressure groups to mould or influence the attitude of democracy.

CHAPTER JG

SOCIAL VALUE

1 Discrimination Against Lower Quartiles

The policy measures outlined in Chapter JF for adoption when the book-fund proves inadequate to fulfil the demands of all the Five Laws in their entirety, are in substance of a discriminating nature. They discriminate against the lower intellectual quartiles. Why is this preferred to making financial stringency visit on the heads of all quartiles alike ? There is only one reason. If we have limited water-supply for irrigation, do we spread it evenly on all the fields however thin the share of each may be? We do not. Because, the thin layer of water can do good to no field. The seeds in all the fields will dry up. None will sprout. We are therefore obliged to pick and choose some fields for favoured treatment. Do we turn the water into the fertile fields or the relatively arid ones ? Into the more fertile fields, certainly. Because, they will add to wealth in a larger measure. With this greater wealth, we may be able to improve irrigation and procure sufficient water to supply all the fields including the less fertile ones. We do not bring in the argument of undemocratic discrimination in this policy measure in irrigation. A similar policy measure in Book Selection is similarly justified.

2 Not Abandonment

Withdrawing money from trashy fiction and light magazines — often forming the main service of public libraries — does not now amount to abandonment of the lower quartiles. For, the public library takes a holistic view. It does not arrogate to itself a monopoly of service to these quartiles. It finds that mass-entertainment and mass-communication have been taken up by other agencies. These agencies are even more effective in result and extensive in coverage. But in the communication of serious thought — be it for mere dissemination or for manuring productive minds to produce more thought — the mass-media are of no avail. It is not enough if serious thought is met with once. It needs to be lived with, for a length of time. It has to be picked up and munched on occasions without end. Mass-media are incapable of providing for this. The public library is the only public medium known so far which can provide for this. If it has to abandon something to cut its service according to finance, it is but proper that it should cut out the service rendered elsewhere. As shown in Sec JF2, the Third Law has convinced itself of the wisdom of abandoning something else too — service to the specialists — because this service is rendered elsewhere. It is for retaining in the hands of the public library, during periods of poor book-fund, only services not rendered anywhere else. One of such services is the supply of reading materials not light enough for mass-media to take up. Another of such services is the supply of reading materials not heavy enough for academic and business libraries to take up. Because the "general public" — embracing the miscellaneous people, particularly the middle class (in the intellectual sense) — is the irreducible responsibility of the public library.

3 Temporary Supervision

It may be asked "In that case, why not permanently abandon the light as well as the heavy stuff from the public library, intended for the so-called 'general public' — the 'middle class' in the intellectual sense ?" There are reasons for the public library continuing its claim to enter those two regions when its book-fund permits. As already stated in Sec JF32, the public library wishes to use the lighter materials as baits to attract to itself the lower class (in the intellectual sense) in order to lift their intellectual status in gradual steps by accustoming them by slow degrees to enjoy serious reading.

Further, countries which have had public library service for some years find that there is a gradual upgrading in the seriousness of the material being sought by the middle class. It does not want to block this much-desired up-grading of reading interests by withdrawing itself entirely from service of specialised materials. On the other hand, wherever money could be found, public libraries have been finding the value of forming special departments in which specialised materials are collected and served to the "general public" not finding affiliation to academies, learned bodies, and industrial houses possible.

4 Functions of the State

The class of reading material, which should fall the first victim to the financial axe if it becomes inevitable, should in fact, be determined in relation to the total context of the functions of the State, as it has developed today and the scale of priority among those functions. This question has been discussed elaborately in Sec 16 and 161 of my *Library development plan* (1950). Today the functions of the State have gone far beyond the preventive ones — to prevent private violence, interference with life and property, and aggression by aliens. They embrace every act necessary to facilitate the realisation of desires deemed to be common to the great majority of citizens and deemed also not to be anti-social. This vast extension of functions brings itself against financial stringency again and again. The functions have therefore to be arranged according to a scale of priority. The position of any function in this scale should be determined by the nature of the commodity or service with the supply of which the function is concerned. For this purpose commodities and services may be classified on the basis of two characteristics :

1 The extent to which they are essential for national well-being ; and

2 The extent to which each citizen will automatically grasp it and pay for it himself.

On the basis of the first characteristic, facility for perpetual self-education — enrichment of memory, sharpening of intellect, and sublimation of emotions — comes prior to facility for satisfying lower emotions and occupying leisure time. On the basis of the second characteristic, it is believed that intellectual wants and the wants for the sublimation of emotions are less compelling and more fleeting than the lower emotional wants. For this reason also supply of reading materials — calculated to enrich memory, sharpen intellect, and sublimate emotions — is given priority over low class fiction and other materials merely satisfying passion. The resultant scale of priority exposes trashy fiction and kindred reading materials to the consequences of financial stringency, earlier than informing, educating, and elevating reading materials. This inevitably results in discrimination against the lower class and in favour of the middle class (in the intellectual sense). But this is not strictly a violation of democracy. It is only a case of making the limited financial resources do the best for the society. Although, it looks as if the first benefit goes to the middle class, in reality the benefit ultimately goes to the entire society including the lower class. This is one of the subtle situations in respect of which statesmanship would uphold collective social good even against the interests of some individuals. But even this apparently favoured discrimination in its favour, places an obligation on the middle class to use it fairly and with circumspection. We shall examine in the next section the dangers of insensitiveness to this responsibility of the abuse of the apparently favoured discrimination.

5 Responsibility of Middle Class

We have suggested in the preceding section that, in times of financial stringency, the first charge on the book-fund of a public library should be the service of the middle class (in the intellectual sense). In the eyes of the "lower class" this may make it look like a privileged institution. In their eyes, the academic and business libraries should appear more so. But the latter often escape their notice. As it has been said in Sec JG2, the only justification for discrimination by the public library in favour of the "middle class" — the central quartiles — is that it will produce better results for the ultimate good of society. The leaders of the community are usually drawn from this middle-class core of the public library clientele. They have to be the channel through which the results of the work of the upper class (in the intellectual sense) have to be distributed to the lower class. On account of this reason and on account of its potentiality to do ultimate good to society, some kind of halo develops around the public library as a social institution. Wherever halo-effect develops, there is the danger of its becoming a false one sooner or later. When the halo-effect is used as a mask to cover selfish pursuits, it begins to degenerate into a false one. The most shrewd among the lower class begin to suspect the genuineness of the halo. Its falsity gradually becomes visible to more and more. The genuine among the upper class too detest the pretentiousness of the halo-effect. Crisis comes. The false idol behind the halo is pulled down. This has happened in history several times. It happened in the sphere of religion. The priest class entrenched behind the halo was liquidated. It happened in political life. The hereditary royalty entrenched behind the halo was liquidated. It is happening in the economic sphere. The capitalist class behind the halo is being liquidated. It will soon happen in the now current political sphere too. The self-seeking, demagoguish Machiavellian nepotist and bureaucrat behind the halo will be liquidated in due course. Such is the course of events in all social institutions. The public library is a social institution. It must avoid this danger. It can, if the middle class (in the intellectual sense) does not abuse the halo developing round the public library. It should be preserved as a true halo, a symbol of benignness and an index of the radiation emanating from it and bathing and irradiating all alike.

51 MESSAGE 15

The fifteenth joint austerity message of the Laws and Finance in relation to curtailment in the selection of low level fiction, newspapers, and low level magazines is :

> *These austerity measures, forced by inadequate book-fund, are not born out of contempt for the poor or for those lower down in the intellectual scale, but are based on a policy of long-term return of social benefit to the community as a whole.*

CHAPTER JH

BOOK SELECTION AND EMERGENT EVOLUTION

1 Social Phenomenon

Library is a social institution. Its efficiency needs testing from time to time. In the past, what passed for test was the general impression formed by a stray, shrewd librarian or other person, here or there, or now and then. The reliability of such an impression was not known. It was too subjective to be verified by others. The extent of its acceptance depended solely on the force and aggressive nature of the personality of the person expressing the impression rather than on the trustworthiness of his opinion. Indeed, the Tamil poetess Avvai had said almost two thousand years ago :

"A true statement of a person may pass for a false one by lack of force in the way in which he utters it — that is, by poor advocacy.

"A false statement of a person may pass for a true one by the aggressive, arresting, and compelling way in which he utters it — that is, by powerful advocacy."

No method was known for testing results objectively. Unlike inert material objects, plants which are biochemical and probably nothing more, and animals which have not advanced much from the biochemical stage beyond the development of hormones correlated to emotions, the humans have developed free will which generates unpredictable behaviour. Moreover, since the observer and the observed are both humans, emotional disturbance affects both observation and inference therefrom. On account of these factors, social behaviour and phenomena had not for long been brought into the ambit of scientific method.

2 Spiral of Scientific Method

Scientific method in the development of a subject consists of an unending series of stages :

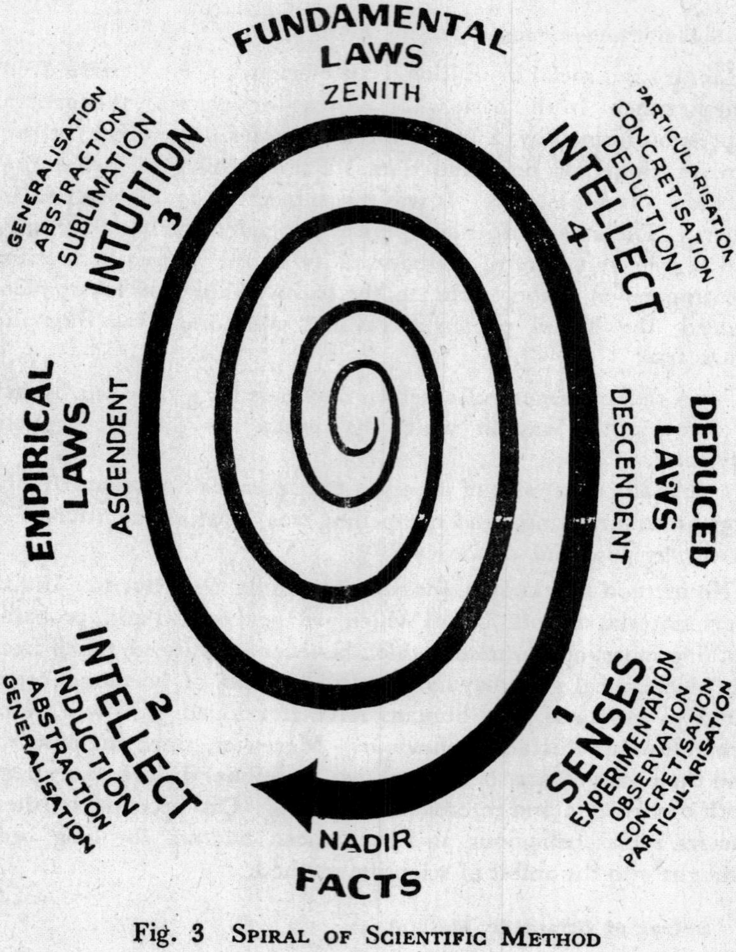

Fig. 3 Spiral of Scientific Method

1 Objective observation with or without experimental manipulation;

2 Empirical generalisation of repeatedly observed facts into empirical laws featuring in exact terms the quantitative or qualitative relation between the factors involved;

3 Intuitive enunciation of a few fundamental laws to which the diverse empirical laws could be reduced;

4 Deriving by deduction from the fundmental laws deduced laws which contain all the empirical laws and also some others of a similar order;

5 Going to observation again with or without experiment and the verification of the new deduced laws by facts;

6 The formation of crisis by disagreement between deduced laws implied in the fundamental laws and the new facts that are observed;

7 Resolution of the crisis by an analysis of the factors involved and the elimination of the faults, if any, in the observation of facts;

8 Inductive generalisation, into empirical laws, of all new facts which, in spite of every possible elimination of faults, are at variance from indications of deduced laws;

9 Intuitive enunciation of fresh fundamental laws to which the facts and the empirical laws known before as well as after the crisis can be reduced; and the repetition of this cycle *ad infinitum*. Once one or two cycles of the spiral of scientific method are completed in a subject, thereafter the study of the subject may begin either with the facts of observation or with the fundamental laws. The former may be described as empirical or pragmatic method and the latter as *a priori* method. It is best to blend the two methods of study and to check up the results of the two methods at suitable stages. The fundamental laws are called Hypotheses in the Natural Sciences and Normative Principles in the Social Sciences.

3 Empirical Laws

For long, the stage marked 1 in the study of social phenomena has been baffling to human capacity. Stage 2 was almost impossible. But today, statistical methods with their technique for random sampling and for estimating the probable error in empirical generalisations are making it possible to bring social phenomena within the ambit of scientific method. It is true that the neutralisation of the deviations from the normal does not take place as easily and with as small a sample in the world of humans as in that of materials, plants, and animals. Perhaps, the normal may never stand out quite sharply. Again, the orbit of indeterminism is very small in the physical world. It is still small in the biological world too. But it is very vast in the social world. Several alternative modes of social behaviour are possible under the same conditions.

4 Normative Principles

Choice between them has to be decided according to their "Values". Thus a Scale of Values becomes necessary in order to replace the chaos of indeterminism by an agreed cosmos. In the world of social phenomena, the laying down of the Scale of Values, best suited to a given context, falls within the sphere of intuition. That is, it belongs to Stage 3 in the spiral of scientific method. Work at this stage turns out to be the formulation of Normative Principles — principles of how facts and behaviours of the entities observed among social phenomena should be — rather than formulation of a hypothesis which can explain or perhaps even predict the facts and behaviour of the entities observed, as in physical and biological phenomena. So long as this difference is not eliminated, scientific method as applied to Social Phenomena will have to be somewhat different from the scientific method as applied to physical and biological phenomena — the so-called Natural Phenomena.

5 Librametry

And yet, the development of statistical methods during the last half a century has enabled scientific method to enter the Realm of Social Phenomena and to help Social Sciences to emerge, though still with considerable limitation. The scientific method being forged for Social Sciences can and should be applied to Library Science. Scientific methods applied to economics is called Econometry. Those applied to Psychology is called Psychometry. We also speak of Educametry. Perhaps, Politicometry may also become possible. Similarly, scientific method applied to Library Science, may be denoted by the term "Librametry". The first occasion in which Librametry was applied in respect of reading interests over a population as large as a nation was brought about in 1946, when the American Library Association proposed to the Social Sciences Research Council the conducting of "a thorough and comprehensive study of the American free public library — as an appraisal in sociological, cultural, and human terms — of the extent in which libraries are achieving their objectives and of the library's potential and actual contribution to American society." This first vast scientific study of the complex of library phenomena was made possible by the appropriation of about a million rupees for the purpose by the Carnegie Corporation of New York.

6 Canons of Book Selection

The first round of the study was completed in 1949. Seven volumes of reports came out by 1951. These are reports of the first scientifically conducted audit of a national system of library service. These volumes have to be scanned carefully to see how far the compromise and austerity policy measures outlined in Chapters JA to JF are on sound lines. The Normative Principles implied in these reports should be distilled out. These principles would be the Canons of Book Selection. Canons of Book Selection have not yet been formulated properly. In their absence, the *a priori* method for Book Selection has to be based on the Five Laws forming the Normative Principles of the whole field of Library Science instead of the Canons specific to the field consistent with the Five Laws, as it already obtains in the subdisciplines of Classification and Cataloguing.

7 Scale of Values

Determination of the Scale of Values is by empirical methods, with the aid of intellect instead of intuition, by democratic vote. This has exposed certain inherent dangers to progress. The Dharma Shastras (= the science of organised society = Social Sciences) of ancient India had sensed this danger. The alternative they had prescribed was to leave the laying down of the Scale of Values to Sat-men (= the superior, enduring, true, unbiased, and far-seeing men, the men in whom intuition shines, the men who are self-centres of illumination). These transcend and elude objective tests. The Dharma Shastras based themselves on this indefinable category — Sat-men. Goethe said that a poet alone can distinguish a true poet from a false one. So also a Sat-man alone can distinguish a true Sat-man from the fraud. The ordinary people cannot. The forceful power-groups are often mistaken by the ordinary people for Sat-men. The power-halo is mistaken for the Sat-halo. The power-halo-men make a combine among themselves to make a Sat-halo-man inaccessible and unacceptable to the ordinary people. They thus mislead and exploit. They adopt tactics and intrigues which Sat-men would never adopt. Democracy thus runs the risk of being beguiled by false idols. This running after demagogues and false idols continues until their misery mounts up to a breaking point and a revolution — often painful — comes at long last. This is responsible for the recurring regression in society and the slowness of over-all progress. This accounts for cultural cycles. The Gita says that God has to create himself periodically to rescue society from the grip of fraudulent power-groups. This is at bottom a conflict between "democratic vote" and "normative principles being laid down by Sat-men". Until the modern methods of social sciences resolve this conflict — can they ever ? — the solution of every problem in any social science will have to stem from halting, tentative, normative principles. It will have to linger in the stage of "emergent evolution", ever uncertain, ever exposed to the danger of being quashed, never knowing what comes round the corner. As Library Science falls within the group of Social Sciences, its problems are exposed to the danger of being quashed, never knowing what comes round the corner. The problems in Book Selection are particularly prone to this difficulty.

Part K

SOURCES FOR BOOK SELECTION

CHAPTER KA

INTRODUCTION

1 Two Factors in Book Selection

Selection of books for acquisition requires judgement. Several factors will have to be borne in mind in deciding the books to be selected and those to be rejected. This work can only be done by persons with mature experience in reference service. Two factors determining maturity of such experience are

1 Knowledge of the Theory of Book Selection ; and
2 Knowledge of the Sources for Book Selection.

The earlier parts of this book have expounded the Theory of Book Selection.

2 Kinds of Sources for Book Selection

The sources for Book Selection may consist of

1 Reader's suggestion ;
2 Review column in newspapers and periodicals ; and
3 Bibliographies.

This part describes and illustrates the various kinds of sources.

3 Kinds of Bibliographies

A Bibliography may be a closed one or a periodical one. Further, a periodical bibliography may be — an

1 Indexing periodical, merely listing documents — that is, bare entries of them ; or

2 Abstracting periodical, giving an abstract at the end of each entry.

Chapter KJ gives a bibliography of abstracting periodicals.

CHAPTER KB

READERS' SUGGESTIONS

1 Mode of Suggestion

Suggestions from readers are bound to be casual. A reader who has heard of a book or read a review of it or has seen it actually somewhere else may suggest its acquisition to the library. The suggestion may be oral or written. If it is oral it should be reduced to writing. If it is written it should be reduced to a standard form.

2 Book Selection Card

The most convenient way of writing out a readers' suggestion is to write it on a book selection card on the basis of "one book, one card". The design for a book selection card is given in Chapter LJ of this book. The headings in the book selection card themselves indicate the information to be furnished. The information may be furnished partly by the reader suggesting it. The rest should be completed by the library.

3 Suggestion Book

Another way is to make readers giving their suggestion write them out in a bound book. It is usually called "Suggestion Book". In either case, the information about the reader who makes the suggestion should be given in each entry.

CHAPTER KC

BOOK REVIEWS IN PERIODICALS

1 An Important Source for Book Selection

The periodicals taken by the library, which have review columns, form an important source of Book Selection. In the selection of periodicals, it is desirable to include some which are rich in reviews. For a general library, for example, the *Times literary supplement* will prove very useful. As already stated in Sec DM3 it may not be wise to defer the selection of every book until a review appears. In practice, the review columns will be of use for :

1 Deciding the selection of doubtful cases ; and

2 Examining whether any important items had been left out by oversight in the process of book selection from primary sources.

The illustrative list given in Sec KC3 mentions some representative organs in which reviews regularly occur.

2 Pattern of Entry

1 For each issue of each periodical, the following data are given in succession :

11 The Colon Class Number ;

12 The title ;

13 The sponsor ;

14 Periodicity ;

15 Year of the first volume ;

16 Size ;

17 Ratio of the number of pages of review to total number of pages (eg 3/52) ;

18 Number of books reviewed ; and

19 Time lag.

2 The entry is made according to the *Classified catalogue code*, Ed 5 (1964).

3 The entries are arranged by Colon Classification Number.

4 Unless otherwise stated, each review begins with a full bibliographical entry of the book reviewed.

5 Unless otherwise stated, the review in a periodical is to be taken as a signed one.

6 Quantitative data are estimated averages.

7 The following abbreviations are used :

A	=	Annual	Q	=	Quarterly
B-M	=	Bi-monthly	S-A	=	Semi-annual
F	=	Fortnightly	W	=	Weekly
M	=	Monthly			

8 Subject is mentioned only when it is not indicated by the title.

3 Periodicals with Reviews

z2m2 **Indology, Periodical, India**

1 *z2m2*,N3 ARYAN PATH, (Indian Institute of World Culture). M. 1930. 24 × 16 cm. Pages 24/160. Books reviewed 16. Time lag 1 year.

2 *z2m2*,N5 ANNALS, Bhandarkar Oriental Research Institute. Q. 1960. 24 × 16 cm. Pages 24/160. Books reviewed 8. Time lag 1 year.

3 *z2m2*,N7 VISHVESHWARANAND INDOLOGICAL journal, (Vishveshwaranand Vedic Research Institute). S-A. 1963. 24×16 cm. Pages 28/124. Books reviewed 14. Time lag 18 months.

z4m3 **Orientalia, Periodical, Great Britain**

4 *z4m3*,N7 ASIAN REVIEW, [Royal India, Pakistan and Ceylon Society (London) and East India Association (London)]. M. 1964. Pages 6/52. Books reviewed 8. Year of publication of the books reviewed is not given.

z4m53 **Orientalia, Periodical, France**

5 *z4m53*,M JOURNAL ASIATIQUE, (Societe Asiatique). Q. 1822. 22.5×14 cm. Pages 4/164. Books reviewed 2. Time lag 2 years.

z4m55 Orientalia, Periodical, Germany

6 z4m55,M5 ZEITSCHRIFT, Deutschen Morgenlandischen Gesellschaft. Irr. (3 parts in a year). 1849. 23×15 cm. Pages 39/224. Books reviewed 17. Time lag 1 year.

z4m73 Orientalia, Periodical, USA

7 z4m73,M9 JOURNAL, American Oriental Society. Q. 1881. 44×22 cm. Pages 44/96. Books reviewed 18. Time lag 12 to 18 months.

8 z4m73,N5 JOURNAL OF Asian Studies, (Association for Asian Studies Inc). Q. 1941. 25×17 cm. Pages 48/134. Books reviewed 49. Time lag 1 year.

9 z4m73,N63 ASIAN SURVEY, (University of California, Institute of International Studies). M. 1963. 22×10 cm. Pages 1/48. Books reviewed 4. Time lag 6 months.

z596m596 Netherlandology, Periodical, Netherlands

10 z596m596,N5 DELTA: Review of arts, life and thought in Netherlands, (Delta International Publications Foundation). Q. 1958. 24×12 cm. Pages 6/96. Books reviewed 4. Year of publication of the books reviewed is not given. Gives a list of recent books.

2m2 Library science, Periodical, India

11 2m2,N5 IASLIC BULLETIN, (Indian Association of Special Libraries and Information Centres). Q. 1956. 24×16 cm. Pages 2/60. Books reviewed 3. Time lag 1 year.

12 2m2,N62 HERALD OF library science, (Sarada Ranganathan Endowment for Library Science). Q. 1962. 24×16 cm. Pages 6/80. Books reviewed 4. Time lag 6 months.

2m3 Library science, Periodical, Great Britain

13 2m3,M9 LIBRARY ASSOCIATION record. M. 1899. 24×18 cm. Pages 2/40. Books reviewed 3. Time lag 1 year.

14 2m3,N5 JOURNAL OF documentation, (Aslib). Q. 1945. 24×17 cm. Pages 10/60. Books reviewed 10. Time lag 18 months. A list of books received is also given.

2m53 Library science, Periodical, France

15 2m53,N5 UNESCO BULLETIN for libraries. B-M. 1947. Pages 6/60. Books reviewed 30. Time lag 1 year.

2m73 Library science, Periodical, USA

16 2*m*73,N1 SPECIAL LIBRARIES, [Special Libraries Association (New York)]. M (Sept to April). B-M (May to August). 1910. 24×17 cm. Pages 4/48. Books reviewed 8. Time lag 1 year. Gives a list of select books.

17 2*m*73,N14 WILSON LIBRARY bulletin. M (except in July and August). 1914. 24×17 cm. Pages 4/80. Books reviewed 20. Time lag 6 months.

18 2*m*73,N3 COLLEGE AND research libraries, (Association of College and Research Libraries). B-M. 1939. 24×16 cm. Pages 6/80. Books reviewed 6. Time lag 1 year.

19 2*m*73,N5 LIBRARY RESOURCES and technical services, [American Library Association, Resources and Technical Services (Division)]. Q. 1957. 23×16 cm. Pages 2/86. Books reviewed 2. Time lag 1 year.

A*m*2 Natural Sciences, Periodical, India

20 A*m*2,N3 CURRENT SCIENCE, (Current Science Association). M. 1932. 24×18 cm. Pages 4/30. Books reviewed 6. Time lag 1 year.

21 A*m*2,N3 SCIENCE AND culture, (Indian Science News Association). M. 1935. 21×14 cm. Pages 4/47. Books reviewed 3. Time lag 3 months.

A*m*3 Natural Sciences, Periodical, Great Britain

22 A*m*3,M7 NATURE. W. 1869. 28×21 cm. Pages 8/100. Books reviewed 8. Time lag 1 year.

23 A*m*3,N1 SCIENCE PROGRESS. Q. 1906. 24×15 cm. Pages 42/170. Books reviewed 40. Time lag 9 months.

24 A*m*3,N20 DISCOVERY. M. 1920. 28×21cm. Pages 3/47. Books reviewed 9. Time lag 1 year.

25 A*m*3,N3 ADVANCEMENT OF science, (British Association for Science). 1939. 24×18 cm. Pages 3/88. Books reviewed 20. Time lag 1 year.

26 A*m*3,N42 ENDEAVOUR, [Imperial Chemical Industries (London)]. Q. 1942. 29×19 cm. Pages 6/50. Books reviewed 30. Time lag 1 year.

A*m*73 Natural Sciences, Periodical, USA

27 A*m*73,M5 SCIENTIFIC AMERICAN. M. 1845. 29×22 cm. Pages 16/296. Books reviewed 48. Time lag 6 months.

28 A*m*73,M9 SCIENCE, (American Association for the Advancement of Science). W. 1880. 28×21 cm. Pages 3/88. Books reviewed 20. Time lag 1 year.

29 A*m*73,N1 AMERICAN SCIENTIST, (Society of the Sigma Xi). Q. 1913. 23×16 cm. Pages 58/262. Books reviewed 40. Time lag 1 year.

B*m*2 Mathematics, Periodical, India

30 B*m*2,N3 MATHEMATICS STUDENT, (Indian Mathematical Society). Q. 1933. 24×16 cm. Pages 3/71. Books reviewed 5. Time lag 2 years.

B*m*3 Mathematics, Periodical, Great Britain

31 B*m*3,M MATHEMATICAL GAZETTE (Mathematical Association). Q. 1894. 21×14 cm. Pages 20/180. Books reviewed 30. Time lag 1 year.

B*m*73 Mathematics, Periodical, USA

32 B*m*73,M AMERICAN MATHEMATICAL monthly, (Mathematical Association of America). M (B-M in June-July, August-Sept). 1894. 25×18 cm. Pages 6/118. Books reviewed 12. Time lag 1 year. A list of books reviewed is also given.

33 B*m*73,N3 SCRIPTA MATHEMATICA, (Yeshiva University). Q. 1932. 25×17 cm. Pages 24/90. Books reviewed 20. Time lag 2 years.

B28*m*73 Statistics, Periodical, USA

34 B28*m*73,M JOURNAL, American Statistical Association. Q. 1888. 24×15 cm. Pages 30/265. Books reviewed 40. Time lag 1 year.

B9*m*3 Astronomy, Periodical, Great Britain

35 B9*m*3,M OBSERVATORY, (Royal Greenwich Observatory). B-M. 1877. 23×14 cm. Pages 3/45. Books reviewed 9. Time lag 1 year.

B9*m*58 Astronomy, Periodical, USSR

36 B9*m*58,N5 SOVIET ASTRONOMY, (American Institute of Physics). [Tr of *Astronomical journal*, (Academy of the

Sciences of the USSR)]. B-M. 1957. 27×21 cm. Pages 3/150. Books reviewed 9. Time lag 1 year.

C*m*3 Physics, Periodical, Great Britain

37 C*m*3,M7 PROCEEDINGS, Physical Society. M. 1874. 26×18 cm. Pages 9/160. Books reviewed 10. Time lag 9 months.

C*m*73 Physics, Periodical, USA

38 C*m*73,N3 AMERICAN JOURNAL of physics, (American Association of Physics Teachers). M. 1933. 27×20 cm. Pages 10/80. Books reviewed 10. Time lag 1 year.

C3*m*3 Sound, Periodical, Great Britain

39 C3*m*3,N5 ACUSTICA, [Physical Society, Acoustics (Group)]. B-M. 1951. 29×27 cm. Pages 2/60. Time lag 1 year.

C3*m*73 Sound, Periodical, USA

40 C3*m*73,N7 SOUND, (Acoustical Society of America). B-M. 1962. 28×21 cm. Pages 2/60. Books reviewed 5. Time lag 1 year.

C5*m*73 Radiation, Periodical, USA

41 C5*m*73,N1 JOURNAL, Optical Society of America. M. 1917. 26×20 cm. Pages 3/110. Books reviewed 4. Time lag 1 year.

C9B3*m*73 Nuclear Physics, Periodical, USA

42 C9B3*m*73,N5 NUCLEONICS. M. 1947. 29×21 cm. Pages 3/100. Books reviewed 8. Time lag 1 year.

D*m*3 Engineering, Periodical, Great Britain

43 D*m*3,M5 ENGINEER. W. 1856. 34×25 cm. Pages 4/40. Books reviewed 10. Time lag 3 months.

D:1*m*73 Applied mechanics, Periodical, USA

44 D:1*m*73,N5 APPLIED MECHANICS review, (American Society of Mechanical Engineers). M. 1948. 29×21 cm. Pages 95. Books reviewed 27. Time lag 1 year.

D1*m*73 Civil Engineering, Periodical, USA

45 D1*m*73, N3 CIVIL ENGINEERING, (American Society of Civil Engineers). M. 1931. 28×21 cm. Pages 2/210. Books reviewed 10. Time lag 1 year.

D2*m*3 Engineering, Building, Periodical, Great Britain

46 D2*m*3,N CONCRETE AND construction engineering. M. 1905. 22×15 cm. Pages 1/40. Books reviewed 2. Time lag 9 months.

D4J*m*3 Engineering, Track, Space, Periodical, Great Britain

47 D4J*m*3,M9 JOURNAL, Royal Aeronautical Society. M. 1895. 29×21 cm. Pages 3/30. Books reviewed 10. Time lag 9 months.

D4J*m*73 Engineering, Track, Space, Periodical, USA

48 D4J*m*73,N63 AIAA JOURNAL, (American Institute of Aeronautics and Astronautics). M. 1963. 28×21 cm. Pages 2/10. Books reviewed 10. Time lag 6 months.

49 D4J*m*73,N64 ASTRONAUTICS AND aeronautics, (American Institute of Aeronautics and Astronautics). M. 1964. 29×21 cm. Pages 1/96. Books reviewed 5. Time lag 1 year.

D6*m*3 Power Engineering, Periodical, Great Britain

50 D6*m*3,N5 CHARTERED MECHANICAL engineer, (Institute of Mechanical Engineers). M. 1954. 27×20 cm. Pages 5/57. Books reviewed 50. Time lag 9 months.

D6*m*73 Power Engineering, Periodical, USA

51 D6*m*73,M7 MECHANICAL ENGINEERING, (American Society of Mechanical Engineers). M. 1879. 28×21 cm. Pages 3/177. Books reviewed 28. Time lag 1 year.

D62*m*3 Hydraulics, Periodical, Great Britain

52 D62*m*3,N47 JOURNAL, Institute of Engineers. 7 issues a year. 1947. Pages 2/84. Books reviewed 3. Time lag 1 year.

53 D62*m*3,N5 WATER POWER. M. 1949. 29×22 cm. Pages 1/43. Books reviewed 3. Time lag 1 year.

D65*m*3 Electronics, Periodical, Great Britain

54 D65*m*3,N INDUSTRIAL ELECTRONICS. M. 1692. 29×21 cm. Pages 1/52. Books reviewed 3. Time lag 1 year.

55 D65*m*3,N3 ELECTRONIC ENGINEERING, M. 1928. 29×23 cm. Pages 2/70. Books reviewed 10. Time lag 1 year.

D65*m*73 Electronics, Periodical, USA

56 D65*m*73,N1 ELECTRONICS WORLD. M. 1919. 28×21 cm. Pages 2/106. Books reviewed 7. Time lag 1 year.

D66*m*3 Electrical Engineering, Periodical, Great Britain

57 D66*m*3,NO8 POST-OFFICE ELECTRICAL engineers' journal, (Institution of Post Office Electrical Engineers). Q. 1908. 28×21 cm. Pages 4/72. Books reviewed 10. Time lag 1 year. (Review is scattered in several pages. Contents page gives reference to these pages.)

58 D66*m*3,N5 JOURNAL, Institution of Electrical Engineers. M. 1955. 28×22 cm. Pages 2/62. Books reviewed Time lag 8 months.

59 D66*m*3,N7 ELECTRICAL REVIEW. W. 1962. 28×21 cm. Pages 1/40. Books reviewed 2. Time lag 6 months.

D66*m*73 Electrical Engineering, Periodical, USA

60 D66*m*73,M9 ELECTRICAL ENGINEERING, (Institute of Electrical and Electronic Engineers). M. 1887. 28×21 cm. Pages 2/90. Books reviewed 20. Time lag 1 year.

61 D66*m*73,M9 ELECTROTECHNOLOGY. M. 1892. 28×21 cm. Pages 1/212. Books reviewed 6. Time lag 9 months.

D68*m*3 Nuclear Engineering, Periodical, Great Britain

62 D68*m*3,N5 NUCLEAR POWER. M. 1956. 29×22 cm. Pages 2/100. Books reviewed 4. Time lag 1 year.

D68*m*73 Nuclear Engineering, Periodical, USA

63 D68*m*73,N5 NUCLEAR SCIENCE and engineering, (American Nuclear Society). M. 1956. 27×20 cm. Pages 4/136. Books reviewed 5. Time lag 1 year.

D77*m*3 Engineering, Radio, Periodical, Great Britain

64 D77*m*3,N3 MARCONI REVIEW, (Marconi's Wireless Telegraph Company). Q. 1938. 23×15 cm. Pages 4/15. Books reviewed 7. Time lag 1 year.

D795*m*3 Engineering, Illumination, Periodical, Great Britain

65 D795*m*3,N1 LIGHT AND Lighting, (Illuminating Engineering Society). M. 1908. 28×21 cm. Pages 2/32. Books reviewed 5. Time lag 1 year.

DA:4*m*73 Production Engineering, Heavy Machinery, Design, Periodical, USA

66 DA:4*m*73,N3 MACHINE DESIGN. F. 1929. 28×21 cm. Pages 2/298. Books reviewed 5. Time lag 6 months.

DS*am*3 Production Engineering, Instrument, Periodical, Great Britain

67 DS*am*3,N5 INSTRUMENT REVIEW. F. 1954. 29×21 cm. Pages 5/105. Books reviewed 6. Time lag 1 year.

E*m*3 Chemistry, Periodical, Great Britain

68 E*m*3,M7 ANALYST. M. 1876. 26×17 cm. Pages 3/80. Books reviewed 5. Time lag 1 year.

69 E*m*3,M7 JOURNAL, Royal Institute of Chemistry. B-M. 1877. 28×21 cm. Pages 6/36. Books reviewed 10. Time lag 6 months.

E*m*73 Chemistry, Periodical, USA

70 E*m*73,M7 JOURNAL, American Chemical Society. F. 1879. 28×21 cm. Pages 2/215. Books reviewed 4. Time lag 9 months.

71 E*m*73,N3 CHEMICAL AND engineering news, (American Chemical Society). W. 1923. 28×21 cm. Pages 2/132. Books reviewed 3. Time lag 3 months.

E:*tm*73 Chemistry, Education, Periodical, USA

72 E:*tm*73,N3 JOURNAL OF chemical education, [American Chemical Society, Chemical Education (Division of—)] M. 1924. 28×21cm. Pages 3/55. Books reviewed 8. Time lag 9 months.

E982*m*596 Enzymes, Periodical, Netherlands

73 E982*m*596,N3 ENZYMOLOGIA : Acta biocatalytica. 6 to 12 times a year. 1930. 24×15 cm. Pages 4/40. Books reviewed 4. Time lag 2 years.

E9G*m*73 Biochemistry, Periodical, USA

74 E9G*m*73,N5 ARCHIVES OF biochemistry and biophysics. M. 1942. 25×16 cm. Pages 6/140. Books reviewed 6. Time lag 1 year.

F*m*3 Technology, Periodical, Great Britain

75 F*m*3,N CHEMICAL PROCESS engineering and atomic world. M. 1920. 28×21 cm. Pages 1/65. Books reviewed 3. Time lag 1 year.

76 F*m*3,N3 INDUSTRIAL CHEMIST. M. 1925. 28×21 cm. Pages 4/48. Books reviewed 10. Time lag 1 year.

G*m*3 Biology, Periodical, Great Britain

77 G*m*3,N1 ANNALS OF applied biology, (Association of Applied Biologists). Q. 1914. 25×17 cm. Pages 4/250. Time lag 1 year.

G*m*73 Biology, Periodical, USA

78 G*m*73,N3 QUARTERLY REVIEW of biology, (American Institute of Biological Sciences). Q. 1926. 25×17 cm. Pages 36/110. Books reviewed 36. Time lag 2 years.

G:6*m*2 Genetics, Periodical, India

79 G:6*m*2,N1 JOURNAL OF genetics. Irr. 1910. 24×18 cm. Pages 30/143. Books reviewed 18. Time lag 2 years.

G11:198*m*73 Cell, Staining, Periodical, USA

80 G11:198*m*73,N3 STAIN TECHNOLOGY: Journal for Microtechnic and histochemistry. 24×17 cm. 1925. Pages 3/34 Books reviewed 6. Time lag 1 year.

I*m*3 Botany, Periodical, Great Britain

81 I*m*3,N5 NEW PHYTOLOGIST. 3 times a year. 1902. 24×18 cm. Pages 14/150. Books reviewed 15. Time lag 1 year.

I23*m*73 Fungus, Periodical, USA

82 I23*m*73,N1 MYCOLOGIA, (Mycological Society of America). B-M. 1909. 24×15 cm. Pages 12/150. Books reviewed 8. Time lag 9 months.

J*m*2 Agriculture, Periodical, India

83 J*m*2,N3 INDIAN JOURNAL of agricultural science, (Indian Council of Agricultural Research). Q. 1931. Pages 4/74. Books reviewed 7. Time lag 1 year.

J:(E)*m*73 Agriculture, Chemistry, Periodical, USA

84 J:(E)*m*73,N18 JOURNAL, Association of Agricultural Chemists. Q. 1918. 25×17 cm. Pages 5/206. Books reviewed 5. Time lag 1 year.

L*m*3 Medicine, Periodical, Great Britain

85 L*m*3,M LANCET. W. 1823. 28×20 cm. Pages 2/55. Books reviewed 8. Time lag 6 months.

86 L*m*3,N32 BRITISH MEDICAL journal, (British Medical Association). W. 1932. 28×24 cm. Pages 4/64. Books reviewed 8. Time lag 6 months.

87 L*m*3,N5 BRITISH MEDICAL bulletin, [British Council, Medical (—Department)]. 3 times a year. 1945. 28×21 cm. Pages 2/80. Books reviewed 5. Time lag 9 months.

L:*fm*2 Medicine, Research, Periodical, India

88 L:*fm*2,N1 INDIAN JOURNAL of medical research. (Indian Council of Medical Research). B-M. 1913. Pages 10/160. Books reviewed 12. Time lag 1 year.

L:4:3-Z1*m*73 Diagnosis, Clinical, Periodical, USA

89 L:4:3-Z1*m*73,M9 CLINICAL MEDICINE. M. 1894. 22×10 cm. Pages 3/110. Books reviewed 7. Time lag 1 year.

L:55*m*3 Public Hygiene, Periodical, Great Britain

90 L:55*m*3,N3 BULLETIN OF hygiene, (Bureau of Hygiene and Tropical Diseases). M. 1926. 24×18 cm. Pages 4/140. Books reviewed 4. Time lag 1 year.

L:55*m*73 Public Hygiene, Periodical, USA

91 L:55*m*73,N1 AMERICAN JOURNAL of public health and the nation's health, (American Public Health Association). M. 1911. 24×18 cm. Pages 5/182. Books reviewed 7. Time lag 1 year.

L:(C)*m*3 Medical Physics, Periodical, Great Britain

92 L:(C)*m*3,N5 PHYSICS IN medicine and biology. (Hospital Physicists Association). Q. 1956. 26×18 cm. Pages 5/80. Books reviewed 5. Time lag 2 years.

L3*m*73 Medicine, Circulatory System, Periodical, USA

93 L3*m*73,N5 CIRCULATION: Devoted to clinical research and advances in cardiovascular field, (American Heart Association). M. 1950. 26×20 cm. Pages 10/190. Books reviewed 20. Time lag 1 year.

L35*m*73 Medicine, Blood, Periodical, USA

94 L35*m*73,N5 BLOOD: Journal of haematology, (American Society of Haemotology). M. 1946. 25×17 cm. Pages 3/135. Books reviewed 4. Time lag 9 months.

L4:4*m*73 Medicine, Respiratory System, Disease, Periodical, USA

95 L4:4*m*73,N1 AMERICAN REVIEW of respiratory diseases: Clinical and laboratory studies of tuberculosis and respiratory

diseases, (National Tuberculosis Association). M. 1917. 24×18 cm. Pages 3/135. Books reviewed 5. Time lag 1 year.

L7*m*3 Medicine, Nervous System, Periodical, Great Britain

96 L7*m*3,N3 JOURNAL of neurology, neurosurgery, and psychiatry, (British Medical Association). B-M. 1938. 24×21 cm. Pages 3/124. Books reviewed 8. Time lag 1 year.

L9H:4*m*3 Medicine, Tropical, Disease, Periodical, Great Britain

97 L9H:4*m*3 TROPICAL DISEASES bulletin, (Bureau of Hygiene and Tropical Diseases). M. 1912. 24×15 cm. Pages 4/100. Books reviewed 7. Time lag 6 months.

LX8*m*2 Pharmacy, Periodical, India

98 LX8*m*2,N INDIAN JOURNAL of pharmacy, (Indian Pharmaceutical Association). M. 1939. 24×18 cm. Pages 4/30. Books reviewed 3. Time lag 1 year.

LX8*m*3 Pharmacy, Periodical, Great Britain

99 LX8*m*3,M5 PHARMACEUTICAL JOURNAL, (Pharmaceutical Society). W. 1841. 28×21 cm. Pages 2/115. Books reviewed 4. Time lag 6 months.

LX8*m*73, Pharmacy, Periodical, USA

100 LX8*m*73,N1 JOURNAL OF pharmaceutical science, (American Pharmaceutical Association). M. 1910. 25×18 cm. Pages 2/90. Books reviewed 16. Time lag 1 year.

O111*m*3 Literature, English, Great Britain

101 O111*m*3,N TIMES LITERARY supplement. W. 1902. 42×25 cm. Pages 12/16. Books reviewed 90. Time lag cannot be ascertained.

P:4*m*73 Linguistics, Semasiology, Periodical, USA

102 P:4*m*73,N5 ETC: Review of general semantics, (International Society for General Semantics). Q. 1944. 18×11 cm. Pages 5/125. Books reviewed 7. Time lag 2 years.

S*m*73 Psychology, Periodical, USA

103 S*m*73,N5 CONTEMPORARY PSYCHOLOGY : Journal of reviews, (American Psychological Association). M. 1956. 26×20 cm. Pages 25. Books reviewed 30. Time lag 1 year.

SO*b*T*m*3 Psychology *biased by* Education, Periodical, Great Britain

104 SO*b*T*m*3,N3 BRITISH JOURNAL of educational psychology (British Psychological Society and the Association of Teachers in Colleges and Departments of Education). 3 issues per year. 1931. 24×21 cm. Pages 12/128. Books reviewed 16. Time lag 1 year. (List of books received is also given.)

S:(B28)*m*3 Psychology, Statistics, Periodical, Great Britain

105 S:(B28)*m*,N5 BRITISH JOURNAL of statistical psychology, (British Psychological Society). S-A. 1948. 25×18 cm. Pages 10/136. Books reviewed 8. Time lag 1 year.

T*m*3 Education, Periodical, Great Britain

106 T*m*3,N1 TIMES EDUCATIONAL supplement. W. 1910. 42×25 cm. Pages 2/48. Books reviewed 12. Time lag 3 months.

U*m*3 Geography, Periodical, Great Britain

107 U*m*3,N1 GEOGRAPHY: Journal. Geographical Association. Q. 1906. 24×16 cm. Pages 16/204. Books reviewed 28. Time lag 1 year.

U28*m*2 Meteorology, Periodical, India

108 U28*m*2,N5 INDIAN JOURNAL of meteorology, [India, Meteorological (Department)]. Q. 1950. 24×18 cm. Pages 3/137. Books reviewed 4. Time lag 1 year.

U28*m*594 Meteorology, Periodical, Switzerland

109 U28*m*594,N5 W M O BULLETIN, (World Meteorological Organisation). Q. 1952. 24×16 cm. Pages 8/60. Books reviewed 16. Time lag 9 months.

U28*m*73 Meteorology, Periodical, USA

110 U28*m*73,M3 BULLETIN, American Meteorological Society. M. 1920. 26×19 cm. Pages 2/55. Books reviewed 5. Time lag 1 year.

W*m*3 Political Science, Periodical, Great Britain

111 W*m*3,N5 POLITICAL STUDIES Journal, (Political Studies Association of the United Kingdom). 3 times a year. 1953. 22×15 cm. Pages 40/104. Books reviewed 70. Time lag 1 year.

W:19*m*3 Political Science, Foreign Policy, Periodical, Great Britain

112 W:19*m*3,N3 INTERNATIONAL AFFAIRS, (Royal Institute of International Affairs). Q. 1931. 24×16 cm. Pages 84/196. Books reviewed 69. Time lag 9 months.

X*m*2 Economics, Periodical, India

113 X*m*2,N ASIAN ECONOMIC review, (Indian Institute of Economics). Q. 1958. 24×16 cm. Pages 23/150. Books reviewed 12. Time lag 9 months.

114 X*m*2,N5 INDIAN ECONOMIC review, (Delhi School of Economics and Political Science). S-A. 195 2. 24×16 cm. Pages 30/115. Books reviewed 20. Time lag 1 year.

X*m*73 Economics, Periodical, Canada

115 X*m*72,N3 CANADIAN JOURNAL of economics and political science, (Canadian Political Association). Q. 1935. 25×16 cm. Pages 48/146. Books reviewed 50. Time lag 1 year.

X*m*73 Economics, Periodical, USA

116 X*m*73,N1 AMERICAN ECONOMIC review, (American Economic Association). 5 times a year. 1911. 24×16cm. Pages 100/350. Books reviewed 60. Time lag 1 year.

X*m*8 Economics, Periodical, Australia

117 X*m*8,N3 ECONOMIC RECORD (Economic Society of Australia and New Zealand). Q. 1925. 24×15 cm. Pages 5/122. Books reviewed 8. Time lag 1 year.

XX*m*3 Management, Periodical, Great Britain

118 XX*m*3,N3 PUBLIC ADMINISTRATION, (Royal Institute of Public Administration). Q. 1923. 24×16cm. Pages 24/124. Books reviewed 18. Time lag 1 year. (A list of books received with a short note is given.)

XX*m*73 Management, Periodical, USA

119 XX*m*73,N3 MANAGEMENT REVIEW, [American Management (Association)]. M. 1924. 22×15 cm. Pages 3/40 cm. Books reviewed 10. Time lag 6 months.

XXY*m*73 Personnel Management, Periodical, USA

120 XXY*m*73,N5 INDUSTRIAL AND LABOUR relations review, (New York State School of Industrial and Labour Relations).

Q. 1948. 25×17 cm. Pages 22/150. Books reviewed 20. Time lag 1 year.

Y*m*73 Sociology, Periodical, USA

121 Y*m*73,M9 ANNALS, American Academy of Political and Social Sciences. B-M. 1890. 23×16 cm. Pages 70/230. Books reviewed 70. Time lag 1 year.

Y:5*m*2 Demography, Periodical, India

122 Y:5*m*2,N5 POPULATION REVIEW, (Indian Institute of Population Studies). S-A. 1957. 24×18 cm. Pages 3/118. Books reviewed 4. Time lag 1 year.

Y:52:5(Y)*m*2 Family Planning, Periodical, India

123 Y:52:5(Y)*m*2,N5 JOURNAL OF family welfare: Personal, marital, and sociological, (Family Planning Association). Q. 1957. 24×17 cm. Pages 10/69. Books reviewed 12. Time lag 1 year.

Z*m*3 Law, Periodical, Great Britain

124 Z*m*3,M9 LAW QUARTERLY review. Q 1885. 25×16 cm. Pages 26/152. Books reviewed 27. Time lag 1 year.

Z1*m*3 International Law, Periodical, Great Britain

125 Z1*m*3,N5 INTERNATIONAL AND comparative law quarterly, (British Institute of International and Comparative Law). Q. 1952. 25×16 cm. Pages 29/176. Books reviewed 42. Time lag 1 year.

CHPTER KD

BIBLIOGRAPHIES

1 Economico-Bibliographical Chain

Sources for book selection should naturally consist of lists of books, including periodicals. Such lists are generally called Bibliographies. A detailed study of them has been made in part 4 of my *Reference service and bibliography*, (1940), (Madras Library Association, publication series, 9). Those who prepare bibliographies fall into the following chain if arranged in the evolutionary sequence :

1 Producers (Thought)	1 Authors
2 Producers (Material)	21 Printers
	22 Binders
	23 Governments
3 Distributors (Material)	31 Publishers
	32 Booksellers
	33 Bibliophiles
4 Distributors (Thought)	41 Book-selection agencies
	42 Library cataloguers
	43 Reference librarians
5 Consumers	51 Authors
	52 Readers

2 Kinds of Bibliographies

Corresponding to the above makers of lists we have the following bibliographies :

1 Author bibliographies ;
21 Printer bibliographies;
22 Binder bibliographies;
23 Copyright lists;

31 Publishers' catalogues;
32 Booksellers' catalogues;
33 Bibliophilic bibliographies;
41 Book selection lists;
42 Library catalogues;
43 Subject bibliographies;
51 Author's bibliographies; and
52 Reading lists.

3 Primary Bibliography

A bibliography is said to be a Primary Bibliography if the following conditions are satisfied :

1 The agency of producing it is a publisher or the copyright authority; and

2 It is prepared by a physical examination of the books included in it.

Catalogues produced collectively by all the publishers of a country — by the Publishers' Association, for example, is also a primary bibliography, if it is only an aggregate of all the publishers' catalogues as the *Reference catalogue* of Great Britain was in its earlier years.

In some countries such as the United Kingdom and India, the national bibliography replaces the copyright list. Such a national bibliography also is a primary bibliography. In Germany, the *Deutsche national bibliographie* is a primary bibliography as it is based upon a physical examination of all the German books included in it.

4 Secondary Bibliography

A Secondary Bibliography is one which does not list books at the point of its production by a physical examination of them. Except library catalogues, bibliophilic bibliographies, printer's bibliographies, and binder's bibliographies, the others might have been prepared from primary bibliographies without physical examination of books. Though printer's bibliographies and binder's bibliographies are prepared by the physical examination of books, they are not common nor much used in book selection. Therefore, the oft-used secondary bibliographies are the following :

1 Bookseller's catologue;
2 Bibliophilic bibliographies;
3 Book selection lists;
4 Library catalogues;
5 Subject bibliographies;
6 Author bibliographies; and
7 Reading lists.

There will be some time-lag between the appearance of secondary bibliographies and of the books included in them. This will detract from their value. However, some amount of judgment would have gone in their preparation. This might add to their value.

5 Value for Book Selection

While lists of any of the twelve kinds mentioned in Sec KD2 can be pressed into service for book selection the degree of their value will depend upon various factors. In *Reference service and bibliography*, I had examined the reference value of these twelve kinds of bibliographies and given the first place to subject bibliographies of an exhaustive annotated or abstracting kind published periodically at regular intervals. The second place was given to select bibliographies like book selection lists, reading lists such as those published by the National Book League of Great Britain and bibliographies furnished by authors in their own books. Library catalogues came next in order. Then followed the exhaustive national bibliographies often equivalent to copyright lists and the selective bibliographies produced as catalogues by the several book trades. The characteristics on which the book-selection-value of the twelve kinds of bibliographies may be based are :

1 Mode of arrangement of the entries ;
2 Producing agency — which is equivalent to the purpose for which produced;
3 Up-to-dateness;
4 Regularity of production; and
5 Completeness.

6 Mode of Arrangement

From the point of view of book-selection-value, the following is the sequence of preference for modes of arrangement of entries in a bibliography :

1 Minutely classified and provided with an alphabetical index ;
2 Arranged as in a dictionary catalogue ,
3 Divided into broad subject groups with alphabetical arrangement in each group ; and
4 Arranged in a single alphabetical sequence.

7 Agency of Production

From the point of view of book-selection-value the bibliographies, designated in Sec KD1 by the names of the producing agencies and correspondingly named in Sec KD2, will fall more or less in the following sequence of preference :

1 Copyright lists ;
2 Publisher's catalogues ;
3 Bookseller's catalogues ;
4 Book selection lists ;
5 Library catalogues ;
6 Subject bibliographies ;
7 Reading lists ;
8 Author's bibliographies ;
9 Author bibliographies ;
10 Bibliophilic bibliographies ;
11 Printer's bibliographies ; and
12 Binder's bibliographies.

8 Bibliography of Bibliographies

Books such as Winchill's *Guide to reference books*, Ed 7 (1951) and its supplements, Walford's *Guide to reference materials* (1959), and my *Bibliography of reference books and bibliographies*, (Madras Library Association series, 10) (1941), give lists of primary bibliographies of several countries which can be used as sources for book selection.

CHAPTER KE

NATIONAL BIBLIOGRAPHY

1 Definition

A general definition of the term "National Bibliography" is "A list of books, periodicals, and of their reprographs published in a country, or on the country, or the citizens of the country or in the language of the country, or written by any citizen of the country irrespective of the country of publication."

In the restricted sense, it may include only any one of the above five categories or any combination of them.

Though the intention is to make the list exhaustive, the policy may be to omit certain categories of publications. As publications come out continuously, a national bibliography has necessarily to be brought out in weekly, monthly, or quarterly, or other fascicules and cumulate once in a year or at other intervals. The agency of publication has been for long set up by the book trade in many countries. The present trend is to make the National Central Library or an auxilary of it as the agency for the national bibliography. This is now happening in Australia, France, India, Italy and the United Kingdom. In Germany, on the other hand, the agency is an *ad hoc* body.

11 ILLUSTRATIVE LIST

Note.

1 The entries are arranged according to Colon Classification Numbers.

2 The entries are made according to the *Classified catalogue code*, Ed 5 (1964).

***a*,12-*z*2*m*2 Generalia, Bibliography, National Bibliography, India, Periodical, India**

1 *a*,12-*z*2*m*2,N58 INDIAN NATIONAL Bibliography, [Central Reference Library (Calcutta)]. Q. 1958. M. (Since 1964).

Cumulation : Annual

Covers Indian Publications including government publications in 14 languages.

Arrangement : The bibliography has two major parts :

1 Non-government publications ; and
2 Government publications.

Each of these major parts have two sections : 1 Classified Section ; and 2 Alphabetical Section. The classified section is arranged by DC numbers. CC numbers are also given.

Each entry gives the DC number, author, title, sub-title, imprint, collation, series, and previous editions, if any, and the language of the books, and the title in the original language.

***a*,12-*z*3*m*3** **Generalia, Bibliography, National Bibliography, Great Britain, Periodical, Great Baitain**

2 *a*,12-*z*3*m*3,N5 BRITISH NATIONAL Bibliography, (Council of British National Bibliography). W. 1950.

Cumulation : 3, 6, 9 and 12 months, and five years.

Cumulation of author index every month.

Lists new publications of the week in Great Britain.

Classified arrangement by DC with an alphabetical index of author, title, and subject.

Each entry gives DC number, the name of the author, title, imprint, collation, series, and previous editions, if any.

***a*,12-*z*52*m*52** **Generalia, Bibliography, National Bibliography, Italy, Periodical, Italy**

3 *a*, 12-*z*52*m*52, N5 BIBLIOGRAPHIA NAZIONALE Italiana, (Biblioteca Nazionale Centrale). M. 1958.

***a*,12-*z*53*m*53** **Generalia, Bibliography, National Bibliography, France, Periodical, France**

4 *a*,12-*z*53*m*53,N BIBLIOGRAPHIE DE la France, (Cercle de la Librarie). W. 1911.

***a*,12-*z*55*m*55** **Generalia, Bibliography, National Bibliography, Germany, Periodical, Germany**

5 *a*,12-*z*55*m*55, N31 DEUTSCHE NATIONAL bibliographie : Gesamtverzeichnis des in Deutschland erschnienenen schrifttums und der deutschsprachigen schriften des Auslands, (Deutsche Bucherei und Borsenverein der Deutschen Bucchandler). Reihe A. W. 1931. Reihe B. F. 1931. (Formerly known as *Wochentliches verzeichnis*. 1842.)

Annual cumulation is called *Jahresverzeichnis des deutschen Schrifttum.* It is an author catalogue with a catch-word index.

Raihe A aims to list all the books published in Germany, Switzerland, Austria, and elsewhere available through trade. Reihe B lists material not available through trade — thesis, institutional publications, offprints, Government publications, such as patents etc.

Both "A" and "B" are arranged in 24 classes. Reihe "A" includes maps, but not music or art reproductions. Both "A" and "B" have author and catch-word indexes, cumulated quarterly.

a,12-*z*8*m*8 **Generalia, Bibliography, National Bibliography, Australia, Periodical, Australia**

6 *a*,12-*z*8*m*8, N7 AUSTRALIAN NATIONAL Bibliography, (National Library of Australia). A. 1962.

2 State Bibliography

The general definition of "State Bibliography" is similar to that of a "National Bibliography" except that the term "country" should be replaced by the term "Constituent State" of a country.

3 Policy for India

In a polyglot country, such as India, the listing of the publications in all the languages in a single sequence and publishing that list as a national bibliography makes the fascicules and the cumulative volumes too costly for their respective Constituent States; and in the case of the all-India languages such as English and Sanskrit, for those interested only in the publications in any one of the languages it is costly. The majority of the buyers will be interested in the publications in one language; for example, the public libraries and the general scholars in a Constituent State will belong to this category. This pattern may change slightly in a generation or two. But even then the number of languages in which the public libraries and the general scholars in a Constituent State will not exceed three or four out of the fourteen languages in which books are published in India.

It is not fair to make them all pay for an omnibus fascicule or volume listing in one sequence the publications in all the fourteen languages. Therefore, since 1947, I have been urging that each

Constituent State should produce its own State Bibliography of the publications in its own language and that an all-India agency such as the National Central Library should publish the bibliographies of the publications in English and Sanskrit, for the time being, irrespective of the State in which they are published. Then the Indian National Bibliography will consist of an ensemble of the above-mentioned State and All-India bibliographies. This will be similar to a World Bibliography consisting only of an ensemble of the national bibliographies of different countries. Even years before the *Indian national bibliography* was started, this policy has been advocated by K D Puranik and S P Phadnis in their paper *State and national bibliographies : estimate* published in the *Public library provision and documentation problems* (1951), Ed by S R Ranganathan. The above-mentioned policy would give great relief to the majority of buyers and will increase the sale of the bibliography. At the same time this policy will not add appreciably to the cost to the few scholars and to the fewer number of libraries anywhere in the world likely to be interested in the bibliography of the publications in all the fourteen languages of India. Nor will this policy in any way detract from India making an impact on other countries with regard to its annual output of publications. In other words, this will not in any way affect the promotion of cultural contact between India and other countries.

4 Current Practice in India

In 1957, India began with an omnibus National Bibliography. The disadvantages of the policy both in production and marketing were pointed out by me in my article *Indian national bibliography* (An lib sc. 4 ; 1957 ; 65-72). Subsequently, an additional cost is being incurred in the production of State Bibliographies too in addition to the omnibus bibliography covering all the languages of India.

5 Future

It is hoped that this duplication of cost will be avoided and that the policy outlined in Sec KE3 will be adopted in the future. When this is done, book selection in the libraries in India — particularly in the Public Library System will be greatly facilitated at a less cost to the nation. With this in view the Public Library Acts of the Constituent States, which have adopted library legislation, have made provision for the publication of State Bibliographies. They also make further provision for co-operation and co-ordination between the National Central Library and the different State Central Libraries in the production of such bibliographies. Under this provision it should be possible for all the fascicules and volumes, whose ensemble will form the Indian National Bibliography, to be produced in an agreed uniform, internal pattern, and external format.

6 Illustrative List

Note: 1 This is an illustrative list of State Bibliographies current in India. (*See* Sec KE2 to KE4).

2 The entries are arranged by Colon Class Numbers.

3 The entries are made according to the *Classified catalogue code*, Ed 5 (1964).

***a*,12-*z*211*m*211 Generalia, Bibliography, State Bibliography, Madras, Periodical, Madras**

1 *a*,12-*z*211*m*211,N5 Intiya Teciya nul Vivarappattiyal, Tamilppakuti, (Madras). A. 1959—

Covers books published in Tamil language.

Arrangement by Dewey Decimal Classification. Gives also Colon Class Numbers.

Six volumes, covering the period 1958-63, have been published.

***a*,12-*z*212*m*212 Generalia, Bibliography, State Bibliography, Kerala, Periodical, Kerala**

2 *a*,12-*z*212*m*212,N5 Desiya granthasuci, Malayala Vibhagam, (Kerala). A. 1958—

Covers books published in Malayalam language.

Arrangement by Decimal Classification. Gives also Colon Class Numbers.

Six volumes, covering the period 1958-63, have been published.

***a*,12-*z*213*m*213 Generalia, Bibliography, State Bibliography, Mysore, Periodical, Mysore**

3 *a*12,*z*213*m*213,N5 Rastriya granthasuci, Kannada Vibhaga, (Mysore). Q. (from 1963). 1958—

Covers books published in Kannada language.

Arrangement by Decimal Classification.

Three volumes, covering the period 1958-60, have been published.

***a*,12-*z*235*m*235** **Generalia, Bibliography, State Bibliography, Maharashtra, Periodical, Maharashtra**

5 *a*,12-*z*235*m*235,N5 RASTRIYA GRANTHASUCI, Marathi Vibhag, (Maharashtra). A. 1958—

Covers books published in Marathi language.

Arrangement by Decimal Classification. Gives also Colon Class Numbers.

Three volumes, covering the period 1958-63, have been published.

***a*,12-*z*236*m*236** **Generalia, Bibliography, Gujarat, Periodical, Gujarat**

6 *a*,12-*z*236*m*236,N5 RASTRIYA GRANTHASUCI, Gujarati Vibhag, (Gujarat). M. (from 1964 onwards). 1958—

Covers books published in Gujarathi language.

Arrangement by Decimal Classification. Gives also Colon Class Numbers.

Four volumes, covering the period 1958-65, have been published.

***a*,12-*z*243*m*243** **Generalia, Bibliography, State Bibliography, Punjab, Periodical, Punjab**

7 *a*,12-*z*243*m*243,N5 RASTRIYA PUSTAKSUCI, Punjabi Bibhag, (Punjab). A. 1958—

Covers books published in Punjabi language.

Arrangement by Decimal Classification. Gives also Colon Class Numbers.

Three volumes, covering the period 1958-62, have been published.

***a*,12-*z*252*m*252** **Generalia, Bibliography, State Bibliography, Uttar Pradesh, Periodical, Uttar Pradesh**

8 *a*12-*z*252*m*252,N5 RASTRIYA GRANTHASUCI, Hindi Vibhag (Uttar Pradesh). A. 1958—

Covers books published in Hindi language.

Arrangement by Decimal Classification. Gives also Colon Class Numbers.

Four volumes, covering the period 1958-61, have been published.

***a*,12-*z*271*m*271 Generalia, Bibliography, State Bibliography, Orissa, Periodical, Orissa**

9 *a*,12-*z*271*m*271,N5 JATIYA GRANTHASUCI, Odia Bibhaga, (Orissa). S-A. 1958—

Covers books published in Oriyan language.

Arrangement by Decimal Classification. Gives also Colon Class Numbers.

Four volumes, covering the period 1958-63, have been published.

***a*,12-*z*275*m*275 Generalia, Bibliography, State Bibliography, West Bengal, Periodical, West Bengal**

10 *a*,12-*z*275*m*275,N5 JATIYA GRANTHAPANJI, Bengali Bibhag, (West Bengal). Q. (from 1964). 1958—

Covers books published in Bengali language.

Arrangement by Decimal Classification. Gives also Colon Class Numbers.

Four volumes, covering the period 1958-64, have been published.

***a*,12-*z*277*m*277 Generalia, Bibliography, State Bibliography, Assam, Periodical, Assam**

11 *a*,12-*z*277*m*277,N5 JATIYA GRANTHASUCI, Assamiya Vibhag, (Assam). A. 1960—

Covers books published in Assamese language.

Arrangement by Decimal Classification. Gives also Colon Class Numbers.

Two volumes, covering the period 1959-61, have been published.

CHAPTER KF

TRADE CATALOGUES

Note.

1 This is a short illustrative list.

2 The entries are arranged according to Colon Classification Numbers.

3 The entries are made according to the *Classified catalogue code,* Ed 5 (1964).

***a,z*1N47*m*3 Generalia, Bibliography, Commonwealth, Periodical, Great Britain**

1 *a,z*1N47*m*3,N5 BRITISH BOOK news, (British Council and National Book League). M. 1940.

Cumulation: Index only. Covers 200 Commonwealth books each month.

Classified arrangement.

Each entry gives the name of the author, title, series, imprint, collation, price, and a short review.

List of books for children, list of "forthcoming books" for two months. A survey of the literature in a subject is also given each month.

***a,z*2 Generalia, Bibliography, India**

2 N60 IMPEX CATALOGUE: Reference catalogue of Indian books in English language giving full details about books in print in India giving full details regarding author, title, publisher, price etc. 1960.

***a,z*3*m*3 Generalia, Bibliography, Great Britain, Periodical, Great Britain**

3 *a,z*3*m*3, N TIMES LITERARY supplement. W. 1902. Devoted to book reviews only. Most of the books reviewed are British. Emphasis is mainly on general books with an apparent slant towards the humanities. Highly technical subjects are not covered. Reviews are signed and are by specialists. Special issues run into more than a hundred pages.

4 *a,z*3*m*3,N24 WHITAKER'S CUMULATIVE book index. Q. 1924.

Cumulation throughout the year, annual, and once in four years.

Covers all books published in the United Kingdom. Has separate author and title index.

Each entry gives the name of the author, title, imprint, collation, price, and class number.

5 *a,z*3*m*3,N33 BOOK SELLER, W. 1933.

Cumulation : Monthly, 6 monthly, and annual.

Covers all new publications of the week of Great Britain.

Arrangement : Alphabetical by the name of the subject.

6 *a,z*3*m*3,N35 ASLIB BOOK list. Monthly list of recommended scientific and technical books with annotation. M (since March 1948). 1935.

Covers 60 to 70 books on scientific and technical subjects.

Arrangement is by UDC Number.

The titles are graded into four categories : A Elementary, B Intermediate, C Advanced, and D Reference books. Each entry gives the name of the author, title, imprint, collation, and a short annotation.

7 *a,z*3*m*3,M67 REFERENCE CATALOGUE of current literature. 2 V. 1867 ; 1957-61 ; ed. 1962.

Coverage : British books in print.

Arrangement : By the name of the author in vol 1, with title index under each subject headings.

Published at irregular intervals.

a,z73m73 Generalia, Bibliography, USA, Periodical, USA

8 *a,z*73*m*73,N02 PUBLISHERS WEEKLY. W. 1872.

Cumulation : Title index only once in a month. Covers new American publications of the week.

Arrangement : Alphabetical by the name of the author.

Each entry gives the name of the author, title, imprint, collation, annotation. List of "forth-coming books" in January, May, September, Children's books in July.

9 *a,z*73*m*73,N05 BOOK REVIEW digest. M (except in February and July). 1905.

Cumulation : Semi-annual, annual, and five year.

Digest and index of 4,000 book reviews in 70 English and American generalist periodicals.

Arrangement : Alphabetical by the name of the author of the book reviewed with separate title and subject index.

Each entry gives, the name of the author, title, imprint, collation, price, description, annotation, and quotation, from one selected review with the name of host document and its locus. Mentions the number of words in the review and indicates whether favourable or unfavourable. Reference to other reviews is also given.

10 *a,z*73*m*73,N50 BOOKS IN print and subject guide to books in print. A. 1950.

Covers books in print of American origin.

Arrangement : By the name of the author, title, and series.

The Subject Guide lists the titles alphabetically by the name of the author under LC Subject Headings.

Gives a list of about 140 publishers with addresses.

11 *a,z*73*m*73,N56 BOOK LIST and subscription books bulletin, (American Library Association). F. V 53. 1956. (In 1956 the *Book list* and *Subscription books bulletin* were merged.)

Covers books for public libraries.

Classified by DC, with author and subject index.

Annual index for author, title, imprint, series, and collation.

Separate section lists films, forming books, children's books and governmental publications.

a,(ZP111)m73 Generalia, Bibliography, English Language, Periodical, USA

12 *a*,(ZP111)*m*73,M9 CUMULATIVE BOOK indes ; World list of scientific books in English language. M (except July, August, and December). 1898.

Cumulation once in 6 months and once in 2 years.

Covers, from 1928, every month the world publications in English. Government publications, pamphlets and ephemera are excluded.

Arrangement : By the name of the author, name of the subject, title, name of the collaborator, name of series, all in one alphabetical sequence.

Author entry gives the name of the author, title, bibliographic information, price, and the Library of Congress Card number.

A directory of publishers is also included in each issue.

CHAPTER KG

BIBLIOGRAPHIES OF REFERENCE WORKS

Note.

1 This is only a short illustrative list.

2 The entries are arranged according to Colon Classification Numbers.

3 The entries are made according to the *Classified catalogue code*, Ed 5 (1964).

***a*,(CF)*m*53 Generalia, Bibliography, Reference Work, Periodical, France**

1 *a*,(CF)*m*53,N61 BIBLIOGRAPHY, DOCUMENTATION and terminology, [Unesco, Documentation and Archives, Libraries (Division of —)]. B-M. 1961.

***a*,(CF)*m*73 Generalia, Bibliography, Reference Work, Periodical, USA**

2 *a*,(CF)*m*73,M76 LIBRARY JOURNAL, (Bowker & Co) M. 1876. (Particularly the annual compilation of technical books in the 15 May issue : Reference Issue).

3 *a*,(CF)*m*73, N14 WILSON LIBRARY bulletin. M. 1914.

***a*,(CF) Generalia, Bibliography, Reference Work**

4 N41 RANGANATHAN (S R) and SIVARAMAN (K M). Reference service and bibliography. V 2. 1941.

5 N51 WINCHELL (Constance M). Guide to reference books. Ed 7. 1951. Supplement 1 : 1950-52. 1954. Supplement 2 : 1953-55. 1956. Supplement 3 : 1956-58. 1960. Supplement 4 : 1959-61. 1963.

6 N54 SHORES (L). Basic reference sources. 1954.

7 N59 WALFORD (A J), *Ed.* Guide to reference material. 1959.

***a*, (CF)-12-*z*3 Generalia, Bibliography, Reference Work, National Bibliography, Great Britain**

8 N57 ALMAN (Miriam), *Ed.* Aslib directory : Guide to sources of information in Great Britain and Ireland. 1957. 2 V. Amendment List 1 : 1960-61. 1961.

_a_,(CF)-12-_z_4 Generalia, Bibliography, Reference Work, Asia

9 N56 GARDE (P K). Directory of reference books published in Asia. 1956.

_a_,(CF)-ZF58 Generalia, Bibliography, Reference Work, Russian

10 N62 MAICHEL (Karol). Guide to Russian reference books. 1962. V 1. General bibliographies and reference books. *Ed* by J S G Simmons. 1962.

_a_,(CF1) Generalia, Bibliography, Bibliographies

11 N41 RANGANATHAN (S R) and SIVARAMAN (K M). Reference service and bibliography. V 2. 1941.

A_a_, (CF)_m_73 Natural Sciences, Bibliography, Reference Work, Periodical, USA

12 A*a*,(CF)*m*73,N5 SCIENCE REFERENCE notes, (Columbia University, Science Libraries). Irr. 1954.

A_a_,(CF) Natural Science, Bibliography, Reference Work

13 N62 JENKINS (Frances Briggs). Science reference sources: Select list of titles for use in library in science. Ed 2. 1962.

14 N64 STERNBERG (Virginia A). How to locate technical information. 1964.

A_a_,(CF)-_z_5 Natural Sciences, Bibliography, Reference Work, Eastern Europe

15 N62 BATEELLE MEMORIAL INSTITUTE. Guide to the scientific and technical literature of Eastern Europe. 1962.

A_a_,(CF1) Natural Sciences, Bibliography, Bibliographies

16 N59 INTERNATIONAL FEDERATION FOR DOCUMENTATION (The Hague). Index bibliographicus. V 1. Science and technology. Ed 4. 1959.

B_a_,(CF) Mathematics, Bibliography, Reference Work

17 N57 PARKE (Nathan G) (III). Guide to the literature of mathematics including related works on engineering. 1957.

C_a_,(CF) Physics, Bibliography, Reference Work

18 N54 WHITFORD (Robert H). Physics literature: Reference manual. 1954.

D_a_,(CF) Engineering, Bibliography, Reference Work

19 N56 HOLMSTROM (J E). Records and research in engineering and industrial science. Ed 3. 1956.

D66*a*,(CF) Electrical Engineering, Bibliography, Reference Work

20 N59 ASSOCIATION OF SPECIAL LIBRARIES and INFORMATION BUREAU, ELECTRONICS (Group). Hand list of basic reference material for librarians and information officers in electrical and electronic engineering. 1959.

E*a*,(CF) Chemistry, Bibliography, Reference Work

21 N57 CRANE (E J), PATTERSON (A M), and MARR (E B). Guide to the literature of chemistry. Ed 2. 1957.

J*a*,(CF) Agriculture, Bibliography, Reference Work

22 N58 BLANCHARD (J Richard), and OSTVOLD (Harold). Literature of agricultural research. 1958.

23 N62 SINGHVI (M L) and SHRIMALI (D S). Reference sources in agriculture : Annotated bibliographies. 1962.

K*a*,(CF) Zoology, Bibliography, Reference Work

24 N52 SMITH (R C). Guide to the literature of the zoological sciences. Revised. 1952.

L*a*,(CF) Medicine, Bibliography, Reference Work

25 N56 DOE (Janet) and MARSHALL (M L). Handbook of medical library practice with a bibliography of reference works and histories in medicine and the allied sciences. Ed 2. 1956.

SZ*a*,(CF) Social Sciences, Bibliography, Reference Work

26 N59 HOSELITZ (Bert F), *Ed.* Reader's guide to the social sciences. 1959.

CHAPTER KH

BIBLIOGRAPHIES OF PERIODICAL PUBLICATIONS

Note :

1 The list is arranged according to Colon Classification Numbers.

2 Entries are made according to the *Classified catalogue code*, Ed 5 (1964).

***ma*'N7 Generalia, Periodical, Bibliography, 1970s**

1 N63 GREAVES (Eileen C), *Ed.* Ulrich's periodicals directory: Classified guide to a select list of current periodicals foreign and domestic. Ed 10. 1963.

***ma*,12-*z*2'N56 Generalia, Periodical, National Bibliography, India, 1956**

2 N55 NATIONAL INFORMATION SERVICE (Poona). Nifor guide to Indian periodicals, 1955-56. 1956.

3 N62 INDIA, NEWSPAPERS (Registrar of—). Catalogue of newspapers and periodicals published in India. 1962.

***ma*,12-*z*3*m*3 Generalia, National Bibliography, Great Britain, Periodical, Great Britain**

4 *ma*,12-*z*3*m*3,N5 WILLINGS PRESS guide. A. 1946/

***ma*,12-*z*3'N7 Generalia, Periodical, National Bibliography, Great Britain, 1970s**

5 N62 TOASE (Mary), *Ed.* Guide to current British periodicals. 1962.

***ma*,12-*z*73*m*73 Generalia, Periodical, National Bibliography, USA, Periodical, USA**

6 *ma*,12-*z*73*m*73,M N W AYER AND sons' directory: Newspapers and periodicals. A. 1869.

***ma*,12-*z*73Z Generalia, Periodical, National Bibliography, Latin America**

7 N55 UNESCO. Directory of current Latin American periodicals. 1958.

***ma*,2107-73*m*73** **Generalia, Periodicals, Union Catalogue, USA, Periodical, USA**

8 *ma*,2107-*z*73*m*73,N62 NEW SERIAL titles: Union catalogue of serials commencing publication after December 31, 1949, (Library of Congress) M. 1953.
(First 10-year cumulation was issued in 1962.)

***ma*,3D'N5** **Generalia, Periodical, Bibliography, Institution Catalogue, 1950s**

9 N59 UNION OF INTERNATIONAL ASSOCIATIONS. Directory of periodicals published by the international organisations. Ed 2. 1959. Brussels. (FID, publications. 162.)

***ma*,ZE2'N5** **Generalia, Periodical, Bibliography, Japanese Language, 1950s**

10 N59 JAPAN, NATIONAL DIET LIBRARY. Directory of Japanese learned periodicals. Ed 2. 1957-8. (In 3 parts.) (In English.)

A*ma*'N50<-N00 **Natural Sciences, Periodcial, Bibliography, 1900 to 1950**

11 N52 WORLD LIST of scientific periodicals published in the years 1900-1950. Ed 3. .1952. 1958.

A*ma*,12-*z*2 **Natural Sciences, Periodical, National Bibliography, India**

12 N64 INDIAN NATIONAL SCIENTIFIC DOCUMENTATION CENTRE. Directory of Indian science periodicals. 1964.

A*ma*,12-*z*42 **Natural Sciences, Periodical, National Bibliography, Japan**

13 N57 JAPAN, EDUCATION (Ministry of—). Bibliographical list of Japanese learned journals (Natural sciences). 1957.

14 N60 BONN (G). Japanese journals in science and technology: Annotated checklist. 1960.

A*ma*,12-*z*49E **Natural Sciences, Periodicals, National Bibliography, South-East Asia**

15 N55 UNESCO SOUTH-EAST ASIA SCIENCE CO-OPERATION OFFICE (Manila). Scientific and technical journals of East and South-east Asia, (Hongkong, Japan, Indonesia, Macao, Malaya, North Borneo, Philippines, Sarawak, Thailand, Vietnam). 1955.

A*ma*,12-*z*72 Natural Sciences, Periodical, National Bibliography, Canada

16 N62 NATIONAL RESEARCH COUNCIL CANADA, LIBRARY. Directory of Canadian scientific and technical periodicals. 1962.

A*ma*,12-*z*73Z Natural Sciences, Periodical, National Bibliography, Latin America

17 N62 ORGANISATION OF AMERICAN STATES. Guide to Latin American scientific and technical periodicals: Annotated list. 1962.

A*ma*,ZA111 Natural Sciences, Periodical, Bibliography, English Language

18 N63 MARTIN (Ralph C) and JETT (Wayne). Guide to scientific and technical periodicals. Select and annotated list of those published in English. 1963.

A*ma*,(9P111-142) Natural Sciences, Periodical, Bibliography, Translation, Russian to English

19 N60 NATIONAL SCIENCE FOUNDATION (USA). List of Russian scientific journals available in English. (85 cover-to-cover translations.) 1960.

C9B3*ma*'N7 Nuclear Physics, Periodicals, Bibliography, 1970s

20 N61 INTERNATIONAL ATOMIC ENERGY AGENCY (Vienna). List of periodicals in the field of nuclear energy. (STI/DDC/30. D.) 1961.

D*ma*'N5 Engineering, Periodical, Bibliography, 1950s

21 N63 ASSOCIATION OF COLLEGE AND RESEARCH LIBRARIES (USA). Recommended list of basic periodicals in engineering and engineering sciences. 1953. Chicago.

D4J*ma*'N5 Engineering, Track, Space, Periodical, Bibliography, 1950s

22 N60 RIFE (C D). Aeronautics and astronautics. World list of current periodicals. 1960.

E*ma*'N5 Chemistry, Periodical, Bibliography, 1950s

23 N62 AMERICAN CHEMICAL SOCIETY. List of periodicals abstracted by Chemical abstracts. 1962.

J1*ma*'N5 Horticulture, Periodical, Bibliography, 1950s

24 N55 SHEPHARD (S). Bibliography of current horticultural periodicals. 1955.

KX332*ma*'N5 Animal Husbandry, Fish, Periodicals, Bibliography, 1950s

25 N57 UNITED NATIONS, FOOD AND AGRICULTURAL ORGANISATION. World list of periodicals for fisheries sciences. 1957.

L*ma*'N5 Medicine, Periodical, Bibliography, 1950s

26 N61 WORLD MEDICAL ASSOCIATION. World medical periodicals. Prepared by C H A Fleurent. Ed 3. 1961.

LX*ma*'N5 Pharmacognosy, Periodical, Bibliography, 1950s

27 N44 HOCKING (G M). Serials pertaining to pharmacognosy and pharmacology. Ed 2. 1944.

CHAPTER KJ

BIBLIOGRAPHIES OF ABSTRACTING PERIODICALS

Note :

1 This is only a short illustrative list.

2 The entries are arranged by Colon Classification Numbers.

3 The entries are made according to the *Classified catalogue code*, Ed 5 (1964).

a,(CW12) Generalia, Bibliography, Abstracting Periodical

1 N59 BESTERMAN (T), *Comp.* Index bibliographicus: Directory of current periodicals, abstracts, and bibliographies. Ed 4 rev. 1959. 2 V.

a,(CW12)-12-z1N47 Generalia, Bibliography, Abstracting Periodical, National Bibliography, Commonwealth Countries

2 N49 ROYAL SOCIETY (London). A list of periodicals and bulletins containing abstracts published in Great Britain, with appendix giving partial list of journals containing abstracts published in the British Commonwealth. 1949.

Aa,(CW12) Natural Sciences, Bibliography, Abstracting Periodical

3 N63 NATIONAL FEDERATION OF SCIENCE ABSTRACTING AND INDEXING SERVICES (Washington DC). Guide to the world's abstracting and indexing services in science and technology. 1963.

Ca,(CW12) Physics, Bibliography, Abstracting Periodical

4 N50 GRAY (D E) and BRAY (R S). Abstracting and indexing services of physics interest. 1950.

Da,(CW12) Engineering, Bibliography, Abstracting Periodical

5 N55 LANDUYT (M M), *Ed.* Bibliography of engineering abstracting services. 1955.

F191a, (CW12) Metallurgy, Bibliography, Abstracting Periodical

6 N53 MOUNT (T E). Abstracting and indexing sources literature on metals and metal fabrication. 1953.

L*a*,(CW12) Medicine, Bibliography, Abstracting Periodical

7 N50 WORLD HEALTH ORGANISATION. Current indexing and abstracting periodicals in the medical and biological sciences. 1950.

CHAPTER KK

BIBLIOGRAPHIES OF TRANSLATIONS

Note :

1 This is a short illustrative list.

2 The entries are arranged by Colon Classification Numbers.

3 The entries are made according to the ***Classified catalogue code***, Ed 5 (1964).

***a*,(9P)*m*53 Generalia, Bibliography, Translations, Periodical, France**

1 *a*,(9P)*m*53,N48 INDEX TRANSLATIONUM: International bibliography of translations, (Unesco). New Series A. F. 1948.

***a*,(9P) Generalia, Bibliography, Translations**

2 N59 KAISER (Frances F), *Ed.* Translators and translations: service and sources. 1959.

***a*,(9P-28)'N60←MOO Generalia, Bibliography, Translation, From Arabic, 1800 to 1960**

3 122N62 INDEX TRANSLATIONUM arabicum. 1962. (Bibliography of works in arabic translated in foreign language between 1800 and 1960. Prepared in French.)

***a*,(9P-44)'N58-N47 Generalia, Bibliography, Translation, From Indian Languages, 1947 to 1958**

4 N63 INDIA, NATIONAL LIBRARY (Calcutta). Index translationum indicarum : Cumulation of entries for India in index translationum. Vols 2-11. Cumulated by D L Banerjee. 1963.

Lists translations from 28 languages to each one of the 16 Indian languages during the years 1947-58. There are about 2,870 entries. Entries are arranged alphabetically by the name of the languages. Under each language the arrangement is by the surnames of the original authors of the book from which translations have been made. Each entry gives,

1 Name of the author of the original document ;

2 Title of the translation followed in square brackets by the language of the translation ;

3 Name of the translator ;

4 Place of publication, name of the publishers, year of publication ;

5 Number of pages, illustrations etc, price ; and

6 Language and title of the original, in italics.

The Main Class Number of the UDC is given for each entry at its right hand top corner. There is an alphabetical list of translators at the end of each linguistic section with reference to the serial numbers of entries in that section containing information regarding the works translated by them.

There is an author index to the volume. The subject index consists of main classes of UDC.

It is a valuable tool for translated works for Indian libraries.

_a_,(CW1)-(9P111-142) Generalia, Bibliography, Periodicals, Translation, From Russian to English

5 N61 LIBRARY OF CONGRESS, REFERENCE (—Department). List of Russian serials being translated into English and other Western languages. Ed 3 rev. 1961.

A_a_,(9P111)_m_73 Natural Sciences, Bibliography, Translations, English, Periodical, USA

6 A*a*,(9P111)*m*73,N60 TECHNICAL TRANSLATIONS, [U S A, Commerce (Department of—)]. Technical Service [Office of—]. F. 1960.

A_a_,(9P111-142)_m_3 Natural Sciences, Bibliography, Translation, Russian to English, Periodical, Great Britain

7 A*a*,(9P111-142)*m*3,N5 NLL BULLETIN (National Lending Library for Science and Technology). M. 1959.

A_a_,(9P111-142)_m_53 Natural Sciences, Bibliography, Translation, Russian to English, Periodical, France

8 A*a*(9P111-142)*m*53,N60 TECHNICAL RUSSIAN literature, [Organization for Economics and Commerce Division (Paris)]. Q. 1960.

Technical literature available from the Office of Technical Service, the Library of Congress, the Special Libraries Association, co-operating foreign governments, commercial translators and publishers, universities, and other sources. The entries are arranged by subject headings. Each entry indicates, by a symbol, the place from which to order, how to order, and the price (if known). Each issue contains an author, subject, periodical, and translation number index.

C9B3*a*,(9P) Nuclear Physics, Bibliography, Translation

9 N61 STRATON (F E), *Ed.* Translation list and cross reference guide. Rev ed. 1961. Part 1 and Part 2. (United States, Atomic Energy Commission. TID-4025.) Supplement to Part 1. 1963.

This lists, by number, the translations held by the Department of Technical Information Extension up to 31 Dec, 1960. The compilation contains author, host document, and subject indexes. The Department plans to issue annual supplements.

C9B3*a*,(9P111)*m*73 Nuclear Physics, Bibliography, Translation into English, Periodical, USA

10 C9B3*a*,(9P111)*m*73,N5 NUCLEAR SCIENCE abstracts, [United States Atomic Energy Commission (Washington DC)] F. 1948.

C9B3*a*,(9P111-142)*m*5961 Nuclear Physics, Bibliography, Translation, Russian to English, Periodical, Belgium

11 C9B3*a*,(9P111-142)*m*5961,N7 TRANSATOM BULLETIN, [European Atomic Energy Community (Brussels)]. M. 1960.

Contains a list of periodicals translated from cover-to-cover. Reference to translations completed and in process are arranged under broad subject headings, similar to those used in NASA. An author index, and an original document index are given.

D4J*a*,(9P111)*m*73 Engineering, Track, Space, Bibliography, Translation into English, Periodical, USA

12 D4J*a*,(9P111)*m*73,N61 NASA TRANSLATIONS list, [National Aeronautical and Space Administration, Scientific and Technical Information (Office of—)]. Irr. 1961.

CHAPTER KL

SANSKRIT SERIES

Note. Each person may fill in pencil column 4 in his copy and bring it up-to-date from time to time.

S N	*Name of the series*	*Year of Commencement*	*Year and Number of the latest volume*
1	2	3	4
1	Advaita manjari series	1893	
2	Adyar Library series	1910	
3	Agamodaya Samiti publications	1917	
4	Allahabad University, publication, Sanskrit series	1940	
5	Ambadas Chawne Digambara Jain Granthamala or Karanjia Jain series, Karanjia	1931-32	
6	American Oriental series, American Oriental Society, New Haven, Connecticut, U S A		
7	Anandasrama Sanskrit series		
8	Ananthakirti Granthamala		
9	Asiatic Society of Bengal, bibliotheca Indica	1784	
10	Atmakamala Jain Library series, Mahavira Jain Sabha, Cambay		
11	Arnathamataprabhakara, (Bhavanipeth, Poona)		
12	Atmananda Jainagranthamala, Bhavanagar		
13	Balamanorama series, Mylapore	1927	
14	Benares Sanskrit series	1880	
15	Bharati Mandiram Sanskrit series, (Kumbhakonam)	1908-18	

S N	Name of the series	Year of Commencement	Year and Number of the latest volume
1	2	3	4
16	Bharatiya Jnana Pitha series, (Benares)		
17	Bharatiya Vidya series. Bharathiya Vidya Bhavan, (Bombay 7)		
18	Bibliotheca Buddhica	1901	
19	Bibliotheca Jainica	1917	
20	Bombay Sanskrit series	1868	
21	Buddhist Text Society (Calcutta)		
22	Calcutta Oriental series	1920	
23	Calcutta Sanskrit series	1933	
24	Calcutta University series		
25	Chowkhamba Sanskrit series (Benares)	1896	
26	Cochin Sanskrit series, Sanskrit College, Tripunittura, Cochin		
27	Collection of Hindu Law Texts: Dharmasastra-granthamala, (Bombay).	1914-24	
28	Dakshina Bharati series, (Madras)	1922-29	
29	Gaekwad's Oriental series (Baroda)	1916	
30	Gandhi Haribhai, (Devakarana Jaina Granthamala, (Calcutta)	1917	
31	Ganga Oriental series, (Bikaner).		
32	Grantharatnamala (Bombay)	1887-91	
33	Gujarat Puratatwa Mandira Granthavali, Ahmedabad 1921	1921	
34	Haridas Sanskrit series, Benares	1924	
35	Harvard Oriental series	1891	
36	Hemachandra (Acarya) Granthamala (-avali), Patna	1916-28	

S N	Name of the series	Year of Commencement	Year and Number of the latest volume
1	2	3	4
37	Indo-Iran series, Columbia University	1901	
38	International Academy of Indian Culture, Satapitaka Series, (New Delhi)		
39	Jaina Atmananda Grantharatnamala, Jaina Atmananda Sabha, (Bhavanagar)	1911-25	
40	Jaina Vividha Sahitya Sastramala, (Benares)	1916-20	
4	Jaina Dharma Prasaraka Sabha series, (Bhavanagar)		
42	Kashi Sanskrit series: Haridas Sanskrit Granthamala, (Benares)	1915-34	
43	Kashmir series of texts and studies, (Srinagar)	1911	
44	Kavyambudhi (Bangalore)	1893	
45	Kavyamala	1886	
46	Kavya Sangraha, (NS Press, Bombay)		
47	Madras Government Oriental Manuscripts Library series		
48	Madras Sanskrit series		
49	Madras University Sanskrit series		
50	Manikyacandra Digambara Jaina Granthamala, (Bombay)	1915-30	
51	Mysore Sanskrit series	1893	
52	Oriental Translation Fund, Royal Asiatic Society, London	1832	
53	Oriental Publishing Co Ltd series, (Madras)	1905	
54	Oriental Texts Society Publications, (London)	1843-48	

S N	*Name of the series*	*Year of Commencement*	*Year and Number of the latest volume*
1	2	3	4
55	Pali Text Society Chipstead, (Surrey, UK)	1882-1934	
56	Pali Text Society, Translation series (Surrey, UK)	1909-34	
57	Pandit (Benares)	1876-1920	
58	Poona Oriental series		
59	Princess of Wales Sarasvati Bhavana Benares Studies, Texts	1922	
60	Punjab Sanskrit series	1921	
61	Rajasthan Puratan Granthamala, The Rajasthan Oriental Research Institute, (Jodhpur)	1951	
62	Raya Dhanapati (or Dhanapata) Sinha Bhadurka Agama Sangraha, (Benares)	1880	
63	Sacred Books of the East	1879	
64	Sacred Books of the Hindus, (Leipzig)	1907	
65	Sacred Books of the Jainas (Lucknow)		
66	Sacred Books of the Jainas, Central Jaina Publishing House, (Arrah)		
67	Samskrita Sahitya Parishat series, (Calcutta)	1922	
68	Saradakridangranthamala, (Bombay)	1890-1901	
69	Seth Devchand Lalbhai Jain Pustakoddhar Fund series, (Bombay)	1911-32	
70	Scindia Oriental series, (Conjeevaram)		
71	Sastramukthavali series, (Conjeevaram)		

S N	Name of the series	Year of Commencement	Year and Number of the latest volume
1	2	3	4
72	Sanatana Jaina Granthamala, (Benares)		
73	Singhi Jaina Granthamala (formerly from Calcutta, now from Bharatiya Vidya Bhavan, Bombay 7)		
74	Tanjore Saraswati Mahal Library series		
75	Tantric Texts series, Ed by Arthur Avalan	1913	
76	Tibetan Sanskrit Works series, K P Jayaswal Research Institute, Patna		
77	Trivandrum Sanskrit series	1904	
78	Vanivilas Sanskrit series, (Srirangam)	1905	
79	Sri Venkateswara Oriental series, (Tirupati)		
80	Venkateswara Steam Press, (Bombay)		
81	Varendra Research Society, Rajshahi Gauda Granthamala; Savitarai Smritisamrakshana Granthamala	1913	
82	Visistadvaita Vaijayanti series, (Kumbhakonam)		
83	Vizianagaram Sanskrit series	1888	
84	Yasoivjaya Jaina Granthamala	1905	

PART L

ROUTINE OF BOOKS SELECTION

CHAPTER LA

INTRODUCTION

1 Administrative Routine

Parts D to J were on the theory of Book Selection. Part K contained a sample of the sources for book selection. The administrative routine of book selection remains to be described. This is part of general library administration. In the approach to library administration from the side of reading materials, book selection is the first section met with. Therefore, the Book Selection section comes at the very beginning of my *Library administration*, Ed 2 (1959). In order to make this book complete in regard to everything about Book Selection, the relevant sections of that book are extracted here.

2 Theory of Administration

This Part includes also extracts from the Theory of Administration or Scientific Management occupying the first part of that book and forming the framework for each of its other parts.

CHAPTER LB

PRODUCTIVITY IN ADMINISTRATION

1 Inter-Dependence

To be successful and to increase productivity, administration should be characterised by *Ekavakyata* (= Unity). The work of all the Sections in a library should cohere. No Section can model itself or change its routine, records, or time-table without affecting all the other Sections. The organisation of the Book Selection Section of a library should therefore be designed in integral relation with the other Sections. Chapter LG will illustrate the intimate points of contact between the Book Selection Section and the various other sections.

2 Job Analysis

To rationalise administrative routine, a system of job analysis has been laid down in my *Library administration.* There is an advantage in applying that system to the Book Selection Section also. In this system the various factors of book selection are first isolated. Then the items of work belonging to each factor are enumerated. Then a search is made for the jobs involved in each item of work. This is first done on the basis of their period of recurrence. It is helpful to recognise the following periodical groups among jobs :

1	Immediate	5	Weekly
2	Hourly	6	Monthly
3	Casual	7	Quarterly
4	Daily	8	Annual

Thereafter, each job in each periodical group is isolated. A name is given to each job. An analytico-expressive Job Number is also devised for each job. This notational device has been of immense help in making Job Analysis thorough, systematic, and not too exacting. Here is an example of a Job Number 2 : 2 : 58. This number is divided into three facets by the two intervening connecting digits, *viz,* colons. The first facet represents the Factor to which the job relates. The second facet represents the Item of Work to which the job relates. And the third facet represents the Ultimate Job. By a "job" is meant an ultimate piece of work which is best done at a single stretch and whose duration is ordinarily short. The mnemonic nature and the penetrating capacity of the Job Number can be seen by a systematic interpretation of the example given above.

2 : 2 : 58 = Book selection card filing
where 2 is the factor number ;
: indicates change of facet ;
2 is work number ;
: indicates change of facet ;
5 is period number ; and
8 is job number.

2 = The factor "Selection" to which the job relates ;
2 : 2 = Book Selection Carding Work ;
2 : 2 : 5 = Weekly jobs in Book Selection Carding Work ;
2 : 2 : 58 = The job : Book Selection Card Filing

It will take us too far into the theory of classification if we attempt to explain the mnemonic use of the digits in the above Job Number.

Chapter LD gives the job analysis for the work of the Book Selection Section. It may be remarked that in the *Library administration,* book selection occurs as Chapter 1 and so the Job Number begins in that book with 1 : 2 instead of 2 as it does here.

3 Routine

By "routine" is meant those duties of a regular and repetitive nature that are requisite for administrative purposes. The routine is described in the light of experience. Scientific Management requires that the Head of the library should devote his full thought to job analysis and write out the routine for every job, bearing in mind the various operational and mental factors involved. While it is the librarian's duty to give a detailed working paper, it is the duty of the staff to carry it out faithfully.

31 Promptness

The time-table for the performance of different jobs should be strictly observed. Any slackness at any point is likely to affect many other Sections and to result ultimately in delay in serving the public.

32 NEATNESS OF WRITING

Slovenly handwriting and execution should be avoided. The lines should be properly directed. They should be invariably parallel to the edges of the slips, cards, or sheets, as the case may be. It is irritating to find lines making all angles with the edges.

33 ACCURACY

Work must be accurate. Even a small inaccuracy in writing the heading or title of a book will create a situation demanding protracted work to discover and set right the inaccuracy at a later stage. A most trivial mistake in the spelling of the name of an author may lead to unintended duplication of a book.

34 ORDERLINESS

As book selection will require the handling of thousands of loose slips, orderliness of the highest degree should characterise routine work. The loose card system of maintaining records reduces a certain related group of routine work by about 75 per cent. Any apparatus so highly evolved and efficient is bound to be extremely delicate. Without the greatest care and orderliness, confusion and chaos will result.

35 DESCRIPTION AND ENUMERATION

Chapter LE describes in detail the routine of every job in Book Selection, enumerated in Chapter LD. But for the second digits being 2 and 3 respectively, the numbers of the corresponding sub-sections of these two chapters will be similar.

4 Elimination of Waste

Scientific Management requires that every possible care must be taken to eliminate waste — in human personality, mental energy, and physical energy ; and in materials, space, and time. The first step in the elimination of waste is to detect wasteful processes in routine and to re-design the routine suitably.

41 DIARY

A method of detecting wastage is to keep accurate records of turnover in every class of work. The daily diary should be cumulated to the weekly one and the weekly diary to the monthly one, and so on. These diaries must be scrutinised by the librarian or his deputy daily, weekly, monthly, etc. The data given will, by themselves and/or when compared with the corresponding figures of the past, indicate the points needing investigation in order to stop wastage, or a re-design of routine. Chapter LF gives the diaries.

42 Simplification and Standardisation

A method of eliminating wastage is simplifying and standardising every material used and every operation involved in the various jobs. The use of unit card (one book, one card) for Book Selection Work and converting it successively into order-card and accession card and the designing of the readings printed on it to suit such a use has eliminated waste to a considerable extent.

43 Pick-up-Work

A still another method of eliminating wastage is to fill up unavoidable vacant intervals in working hours of the members of the staff by a system of pick-up-work. For example, the counter staff can be asked to write book selection cards as pick-up-work.

44 Photo-routine

The *Library administration* (1935) suggested methods of elimination of waste of man-hours by standardised and simplified methods of operation, rationally planned time-scheme, and properly designed forms and registers. During recent years, gadgets have been designed so as to mechanise the manual labour involved in routine. These gadgets involve the use of electronics, electricity, and photography. To standardise and simplify the methods of operation so as to get the maximum benefit from such gadgets a re-designing of forms and registers will be necessary. I saw them in use in the Library of the Department of Agriculture of the United States of America in 1948. When S Parthasarathy and myself again visited that library in 1950, Ralph Shaw, its librarian, showed us the further progress made and the draft-copy of a book he was writing on the use of gadgets to eliminate waste in the routine of all the Sections of a library. Parthasarathy has shown me the notes he took when he again visited the library later. Here are some extracts from his notes.

45 Main Aspects of Mechanisation

1 Substitution of machine for manual operations without changes in procedure.

2 Revision of procedures to take full advantage of the new mechanism.

A sum of about Rs 85,000 was saved per year by the Library of the Department of Agriculture merely by substituting photographic copying for manual copying and revising.

Saving in binding records. Old procedure used to handle 800 volumes per man-year. New procedure handles 4,300 volumes per man-year. Change from manual to photo-copy saved about Rs 2,000 per year.

46 Time and Cost Studies

Time and cost studies should be made before and after introducing new techniques.

47 Technique

Information is to be duplicated on 125×75 mm slips. Various types of masks are used for copying the required information and for including additional information. The photo-copying method is used by the Department of Agriculture Library in 34 processes. 500 copies per hour can be taken by this method (as against 20 per hour by typing).

L-shaped mask
Name of Source of Information typed on a slip and placed on the mask

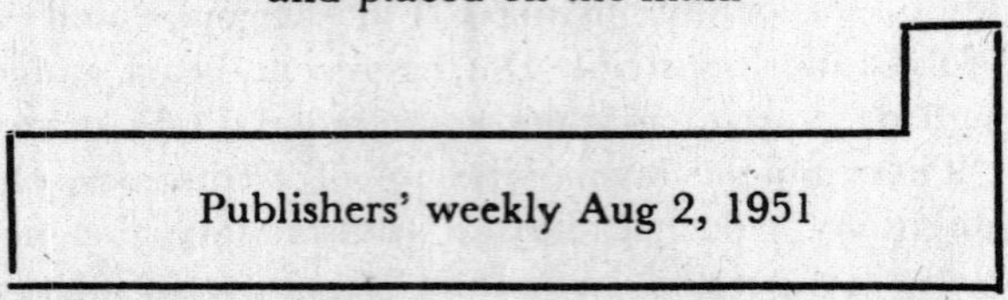

48 Comparative Costs for a Load of 3,000 copies per year :

Manual Procedure		*Photographic Procedure*	
	Rs		Rs
Typing 20 per hour		Exposing 180 per hour	
150 hrs @ Rs 7	1,050	17 hrs @ Rs 6	102
Slips Rs 4 per 1000	12	Paper, developing & cutting	
		@ Rs 0.27 per exposure	80
Actual cost	1,062	Actual cost	182
Add overhead	106	Add overhead	18
Total	1,168	Total	200

Saving Rs 968 per year

481 CONDITIONS FOR SAVING

The annual quantum of work should be sufficient to off-set the capital equipment and its annual obsolescence taken together.

5 Correlation

Every section in a library will have to do with most of the other sections. Chapter LG tabulates the various jobs, involved in Book Selection, bringing the Book Selection Section into relation with the other Sections of the library.

6 Time Scheme

Time is the canvas on which every administrative picture has to be drawn. The canvas is limited. If a library attempts to fulfil the first three Laws of Library Science, it has to face a perpetual time-famine. One of the means of meeting time-famine is to draw up a careful time-table for every job on an hourly, daily, weekly, monthly, and annual basis and not to depend upon a fortuitous adjustment of time from moment to moment. Generally speaking, except in circulation work, the week is the most convenient unit of time. It is particularly so in Book Selection Work. In fact, it will be found that most of the jobs given in Chapter LD are weekly jobs. There are, however, necessarily a few daily, monthly, and annual jobs. Chapter LH gives a model time-table for Book Selection Work. There are certain junction moments in which the Book Selection Work will have to meet the work of other Sections. Unless the time-table of the Section is adhered to within limits of tolerance, the junction moments will be thrown out of gear.

CHAPTER LC

PLANNING

1 Weekly Rhythm

It has been shown in my *Five laws of library science* that considerable economy can be effected by planning most of the work of a library on a weekly basis. It must be remembered that this weekly pulse has to be generated in the Book Selection Section. It is only if the Book Selection Section starts the pulse according to the time-table, the pulse of work can move forward through all the Sections and new books can reach the readers' hands every week without fail. It is wasteful and clumsy to do book selection by fits and starts. It will kill the rhythm of work in the entire library if some weeks are left fallow in the Book Selection Section and other weeks are over-crowded. Announcements about books released by the trade in the course of the week should be carefully scanned and the preliminary selection work should be completed each week without fail. A scheme should be worked out for spreading out the preparation of indents throughout the 52 weeks in the year.

11 Unit Card Principle

It has been shown in the *Five laws of library science* that considerable economy can be effected by writing book selection cards on the "unit card principle" — one title, one card — and pushing that card on into the Order Section along with the sanctioned indents, for use as order cards, and finally into the Accession Section to form the permanent accession register.

12 Effect on Appropriation

Finance too will be better appropriated if indents are prepared on a weekly basis. The wasteful, embarrassing, and ugly habit of leaving money unappropriated for weeks without end and spending it somehow at the end of the financial year, will be fatal to the usefulness of the library.

2 Sources for Book Selection

The sources for book selection are varied. Suggestions can be got not only from the trade lists and National and State Bibliographies, but also from the bibliographies and reviews occurring in books and periodicals. The suggestions from the reading public form another possible source, although this source is likely to be of uneven merit. The Reference Section, the Shelf Section, and the Circulation Section can give much help in this matter.

3 Experts for Help

It should not be presumed that the entire evaluation of Selection can be done by the library itself. It will be a good policy to have the help of experts in different subjects in making the Selection. But, the whole work of selection should not be shifted to experts. The library alone will have access to the greatest number of sources. Therefore, most of the work should be done by the library, leaving the minimum possible work to be done by the experts.

4 Financial Responsibility

Finance is an ultimate deciding factor in the selection of books. No library is likely to have unlimited funds to buy everything published — or even to buy all the most worthwhile publications. Hence, the greatest care is to be exercised in spending the sum available for books. To see that the budget is not exceeded on the one hand and that, on the other, no amount is left unspent at the end of the financial year, the Book Selection Section should exercise the greatest vigilance possible and work hand in hand with the Book Order Section, the Periodical Publication Section, and the Accounts Section. It is also the duty of the Book Selection Section to see that the book fund is distributed in proper proportion among the different subjects in the light of legitimate local demand and that no particular subject usurps far more than its proper share, simply because it happens to be sponsored, for the time being, by an influential person or clique.

5 Subject Cycles

It will help the symmetrical building up of the stock of the library and add to the systematisation of the work of this Section and of the other Sections if the book resources to be added to the library annually in the different subjects are taken up for treatment in systematic cycles. The periodicity for each subject should be adjusted from time to time in the light of supply and demand and with a view to spreading the work of the Section evenly over the different weeks of the year.

6 Factors in Planning

The distinctive work of the Book Selection Section is to be planned with reference to the following factors:

1 Sources;
3 Selection;
5 Indent; and
6 Finance.

CHAPTER LD

JOB ANALYSIS

1 Sources

The work of the Book Selection Section relating to sources in general may consist of the following items :

2 Acquiring the sources for book selection by purchase, or donation, or exchange, which may be referred to as *Sources Acquiring Work* ; and

8 Arranging the sources of book selection, which may be referred to as *Sources Arranging Work.*

1 : 2 Sources Acquiring Work

1 : 2 : 1 Sources Acquiring Work is to consist of the following *immediate jobs* :

1 As and when the names of useful sources for book selection come to notice, jotting down the necessary particulars, which may be referred to as *Sources Noting* ; and

2 As and when specific books of probable interest to the library are brought to notice, jotting down the necessary particulars about them, which may be referred to as *Suggestion Noting.*

1 : 2 : 5 Sources Acquiring Work is to consist of the following *weekly job* :

2 Sending requisition for sources of book selection, which may be referred to as *Sources Requisitioning.*

1 : 8 Sources Arranging Work

1 : 8 : 5 Sources Arranging Work is to consist of the following *weekly job* :

8 Arranging the sources of book selection, as they are received from time to time, in a systematic manner on the sources shelf, which may be referred to as *Sources Shelving.*

1 : 8 : 8 Sources Arranging Work is to consist of the following *annual job* :

8 Weeding out the out-of-date sources from the sources shelf, which may be referred to as *Sources Weeding.*

2 Selection

The work of the Book Selection Section relating to Selection in general may consist of the following items of work :

1 Selecting from the different sources the items worth consideration by the experts in the different subject-fields, which may be referred to as *Book Selection Work* ;

2 Writing out Book Selection Cards for the items selected, which may be referred to as *Book Selection Carding Work* ; and

5 Forwarding Book Selection Cards and other references to experts for an expression of their opinion or for facilitating the preparation of indent, which may be referred to as *Book Selection Consultation Work.*

2 : 1 BOOK SELECTION WORK

2 : 1 : 3 Book Selection Work is to consist of the following *casual job* :

1 Marking in the sources the items worth being sent up for consideration by the experts in the different subject-fields, which may be referred to as *Preliminary Selection* ; and

8 Checking the marked items with the stock in the library, which may be referred to as *Preliminary Checking.*

2 : 1 : 5 Book Selection Work is to consist of the following *weekly jobs* :

1 Forwarding the marked sources for the consideration of the librarian, which may be referred to as *Marked Sources Forwarding.*

2 : 2 BOOK SELECTION CARDING WORK

2 : 2 : 3 Book Selection Carding Work is to consist of the following *casual jobs* :

1 Writing out Book Selection Card for each of the approved items, which may be referred to as *Book Selection Card Writing* ;

5 Tentatively classifying each Book Selection Card, which may be referred to as *Book Selection Card Classifying* ; and

7 Filling up the bibliographical gaps in the Book Selection Cards, which may be referred to as *Book Selection Card Completing.*

2 : 2 : 5 Book Selection Work is to consist of the following *weekly jobs* :

1 Comparing and verifying the entries in the Book Selection Cards with the sources, which may be referred to as *Book Selection Card Revising* ; and

8 Filing the revised Book Selection Cards in the Selected Cards Tray, which may be referred to as *Book Selection Card Filing.*

2 : 5 Book Selection Consultation Work

2 : 5 : 4 Book Selection Consultation Work is to consist of the following *daily job* :

5 When the acquisition of a book has to be urgently considered, sending a reference to the expert concerned and asking for his advice, which may be referred to as *Urgent Book Selection Consulting.*

2 : 5 : 5 Book Selection Consultation Work is to consist of the following *weekly jobs* :

1 Forwarding the accumulated Book Selection Cards to the experts concerned asking for their recommendations, which may be referred to as *Book Selection Card Forwarding* ;

3 Making a list of the approved items, which may be referred to as *Indent Copying* ; and

8 Sorting the Book Selection Cards returned by the experts and disposing of the cards not recommended, which may be referred to as *Unrecommended Card Filing.*

3 Indents

The work of the Book Selection Section relating to indents in general may consist of the following items of work :

1 Scrutinising the indents for books received from the experts or the authorities concerned, which may be referred to as *Indents Scrutinising Work* ; and

3 Getting the necessary sanction for the indents, which may be referred to as *Indents Passing Work.*

3 : 1 Indents Scrutinizing Work

3 : 1 : 5 Indents Scrutinising Work is to consist of the following *weekly jobs* :

1 Checking the indents received with the stock, the order tray, and the bills on hand, which may be referred to as *Indents Checking* ;

23 Preparing Book Selection Cards for such of those items in the checked indent as have not been already carded, which may be referred to as *Supplemental Book Selection Carding* ;

25 Tentatively classifying the Supplemental Book Selection Cards, which may be referred to as *Supplemental Book Selection Card Classifying*;

27 Filling up the bibliographical gaps in the Supplemental Book Selection Cards, which may be referred to as *Supplemental Book Selection Card Completing*;

28 Merging the Supplemental Book Selection Cards with the Book Selection Cards already existing in relation to the indents concerned, which may be referred to as *Supplemental Book Selection Card Merging*;

4 Clearing up doubts and difficulties in consultation with the experts concerned, which may be referred to as *Indents Doubts Clearing.*

5 Obtaining information about the cost of the items wherever necessary, which may be referred to as *Cost Ascertaining*; and.

6 Estimating the cost of the indents, which may be referred to as *Indents Estimating.*

3 : 3 INDENTS PASSING WORK

3 : 3 : 5 Indents Passing Work is to consist of the following *weekly jobs*:

1 Preparing the necessary notes for the sanctioning authority, which may be referred to as *Indent Noting*;

11 Forwarding the indents to the sanctioning authority, which may be referred to as *Indent Forwarding*;

2 Passing the sanctioned indents on to the Order Section, which may be referred to as *Sanctioned Indent Forwarding*; and

8 Taking the necessary action on such of the items of the forwarded indents as have not received the sanction of the authority concerned, which may be referred to as *Rejected Items Disposing.*

6 Finance

The work of the Book Selection Section relating to finance in general may consist of the following items of work:

6 Taking the necessary steps to fix the annual allotment for books and periodicals in different subject-fields, which may be referred to as *Allotment Work*; and

7 Advising the experts responsible for the preparation or approval of indents for books about the financial position in regard

to the different subject-fields from time to time, which may be referred to as *Allotment Watching Work.*

6 : 6 ALLOTMENT WORK

6 : 6 : 8 Allotment work is to consist of the following *annual jobs* :

1 Ascertaining from the expert advisers in different subjects if they desire to have any change in the annual allotment to their respective subjects, which may be referred to as *Expert Opinion Obtaining* ;

22 Estimating the cost of the indents awaiting ordering in each subject-field, which may be referred to as *Arrear Indents Estimating* ;

23 Estimating the cost of Outstanding Orders for ordinary books in each subject-field, which may be referred to as *Outstanding Orders Estimating* ;

24 Estimating the probable cost of Standing Orders of various kinds in each subject-field, which may be referred to as *Standing Orders Estimating* ;

3 Ascertaining from the Periodical Publications Section the probable cost of the current periodical publications in each subject-field, which may be referred to as *Periodical Publications Subscription Estimating* ;

6 Ascertaining from the Finance Section the total Book Fund likely to be sanctioned for the year, which may be referred to as *Budget Ascertaining* ;

7 Ascertaining from the Accounts Section the Actual Expenditure on books and periodical publications in each subject-field, for each of the three preceding years, which may be referred to as *Actuals Ascertaining* ;

8 Preparing in the light of the data obtained by the foregoing routines, the Schedule of Allotment for the different subject-fields, which may be referred to as *Preliminary to Allotment* ; and

91 Forwarding the Schedule of Allotment to the sanctioning authority and obtaining the necessary sanction, which may be referred to as *Allotment Sanctioning.*

6 : 7 ALLOTMENT WATCHING WORK

6 : 7 : 7 Allotment Watching Work is to consist of the following *quarterly jobs* :

The jobs under this section will be similar to the annual jobs 22, 23, and 24 under 6 : 6 Allotment Work and in addition the following :

3 Ascertaining from the Periodical Publications Section the annual subscription that will have to be incurred during the current financial year on any new periodical that might have been sanctioned in the year, which may be referred to as *New Periodicals Cost Ascertaining*.

7 Ascertaining from the Accounts Section the actual expenditure on books during the current financial year, which may be referred to as *Spent Amount Ascertaining*.

8 Advising the experts in the different subject-fields, about the amount remaining unappropriated, which may be referred to as *Allotment Balance Advising*.

6 : 7 : 8 Allotment Watching Work is to consist of the following *annual job* :

1 Advising the expert in each subject-field, about the Annual Allotment for the subject-field, which may be referred to as *Allotment Advising*.

CHAPTER LE

ROUTINE

1 Source

1 : 2 SOURCES ACQUIRING WORK

1 : 2 : 1 *Immediate jobs*

1 : 2 : 11 Sources Noting

The Book Selection Section is likely to come across information regarding sources that may be of use in Book Selection Work at any moment. This may happen either in the course of the section's systematic perusal of the printed materials, or in their conversation or correspondence with persons or bodies competent to give advice in the matter. It may even happen in a very unexpected and unusual way while engaged in some other work. As soon as the information is spotted out, note down all the necessary particulars as far as they may be available with regard to the source that should be acquired to aid book selection. It will be convenient to use a *Source Selection Slip* with similar headings as the book selection card for noting down the particulars. File all such source slips in the *Source Slips Tray* in a classified sequence on the basis of the subject to which the source relates.

1 : 2 : 12 Suggestion Noting

Books of probable interest to the library are likely to be brought to the notice of the Book Selection Section either by the other sections of the library or by the users of the library or when the Book Selection Section peruses different books and periodicals.

When the suggestion reaches the Book Selection Section, prepare a *Book Selection Card* for it and file it in the *Suggestion Tray*, in the classified sequence.

1 : 2 : 5 *Weekly jobs*

1: 2 : 52 Sources Requisitioning

On the appointed day of the week, pick out from the source slips tray the outstanding source slips and send requisition to the appropriate party for the supply of the source.

1 : 8 Sources Arranging

1 : 8 : 5 *Weekly jobs*

1 : 8 : 58 Sources Shelving

On the appointed day of the week, insert all the sources of book selection received in the course of the week, in the appropriate places in the *Sources Shelf*. While shelving a source, if there is an earlier edition or copy of it, weed that out.

It will be convenient to have the following three characteristics for the classified arrangement of the sources :

1 Subject ;
2 Vendor or publisher, as the case may be ; and
3 The date of the source.

These characteristics may be taken in the sequence given.

A result of this will be that on the sources shelf all the source materials relating to a specified subject will be found together. Among the sources relating to a specified subject, all those issued by a specific vendor or publisher will be found together and arranged chronologically in the order of the date of issue.

As book selection will have to proceed subject by subject, it can be easily seen that this is the most convenient arrangement for shelving the sources :

1 : 8 : 8 *Annual job*

1 : 8 : 88 Sources Weeding

At the appointed time each year, scrutinise the sources shelf carefully and weed out all unwanted materials.

The sources for book selection accumulate in a library at a very rapid rate. They also grow out of date with equal rapidity. If the weeding out is not done systematically, one is likely to be snowed down by useless rubbish and the sources shelf may prove to be an obstruction rather than a help.

2 Selection

2 : 1 BOOK SELECTION WORK

2 : 1 : 3 *Casual jobs*

2 : 1 : 31 Preliminary Selection

Mark in pencil in the source for book selection each item that in your opinion deserves consideration by the experts who help the library in book selection work. The marking should be done as follows :

Guess the main subject of the item and put in the left hand margin opposite to the heading of the item the digit symbol for the main subject and any additional digits of which you are reasonably certain.

2 : 1 : 38 Preliminary Checking

Take each of the marked sources in hand and check the marked items with the library catalogue as well as the book selection cards in the selected cards tray and the order tray. Score out the items that are already represented in the library catalogue or in the selected cards tray or in the order tray.

2 : 1 : 5 *Weekly jobs*

2 : 1 : 51 Marked Sources Forwarding

On the appointed day of the week, forward to the Librarian all the marked sources which have been preliminarily checked.

2 : 2 Book Selection Carding Work

2 : 2 : 3 *Casual jobs*

2 : 2 : 31 Book Selection Card Writing

As soon as the marked sources are received from the librarian, write out a *Book Selection Card* for each of the items approved by him.

Use the library hand for writing the book selection card. Remember in particular that the book selection card written by you is going to be transformed successively into the indent card, order card, and accession card and that the last forms a permanent record of the library.

Give in the left hand bottom corner of the book selection card the exact reference to the source from which the book is selected, *e.g.* PC (meaning *Publisher's circular*) V 38, P 55.

2 : 2 : 35 Book Selection Card Classifying

As far as can be judged by the title, author and review notes, if any, found in the book selection card, classify the book as closely as possible and enter in pencil the class number in the appropriate place in the book selection card. Whenever necessary, consult the technical section.

2 : 2 : 37 Book Selection Card Completing

If the necessary bibliographical details are not to be found in the source, secure them from any other available source and make the book selection card as complete as possible.

2 : 2 : 5 *Weekly jobs*

2 : 2 : 51 Book Selection Card Revising

On the appointed day of the week, take out all the book selection cards written and completed in the week and compare the entries with the sources from which they were taken. Carry out all the corrections found necessary.

2 : 2 : 58 Book Selection Card Filing

As soon as the revision work is over, insert the cards in the *Selected Cards Tray* in the appropriate classified sequence. While inserting a card, if a card is already found for a particular book take away and score out the card which is less full in details.

2 : 5 Book Selection Consultation Work

2 : 5 : 4 *Daily jobs*

2 : 5 : 45 Urgent Book Selection Consulting

The routine for this job is similar to the routine given in 2 : 5 : 5, except that it will have to be done urgently.

2 : 5 : 5 *Weekly jobs*

2 : 5 : 51 BOOK SELECTION CARDS FORWARDING

On the appointed day of the week, pick out, from the selected cards tray and the deferred cards tray, the book selection cards pertaining to the subject or subjects which fall due to be dealt with in the week in the light of the suggestions contained in the introduction to this chapter and forward them to the experts who help the library in book selection work. In the forwarding letter, mention the number of cards sent, the amount allotted to the subject for expenditure within the year, the amount already spent, the amount still unspent and an estimated cost of the items included in the book selection cards sent. Request the experts to sort the book selection cards into three groups, as "approved", "rejected" and "deferred". If necessary, mention also the date by which the reply is expected. A more satisfactory practice will be to persuade the experts to call at the library and get the work done jointly by the expert and the librarian.

2 : 5 : 53 Indent Copying

Sort the cards in the approved group by the main subjects. Separate out the cards that require standing order, prepayment etc. Sort the remaining cards pertaining to a specific main subject by the standing vendor with whom the order is to be placed so far as can be ascertained from the book order section. Arrange the cards in each vendor group alphabetically using the heading as the basis. After the arrangement is over, send them to the correspondence section for the indents to be typed. It will be an advantage to get four copies to be typed. One copy is to be used as the indent, the second as the order, the third as the office copy of the order and the fourth for the file of the reference section.

2 : 5 : 58 Unrecommended Cards Filing

As soon as the cards come back from the experts, file the deferred cards in the appropriate classified sequence in the selected cards tray and file the rejected cards in the appropriate classified sequence in the rejected cards tray. If the expert had not already sorted the cards as desired but had merely noted on the cards his opinion, the cards will have to be sorted out into the three groups as a preliminary step before the unrecommended cards are filed.

It is a matter for consideration whether the finally rejected cards may not be straight away destroyed. But experience shows that it may be helpful to preserve them for some time and pass them on to other libraries which are less organised and seek our help in book selection work. If, however, there is no chance for this, the rejected cards may be destroyed periodically, say, once in a year.

3 Indents

3 : 1 Indents Scrutinising Work

3 : 1 : 5 *Weekly jobs*

3 : 1 : 51 Indent Checking

On the appointed day of the week, check each indent received in the week carefully with the catalogue, the order tray, and the bills on hand awaiting payment. Check each item not only with reference to the heading but also with reference to the title, if it is one that is likely to have received a title entry. Check also with reference to the series entry, if the book belongs to a series. Check also the names of translator, editor, etc, and in every other possible way to see that no item is unnecessarily duplicated ; in cases of doubt go to the shelf and examine such of the books as you have reasons to suspect might have been wrongly entered in the indent. If, in your opinion an attempt should be made for securing any item as a donation, put the letter "G" against it. If any item raises issues which cannot be settled without a reference to the expert, put the letter "E" against it. Score out the items which are not wanted. As soon as the checking is over, write the word "checked" at the left hand bottom corner of the last sheet of the indent, initial and date it.

3 : 1 : 523 Supplemental Book Selection Carding, etc.

Supplemental book selection process : The routines for these jobs are similar to the routines of the corresponding jobs given under 2 : 2 Book Selection Carding Work.

3 : 1 : 54 Indents Doubts Clearing

On the appointed day of the week, scrutinise the indents checked in the week and refer all the items against which the letter "E" has been put to the expert concerned setting forth clearly the issues that require to be examined by the expert and asking for a definite decision by him.

3 : 1 : 55 Cost Ascertaining

If against any of the items in the indent, the cost is not given, write to the publisher or vendor, as the case may be, asking for a quotation. In some cases the cost may be estimated and the further work with the indent may be taken on hand. In cases where the cost is likely to be very high or the cost is likely to go beyond the amount allotted for the subject, it is desirable that the cost is ascertained before further action is taken.

3 : 1 : 56 Indent Estimating

After all the processes that are mentioned under indents scrutinsing work are over, estimate the cost of the indents as closely as possible and write the figure in pencil opposite to the word "checked" at the bottom of the last sheet of the indent. The estimate should be given both in foreign and local currency to facilitate the work of the ordering section.

3 : 3 Indents Passing Work

3 : 3 : 5 *Weekly Jobs*

3 : 3 : 51 Indent Noting

On the appointed day of the week, for each of the scrutinised indents, prepare an indent note, filling up all the columns as fully as possible, taking care to get the exact amount already spent in the subject and the estimated cost of the outstanding orders from the accounts section and the order section respectively.

As soon as the notes are filled up, forward it to the librarian for his approval and remarks, if any.

3 : 3 : 511 Indent Forwarding

On the appointed day of the week, collect all the indents on which notes have been prepared in the week, including the urgent indents also, if any. Arrange them in the sequence of the subjects and forward them to the Committee Section for inclusion in the papers that are to be sent up to the sanctioning authority during the week.

3 : 3 : 52 Sanctioned Indent Forwarding

On the appointed day of the week, take up each of the sanctioned indents received from the Committee Section and deal with it as follows:

Pick out the three other copies of the indent (vide routine 2: 5: 53 which provides for four copies of the indents being made at the time of indent copying) in the case of indents copied by the Section and score out in them such of the items as have not received the sanction. Score out similarly in the case of indents received in the form of lists from outside. Attach a transmission sheet to one of the copies or the original as the case may be and copy in it relevant extracts from the indent noting sheet. Remember, particularly, to note down the date of sanction and the remarks, if any, of the sanctioning authority and then transmit the three copies of the indent to the ordering section.

Along with the copies of the indent or the original as the case may be, transmit also the book selection cards of the sanctioned items.

Note down in the indent note sheet, the date of transmission of the copies to the Order Section and get the dated initials of the head of the Order Section as a token of the Section having taken charge of the copies of the indent and of the related book selection cards.

3 : 3 : 58 Rejected Items Disposing

After the transmission of the copies to the Order Section, pick out the book selection cards of the rejected items and insert them in the proper place in the *Rejected Cards Tray or Deferred Cards Tray*, as the case may be. If, however, the instruction of the sanctioning authority is that the item should be brought up definitely at a later meeting, transfer the cards to the selected cards tray with a slip attached to the cards showing the time when they should be sent to the sanctioning authority.

6 Finance

6 : 6 ALLOTMENT WORK

6 : 6 : 8 *Annual Jobs*

The different jobs of the allotment work should be done for each subject separately.

6 : 6 : 81 Expert Opinion Obtaining

At the appointed time each year, write to the experts helping the library in book selection work in different subjects, seeking their advice as to whether the annual allotment for their respective subjects would require any change. In the letter, state the total annual allotment for the preceding year, the amount spent on current periodicals, and the balance available for books and back volumes of periodicals. Ask also if they would suggest the acquisition of the back volumes of any periodical or any other kind of reading material in the ensuing financial year.

6 : 6 : 822 Arrear Indents Estimating

At the appointed time each year, pick out the indents that are either awaiting sanction or having been sanctioned, have not yet been transmitted to the Order Section. Estimate which of these indents could be purchased within the financial year and eliminate them. Estimate the cost of the indents that will have to be purchased in the next financial year. This amount may be referred to as *Arrear Indent Cost*.

6 : 6 : 823 Outstanding Orders Estimating

Find out from the Order Section the items for which an order had been sent but whose supply could not be expected within the financial year and get an estimate of their cost. This amount may be referred to as *Outstanding Order Cost*.

6 : 6 : 824 Standing Orders Estimating

Find out in consultation with the Order Section, how many volumes are likely to be received in the next financial year under the different standing orders which are current. Estimate their cost. This amount may be referred to as *Standing Order Cost*.

6 : 6 : 83 Periodical Publications Subscription Estimating

Get from the Periodical Publications Section an estimate of the annual subscription for the periodicals current in each of the subjects. Find out also if there is any probability of any back volumes of periodicals being acquired and if so get their probable cost.

Ascertain in this way the total amount that is to be spent on periodicals for each subject in the next financial year. This amount may be referred to as *Periodical Publications Cost*.

6 : 8 : 86 Budget Ascertaining

Find out from the Finance Section the probable amount that is likely to be available for purchase of books and periodicals in the next financial year. This amount may be referred to as the *Budget Amount*.

6 : 6 : 87 Actuals Ascertaining

Find out from the Accounts Section the actual expenditure on books and periodical publications in each subject for each of the three preceding financial years. Estimate from these data the average or the normal amount spent on each subject per year. This amount may be referred to as the *Actuals*.

6 : 6 : 88 Preliminary to Allotment

In the light of the data obtained by the foregoing routines, prepare a schedule of allotment for the different subjects.

6 : 6 : 891 Allotment Sanctioning

Forward the schedule of allotment with the necessary notes to the Committee Section for inclusion in the papers that are to be sent to the sanctioning authority.

6 : 7 Allotment Watching Works

6 : 7 : 7 *Quarterly Jobs*

6 : 7 : 722, 6 : 7 : 723, 6 : 7 : 724

These routines are similar to the corresponding annual routines in Allotment Work.

6 : 7 : 73 New Periodicals Cost Ascertaining

Find out from the Periodical Publications Section, if any new periodicals have been sanctioned during the year and if so how much amount should be set apart for meeting their subscription in the current financial year.

6 : 7 : 77 Spent Amount Ascertaining

Find out from the Accounts Section the amount actually spent on books during the financial year.

6 : 7 : 78 Allotment Balance Advising

Find out the total of the amount ascertained by the foregoing routines and subtract it from the annual allotment to the subject. Write to the expert in the subject specifying the amount that is still unappropriated.

6 : 7 : 8 *Annual Job*

6 : 7 : 81 Allotment Advising

As soon as the sanction for the schedule of annual allotment is received from the Committee Section, advice the experts in each subject about the amount allotted to the subject for expenditure during the financial year and also the distribution of the amount under different heads such as books, standing orders on books, periodicals and back volumes of periodicals.

CHAPTER LF

ELIMINATION OF WASTE

1 Division of Work

If the turnover in the Section demands the assignment of several members to it, the distribution of work among the assistants of the Section should proceed along the lines of subject specialisation. This will enable each member to acquire an intensive acquaintance with the bibliography of certain subjects or groups of subjects and an intimate knowledge of the resources of the library in those subjects.

2 Responsibility of the Head of the Section

The Head of the Section should review the work of the assistants carefully, so that books of a border line nature do not get duplicated by different assistants. This can be done by the scrutiny of the provisional class numbers assigned, as well as by an alphabetical comparison of the different groups of book selection cards. It is desirable that the Annual Allotment Work and the quarterly Allotment Watching Work be done by the Head of the Section himself.

Monthly meetings and reviews are necessary to check up smoothness of the progress and efficiency.

3 Diary

Two diaries are necessary for the Section.

1 General Diary ; and
2 Book Selection Cards Diary.

31 General Diary

The General Diary is to be on a *daily basis* and is to have the following headings:

11 Letters received
121 Letters replied
122 Letters filed

141 Letters drafted
142 Routine letters issued
15 Reminders sent
21 Indents called for
22 Indents received
31 Book selection cards checked with selected cards tray
32 Book selection cards checked with order tray
34 Book selection cards checked with bills on hand
35 Book selection cards checked with catalogue.

35 Book Selection Cards Diary

The diary is to be on a *weekly basis* and is to show the number of book selection cards written. Its headings must consist of the symbols for the main divisions of the classification scheme used or some suitable modification of them as determined by the context of the library.

CHAPTER LG

CORRELATION

1 Avoiding Duplication

Much internal correlation will be necessary to avoid the duplication of the same book by different assistants. Further, in the case of books in unfamiliar languages, the assistant who knows the languages will have to give a helping hand in the selection of books in those languages, although the subject of the books may be different from the ones he specialises in.

2 Table of Correlation

The following table of correlation shows the jobs that bring the Section into contact with other sections :

1 All Sections
1 : 2 : 12 Suggestion noting

2 Book Order Section
2 : 1 : 38 Preliminary Checking ;
3 : 1 : 51 Indent Checking ;
3 : 3 : 52 Sanctioned Indent Forwarding ;
6 : 6 : 823 Outstanding Orders Estimating ;
6 : 7 : 723 Outstanding Orders Estimating ;
6 : 6 : 824 Standing Orders Estimating ; and
6 : 7 : 724 Standing Orders Estimating.

3 Periodicals Publication Section
6 : 6 : 83 Periodical Publications Subscription Estimating ;
6 : 7 : 73 New Periodicals Cost Ascertaining.

4 Accession Section
3 : 1 : 51 Indent Checking.

5 Technical Section
3 : 2 : 35 Book Selection Card Classifying.

91 Committee Section
3 : 3 : 511 Indent Forwarding (Tuesdays, 12 noon) ;
6 : 6 : 891 Allotment Sanctioning.

96 Finance Section

6 : 6 : 87 Actuals Ascertaining ;

6 : 7 : 77 Spent Amount Ascertaining.

3 Meeting Other Sections

Periodical meetings with other sections should be held to revise and improve routine.

CHAPER LH

ILLUSTRATIVE TIME SCHEME

5 Weekly Jobs

Saturday

1 : 8 : 58 Sources Shelving; and
3 : 1 : 51 Indent Checking

Sunday

3 : 1 : 51 Indent Checking;
3 : 1 : 523 Supplemental Book Selection Carding;
3 : 1 : 525 Supplemental Book Selection and Cards Classifying;
3 : 1 : 527 Supplemental Book Selection Cards Completing;
3 : 1 : 528 Supplemental Book Selection Cards Merging;
3 : 3 : 4 Indents Doubts Clearing; and
3 : 1 : 55 Cost Ascertaining

Monday

2 : 1 : 51 Marked Sources Forwarding;
2 : 2 : 31 Book Selection Card Writing; and
2 : 5 : 53 Indent Copying

Tuesday

1 : 2 : 52 Sources Requisitioning;
3 : 1 : 56 Indent Estimating;
3 : 3 : 51 Indent Noting; and
3 : 3 : 511 Indent Forwarding (12 noon).

Wednesday

2 : 2 : 31 Book Selection Card Writing; and
2 : 2 : 51 Book Selection Card Revising.

Thursday

2 : 2 : 58 Book Selection Card Filing;
2 : 5 : 51 Book Selection Cards Forwarding;
2 : 5 : 58 Unrecommended Cards Filing;
3 : 3 : 52 Sanctioned Indents Forwarding; and
3 : 3 : 58 Rejected Items Disposing.

7 Quarterly Jobs

The last week of each quarter

1 : 7 : 7 The jobs of the Allotment Watching Work.

8 Annual Jobs

January

1 : 8 : 88 Sources Weeding ; and
6 : 7 : 81 Allotment Advising

September

Second week

6 : 6 : 81 Expert Opinion Obtaining ; and
6 : 6 : 822 Arrear Indents Estimating.

Third week

6 : 6 : 823 Outstanding Orders Estimating ; and
6 : 6 : 824 Standing Orders Estimating.

Fourth week

6 : 6 : 83 Periodical Publications Subscription Estimating

October

First week

6 : 6 : 86 Budget Ascertaining

Second week

6 : 6 : 87 Actuals Ascertaining

November

First week

6 : 6 : 88 Preliminary to Allotment

December

First week

6 : 6 : 891 Allotment Sanctioning.

CHAPTER LJ

FORMS, REGISTERS, AND EQUIPMENT

ABBREVIATIONS USED :

C = Card size = 125 × 75 mm.

Q = Quarto size = 215 × 170 mm.

S = Super size or Folio size = 340 × 215 mm.

C12 Book Selection Card. Printed. 6 pt. Bristol board. White Tray. The text of the form is as follows :

(Front side)

Ac M		**Don N**	**Wl N**
Auth			
Title			
Size	**Colln**	**Edn**	**Yr**
Pub		**Pub Price**	
Series, etc			
Review			
Reference			

(Back Side)

Vendor

	Date	*Initials*		
Sein			Dost	Indian Foreign
Apprd				
Order			Order N	
Recd			Voucher N	
Paid				

Accnd			*Cum N of Vols in*	*Cur Yr*		*Total*	
Cut							
Class			Sub				
Cat			Lang				
Shld			Cump Cost	Rs	P	Rs	P
Bound			Sub				
Wl			Total				

Q12 *Book Selection Consultation Letter Form.* Stencil 21 lb Printing paper. White. The text of the form is as follows :

Subject : Book Selection

Number book selection cards in (subject) are enclosed herewith for your consideration. Please be good enough to sort them into the three groups, "approved", "deferred", and "rejected". The three groups may be separately bundled and sent to me along with a covering letter embodying your recommendation.

The balance available for purchase of books in your subject-field within the current financial year is Rs...

Expecting your reply within a week,

S13 *Indent Noting Form.* Stencil. 21 lb Printing paper. White. The text of the form is as follows :

Outside N.. Dated
File N.. Date of receipt
From..
Subject : Indent for Books

Librarian's Note	*Office Note*
	N of items recommended ..
	N of items already available or on order ..
	N of items recommended for duplication ..
	Estimated cost of the items not in library ..
	Estimated cost of the duplication recommended ..
	Total estimated cost ..
	Allotment for books ..
	Amount already appropriated Balance available ..
	Remarks

Library Committee's decision

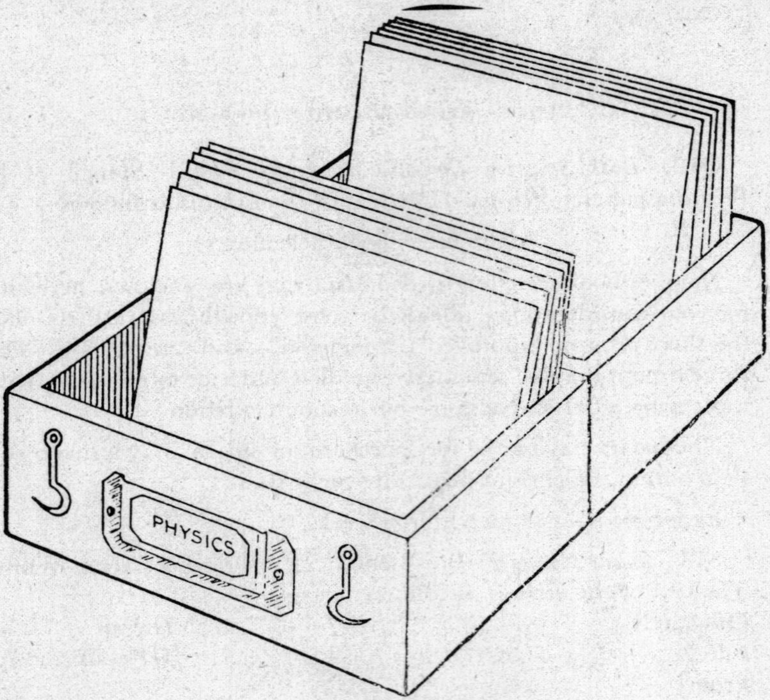

WORK BOX

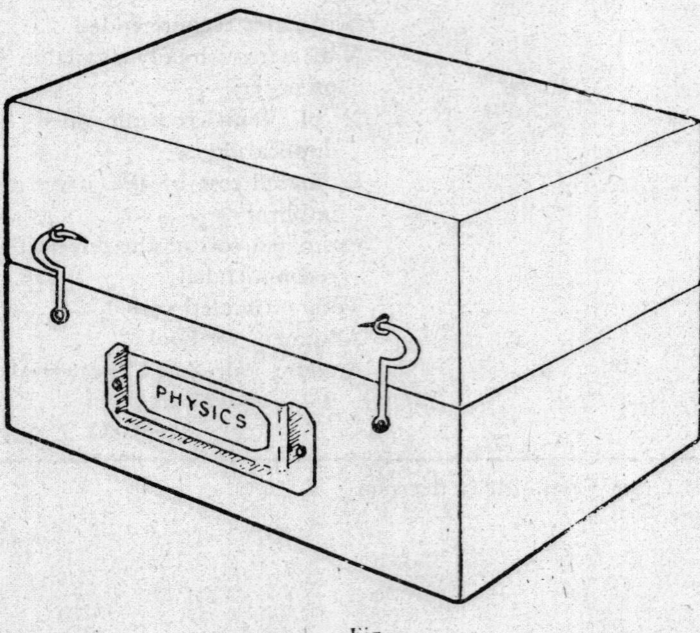

Fig.

If the librarian is the sanctioning authority, the first column should have the heading "Note by Head of Section"; and the bottom line should read "Librarian's decision".

W Work Box

In modern library practice, 125×75 mm cards are widely used in the different sections of a library. In particular, they are used for Book Selection. One card contains one and only one title. Successively a Book Selection Card becomes a Book Indent Card, a Book Order Card, an Accession Card, and a Withdrawal Card. The cards of the three-card system of the periodicals work, the Catalogue Cards of the Technical Section, the Shelf Register Cards of the Maintenance Section are also 125×75 mm. Till the cards are filed in their permanent cabinet, they have to be temporarily passed on from one member of staff to another. To ensure safety and security for the cards, a Work Box was designed by me in 1925. It is made of thin teak wood planks 8 mm thick. When closed, its internal dimensions are 134×84×84 mm. The lower part and the lid are of equal height so that when fully opened each of them rests on the table top. The lower part is provided with a brass label holder and a pair of flat brass hooks. The lid has the eyes to take the hooks. (*See* the illustration). This Work Box has been included by the Indian Standards Institution in the *Indian standard specification for library furniture and fittings, Part I: Timber*. [Is : 1829 (Part 1)—1961].

FILES

Name	Class Number	Amplifying device	Filing characteristic	Year of transfer to record sequence after the file is closed	Year of destruction after transfer to the record sequence
Sources	11	Subject Device or/ and Language Device	Correspondent	1 Year	III year
Selection	12	Subject Device	do	do	V year
Indent	13	do	do	do	X year
Allotment	16	do	do	do	do
Outward enquiries	191	do	do	do	III year
Inward enquiries	192	do	do	do	do

INDEX

Note.

1 The index number is the number of the part, chapter, or section of the occurrence of the item indexed.

2 For example, the index number JG2 means Sec 2 of Chapter JG in Part J.

3 The following contractions are used.

def = Definition
irt = in relation to
qirt = quoted in relation to